D

ISBN: 0615821936
ISBN-13: 9780615821931

DEDICATION

For Maria Ester Gomez de Ramirez

CONTENTS

FOREWORD

By Carlos Conde

The sixties and the seventies were tumultuous years for Chicanos. After decades of being held hostage by a prejudiced US society, we finally found the courage and the will to seek our rightful role and participation in a country in which we had given so much and received so little.

Mexican Americans had historically lived primarily in the southwest regions from Texas to California along the US-Mexico border. Southern California and Los Angeles were large Chicano enclaves, as was the Texas region; the community extended to Chicago and western states.

Whatever our geography, we lived as an isolated group, socially and politically.

Puerto Ricans and their politics were confined to their New York and East Coast habitats. The Cuban American Diaspora was just evolving.

The awakening of this "sleeping giant," as the Chicano movement was called, came after World War II—in which Mexican Americans and Puerto Ricans loyally served their country and distinguished themselves in combat, as attested by their Medal of Honor decorations. Our GIs returned home to lead the quest for acceptance and the participation of the Spanish-speaking minority in our country's socioeconomic process.

It wasn't easy or quick. We had not yet mastered the process of articulating our grievances to our country's leaders, many of whom regarded us mostly as political chattels.

Despite our growing population and potential political strength, we continued to be an isolated and deprived community into the early sixties, when we realized that to break into our country's socioeconomic process, we needed to participate directly and be more assertive in the political process.

In 1960, Americans barely chose John F. Kennedy as president over Richard M. Nixon. The Democrat, with the help of the "Viva Kennedy" clubs, won the Mexican American vote—which was pivotal to his victory. Kennedy, with only token knowledge or interest in the Mexican American community except for its political potential, did not reciprocate its support. Lyndon B. Johnson, who assumed the presidency after Kennedy's assassination, had grown up among Mexicans in his native Texas but wasn't much better.

It was left to Nixon to address and redress the grievances and petitions of the Mexican American minority and include them in his national governance. He chose Henry Ramirez for the job after Nixon's first ombudsman, Martin Castillo, left after a brief tenure.

In *A Chicano in the White House,* Henry passionately articulates the events leading up to the Watergate scandal that cut short the administration of President Nixon. But the impetus his leadership gave to the Latino involvement in federal and national affairs survived and prospered. He does an excellent job describing the Latino involvement that had been spurred by the southwest's Chicano movement and now included the US's Puerto Rican community and disenfranchised Cubans fleeing Castro's Cuba.

Growing up in Pomona, California, in a family of eleven, Henry lived the Mexican American drama. He worked in the agricultural fields in his youth. He then spent ten years in seminary studies but left to pursue a university degree after deciding he was not meant for the priesthood.

He became an educator, developing a deep interest in the Mexican American genesis and its social revolution. He aptly details the events that led to his role in the Nixon administration as the Latinos' chief lobbyist and defender of the ethnic minority.

I met Henry when I did short stints in a Latino presidential committee and the US Commission on Civil Rights before becoming a White House communications aide. Henry was a man possessed, leading a Commission studies team that interpreted the sociocultural background and the potential of this minority group.

Henry's *padrino* in the White House was Counselor Robert Finch, who helped shepherd Henry's agenda after Nixon appointed him chairman of the Cabinet Committee on Spanish Speaking Affairs. And, contrary to what Henry's critics say, he enjoyed access to the president and his inner circle. The president held Henry in sufficiently high regard to accord him his five-point agenda on Hispanic inclusion, which earned Henry, me, and others of the White House's "Latino steering committee" appearances before the Watergate grand jury.

Henry was a demanding advocate of US Latino interests, which by then included all Spanish-speaking minority groups. Some battles he won, others he lost; but he never lost sight of his roots, his mission, and his commitment to *la causa,* that grand mission to integrate Latinos into American society with all its citizens' rights, privileges, and opportunity.

Henry's tome tells it well.

ACKNOWLEDGMENTS

My spirit yearns to thank personally all who made this book possible. But that is not possible; they are just too numerous. And many are no longer in the finite.

So, I commence with the two who did God's Will, giving me my body while God gave me my soul. Then, in the face of the hardships of life in a foreign land, they gifted me with the knowledge of God, who favored me with Faith.

They, in turn, were the beneficiaries, through their Nahuatl-speaking ancestors, of the *Nican Mopohua*, the precious and delicate dialogue of the Mother of Jesus with a man atop the hill called Tepeyac, in Anahuac. Tepeyac was the hill that Aztecs dedicated to the mother of their god, Teotl, and where Our Lady of Guadalupe divinely appeared several times and conversed ever so tenderly with an indigenous man named Juan Diego, in the area today known as Mexico City. Within ten years, most of the Mexico of that time was Christianized.

I express unending gratitude to Pascual and Romana, my parents, for the private schooling they acquired for their children in the 1930s and 1940s at Saint Joseph's Grammar School in Pomona and at Catholic high schools, and for the Christian formation with which they endowed their family of eleven. They had us earn money for our school expenses as seasonal migrant workers in Santa Clara County, in the Fresno area, and in Southern California. We learned how to harvest apricots, prunes, cotton, grapes, lemons, oranges, grapefruit, tomatoes, cucumbers, potatoes, walnuts, and maybe several more edibles I've forgotten. Mom and Dad cared not a whit (or did not realize) that the public schools of California segregated Mexican children. They had fled from militant secularism, Protestant influences, Masonic intrigues, Marxism, and the bloody French-Revolution style persecution of the Catholic Church. They would have nothing to do with anything close to paganism or education that failed to teach Christianity.

Very special gratefulness is prayed to and for the thousands of unknown Catholic families who financed my almost ten years of seminary education and formation for the Roman Catholic priesthood.

And, what can I say to the Vincentian priests, my professors, for the knowledge and spiritual formation they pounded into me? They taught me the histories of humanity, from the Sumerian civilization to the Hellenistic, to the Roman, to the Christendom of Europe, to the modern times dating from the printing press and its myriad consequences. They filled my reluctant mind with algebra, geometry, calculus, and trigonometry; physics, chemistry, human anatomy, botany, and biology; Greek, Latin, Spanish,

English, and some Italian language and literature; Aristotelian, Scholastic, and European philosophy, including that of Descartes and his followers; moral theology, biblical studies, and exegesis; plus the histories of major religions. They tried their best to prepare me for giving and sharing so that I would have what it takes to be ready to live and die for my belief in God.

My deep appreciation goes out to my seminary colleagues, with whom I lived in residential halls for almost ten years. After twelve years, some became priests; others left the seminary after six or seven or ten years, as did I: Bernie, Charlie, Paul, Edmund, Paco, Denny, Diamond Jim, James S., Gene, Tom, and hundreds of others. They taught me so much of their Irish, French, German, English, Lebanese, Italian, Iberian, and European American cultures and *modus vivendi*.

For Father Martinez, my Professor Higgins, my prayers. He patiently introduced me to my own New Horizons beyond the barrios of Pomona, California. He did not give up after my first lesson: One summer Sunday morning after Mass in Pomona, he invited me to a 5:00 p.m. dinner at Romanoff's Restaurant in Hollywood. I still recall vividly the look on his face that evening as I cautiously and hesitantly asked the person at the door if I could enter. I had dressed in my summer best: A clean white T-shirt, "pachuco"-style trousers held up with a thin belt, and shoes with thick soles. Father's glance was aghast and vexed but he voiced no concern. I learned about menus, waiters who vigilantly refreshed my water glass after every gulp, and how to dine at a fancy restaurant at Hollywood and Vine. Father taught me that priests must know "how to" with the rich as well as with the poor. This lesson was followed by many more as he labored to take me out of the barrio.

Soon after my departure from priestly studies, I volunteered for the army in 1953—specifically, for the National Security Agency. But an army major informed me in 1954 that it did "not exist." The draft was next. Despite encouragement to enter officer training, as a soldier with postgraduate education I was in a hurry to acquire a profession. I also knew too much about the science of the military from my comprehensive studies of warfare in Europe across the centuries. I had translated the wars between the Greeks and the Persians, and the wars of Caesar. The European wars were a constant historical variable. The purpose of war was to destroy and kill, and that, generally, by inflicting some object on the body of the enemy. I did my duty and served honorably. The artificiality of officer privileges held no fascination.

Since I had no interest in celibacy, I searched for the best person to be my wife and mother for our children. God helped me find Maria Ester Gomez Bernal. What an eternal gift! Her dad and I became friends and buddies. Her family was wonderful! I thank God for the best discovery of my life. At our wedding, I promised my wife that I would do my best to ensure that we both arrived in heaven when death us did part.

I owe so much to Loyola University and also to Claremont Graduate School for preparing me to be a good high school teacher. Loyola gets my highest gratitude. I was awarded a PhD in 1971 and won Alumnus of the Year in 1972. I was accepted to Loyola Law School and successfully achieved one year. My study of law equipped me to become an innovative educator.

I would fail utterly were I not grateful for my New Horizon students at Whittier High School. They proved that educational transformation is feasible. Their academic success in five measurable outcomes of high school experience showed what a community like Whittier can achieve.

I wish to thank in a most special way these educators, who were invaluable to me in my professional life: Cy Jackson, dean of students at El Rancho High School; Seabron Nolin, Whittier High School principal; H. Holloway, superintendent of Whittier Union High School District; and Manuel Ceja, consultant at the California Department of Education.. Deep appreciation also goes out to those who were instrumental in hiring me to the US Commission on Civil Rights, transferring my family to Washington, DC and teaching, guiding, and showing me the ways of Washington

Very special gratitude and appreciation is hereby acknowledged for "Bob" Finch, presidential counselor; Mo Garcia, my deeply loyal and faithful Achates; Martin Castillo; congressmen and senators who abided in my efforts; my FBI liaison (who will remain anonymous); The "Brown Mafia;" El Mayor Manuel Levi Peza, former military personal assistant to two Mexican Presidents; and so many more.

Deep appreciation goes out to my grandson, Ruben Brown Ramirez, for his ever present instructions on the "how to's" of the digital age.

I first outlined this book in August 1974. I knew of key writings of mostly unknown authors who participated in making history in their times and countries; these motivated me to try to fill in the gaps of history between 1971 and 1974 from the perspective of a Mexican Mestizo.

To all of you known only by God who helped me in this endeavor and in my life, receive my devout prayers and deep agape.

INTRODUCTION

A Chicano in the White House is the first book to tell the unknown story of President Richard M. Nixon and the Chicanos. Nixon found us. He made us known and famous. Only Nixon or I could have written this book. He and I are the only ones who knew what visions we discussed and planned in the Oval Office. It is a disclosure of how his visionary actions brought an unknown, forgotten, and conquered *raza* into mainstream America.

I present details of the first "exodus" through the 1920s of almost two million rural and illiterate, landless peasants from a feudal society to the Midwest and Southwest of the United States, where they established "little Mexico's" called barrios. The Mexican Revolution of 1910 turned ugly after 1913 when the leaders of the Marxist Union named International Workers of the World, (I.W.W.) of Baltimore, Maryland, imposed a quasi-Stalinist regime and proceeded to persecute and attempt to eliminate the Catholic Church in Mexico. The atrocities against Catholics caused frightened flight on empty boxcars to *"El Norte."*

In a monologue, President Nixon ruminated about the rationale for the Great Wall of China, pounding his fist as he declared, "And we Anglos have built a similar wall, but it is an invisible wall of discrimination against you Mexicans." Tersely, he bellowed, "You, Henry, and I, the president, are going to tear it down!" I instantly understood that he, the president, and I working together on our visions would diminish discrimination against Chicanos.

On the day he dedicated his presidential library in the presence of hundreds of us, members of his inner White House circle, he spotted me with my nephew Damien Miranda in the hallway as he exited the auditorium. He approached me with serious intent on his countenance, and with vigor he jabbed my chest with his index finger, declaring: "You have not written *our chapter*. You will note in my books, I have not written about it; I left it up to you. Well, now—" (here he uttered a few impolite words) "—write it!" Then he turned to my young nephew and eagerly chatted with him, as President Nixon appeared somewhat dismissive of me.

A Chicano in the White House is the first book to reveal Richard Nixon as the warm-hearted person who really knew and liked us. For the first time, the world will discover the five visions he implemented to advance and make visible the Mexican Americans and other Spanish-speaking groups, namely, the Cubans and the mainland Puerto Ricans.

Richard Nixon was once a poor white man who worked alongside poor Mexicans in the orchards and fields of two ranches adjacent to his parents' gas station and grocery store—the Leffingwell and Murphy ranches of East Whittier in Southern California. He learned more about his Mexican customers as he tended his parents' little businesses on the corner of Santa Gertrudes and Highway 101 (locally known as Whittier Boulevard).

Nixon was the only US president born in California. He got to know us in the hot, dusty, and dirty fields and orange groves where hard physical work was requirement number one and reality and authenticity are clearly manifest. He got to know us while we lived our culture in accord with our values: God, family, hard work, respect for the law, and an aversion to hand-outs. He got to know us as we really were—not as stereotyped by Hollywood, dressed sloppily in dark clothing, with unkempt hair and an unruly mustache smeared with food and saliva and sleeping under a *nopal* (a cactus).

I'll tell you how Hispanic Week got started: Congress voted in a law that made it possible, but Nixon was the first president to act on it and proclaim Hispanic Week (now expanded to a month). Those interested in political science will discover how and why Nixon went from 5 percent of the Mexican vote in previous elections to almost 30 percent in 1972.

Not only will academics acquire new knowledge of the Nixon era, but once this book is published, librarians will be able to direct students to its information on factors leading to the advancement of Mexican American Mestizos. Chicano civil rights activists and Chicano history professors will finally get the rest of the story from the only primary source who could write it: I and the president made this history. Research on the beginning and history of the Chicano and Puerto Rican civil rights movement will improve. UCLA will no longer give Lyndon Johnson the credit for proclaiming Hispanic Week. Writers will give credit to Nixon for signing the law enabling the Cabinet Committee on Opportunities for the Spanish Speaking People (CCOSSP) and for meeting with his cabinet in the Cabinet Room and Roosevelt Room over Mexican Americans matters. A myriad of historical firsts will be revealed. The book is a *sine qua non* for understanding the rise of the Chicanos and Nixon's part in it.

PART I:

NIXON WANTS IT DONE

In January 1971, Finch introduced the topic: "You do national research, right?" Then, he got to the point. "We want you to find out what Mexicans think of this White House."

CHAPTER ONE

FINCH WANTS A STUDY ON MEXICAN AMERICAN PERSPECTIVES OF THE NIXON WHITE HOUSE

August 5, 1971, started as just another hot, humid day in Washington, DC, but it was to end as a momentous day. The president of these United States would discuss in the Oval Office and in the Cabinet Room what he wanted done for Mexican Americans and Spanish-speaking people. And on that early morning in my office on the third floor of the US Commission on Civil Rights (USCCR), I wrote five visions that defined how Mexican Americans could be included in the mainstream of American life. After reviewing the five ideas listed on a three-by-five card, I inserted it into my shirt pocket. This was, I mused, just in case the president were to ask me in the Oval Office,

> *"What are we going to do to advance the lives of Mexican Americans?"*

By mid afternoon, I found myself crossing the street between the West Wing and the Executive Office Building (EOB), in deeply ambivalent reflection. On one hand, this had been the place where a little over a century ago, another president, James K. Polk, commanded the military to invade and conquer Mexico, a nation barely independent as of 1823. (1) On the other hand, today, this president, Richard M. Nixon, had commanded systemic changes to assure that the descendants of those Mexicans, now veterans of wars, would become first-class US citizens, enjoying all the rights and duties of all Americans in the land of the free.

How was this to be accomplished? And why did this president want it done?

Soon after Nixon settled in as our thirty-seventh president, he asked Congress to establish an agency for the needs of the Mexican Americans—by law and not by memorandum. A year after Richard Nixon was elected; Congress breathed life into the new agency on the last days of December 1969. Its purpose was to assure that all federal programs were reaching this target population. The senators from Illinois, New York, and Connecticut had approved the House version but with one big "however:" The new agency's name, and its work, would have to include "other," very newly emerging Spanish-speaking people: Cubans and Puerto Ricans. This country now also included Spanish speakers other than just the Mexican Americans.

In its first year, valiant efforts were mounted to achieve the enabling legislation's high goals (see Appendix A), but the agency's leadership was summarily dismissed a year later by the counsel to the president, John Dean, over some scandal that involved him personally. Chairman Martin Castillo had performed most superbly in a hostile and ignorant environment. The agency became a hot potato in the White House and remained somewhat dormant until the day of August 5, 1971.

President Nixon wanted to reach out to Mexican Americans. He was firm and adamant about this effort. So, he charged his trusted friend and counselor, Robert Finch, to lead efforts on behalf of Mexican Americans and of the agency, called the Cabinet Committee on Opportunities for the Spanish Speaking People. It was, by the way, highly maligned by the Democrats on the Hill. Congressman Henry B. Gonzalez of San Antonio, Texas shrieked, "It is a paper tiger!" He had voted against its passage. Senator "Little Joe" Montoya of New Mexico, cried: "The president has not met with his cabinet on opportunities for the Spanish speaking." The jeers from the Democrats and their partisans filled the airwaves. The Puerto Ricans complained to their Senators, "It is still an agency for Mexican Americans, only. It has done nothing for the Boricuas." On the scale of popularity, it ranked at the bottom.

Eight months earlier, in mid-December of 1970, Republican congressman Charles Wiggins of California had invited me for lunch at an exclusive restaurant on Capitol Hill. I was working at the US Commission on Civil Rights as an anonymous public servant. Never had I been called by a member of Congress for any reason, let alone for a private lunch! I was surprised and elated. For me, that call was momentous.

Years before, in Whittier, I had worked for Wiggins's election as a precinct worker. There was nothing remarkable about this; I was just another worker. My little but growing family had lived in

East Whittier, part of his district; I was only one of thousands of supporters that candidates meet in the course of their campaigns.

The lunch was at first chatty. I vividly remember recounting passages from a book I had recently read.[i] It was a compilation of communications between Confederate officers over the activities at Hicks Camp in El Monte, California, also part of his district. It was there that recruits from Southern California had been trained to fight in the Civil War for the Confederate Army. Charlie had been mayor of El Monte, so I felt that this tidbit of historical chatter would be interesting. (2) But the congressman changed the topic, getting to his agenda right away. He wanted my opinion on which candidates President Nixon should consider for appointment to the just-vacated position of chairman of the Cabinet Committee on Opportunities for the Spanish Speaking People (of course, he simply called it the "Cabinet Committee").

I suggested about ten names and, in detail, outlined the pros and cons of each. He did not engage or respond; his disinterest in those I had listed was patent. As I finished describing my candidates, he remarked. "You didn't include yourself, why not?" My response was lengthy. I had been in Washington for three years and had finished the studies I had been recruited to do but for the final writing, and that was in the good hands of my staff. Further, I would be applying for jobs as a superintendent of schools in California. I had been approached by three school districts. In addition, I rejected the possibility of entering the heated maelstrom of partisan bickering. I had my profession and was cognizant of the opportunities in that direction. Besides, I was not comfortable in the DC area. California was where I wanted to live and raise my family.

The lunch was over. We parted with no future plans and with no conclusions to his inquiries. For my part, I gave no further thought to the implications of our discussion; neither did I search for other reasons he had called me. I went on my merry, uncomplicated way back to my office to work on the educational reports over which I had been laboring. We would submit them to the president and to Congress; the first two of six reports were being printed and would soon be released[ii] while we continued work on the rest.[iii]

A month later, I was summoned to the West Wing of the White House. Dr. George Grassmuck called my bosses on behalf of his boss, Robert H. Finch. My bosses at the Commission had no idea why I was summoned. And so, for the first time in my life, I appeared on the grounds of the White House. Every step was novel and a new experience. As I approached the door to the West Wing, an alert marine saluted smartly and briskly opened the door. I identified myself to the receptionist. She nodded, asked me to be seated, and announced my arrival. After a short wait, Dr. George Grassmuck showed up, identified himself and asked me to follow him upstairs to the counselor's office. I was warmly greeted by Mr. Finch's secretary, Carol. George escorted me into a large, warmly decorated office and remained. Mr. Finch arose from his imposing desk and joined us. I was quite nervous but tried to present a picture of total composure.

I was in the presence of a former California lieutenant governor, a former cabinet officer in the then Department of Health, Education, and Welfare (HEW), a famous person who was frequently in the news. This was big-time stuff. He spent no time on pleasantries or small talk. He spoke directly and to the point. He affected a spirit of calmness and of being in control. His attire was impressive. Brooks Brothers must have been his favorite hang-out. It was not until many years later, when I attended a seminar on "How to Make a First Impression" in 1977 in the course of my business, that I learned that silk ties, Gold Toe socks, dark suits, cotton button-down shirts, certain types of shoes, and so on, were a "uniform." Many times since then, I have reflected back on that day and wondered if Counselor Finch had judged my clothing a little out of step with White House norms. My outfit must have momentarily raised his eyebrows. I was dressed in my usual Southern California casual: colorful ties, sport jacket, and J. C. Penney shoes and shirts. I certainly did not belong with the Washington DC "suits." I was oblivious to their existence and the standards of dress they required to denote that you were "in the know."

Counselor Finch proceeded as if he were doing a legal deposition. He was businesslike, frank, and straight to the point, as if the assumption were that someone else had already done the vetting. I saw no similarity between the lunch interview with Charlie Wiggins and this event. "Since you excel at the Commission on doing national studies, we want you to do a study for us," he announced. "We want the study to dwell on what the Mexican Americans think about this administration. What are their perceptions of this presidency? What do they feel about the Cabinet Committee? What qualifications should the new chairman for the Cabinet Committee on Opportunities for the Spanish Speaking have?"

"Mr. Counselor, that is a big job," I whispered. I was taken aback! "Do you really mean what you are saying? You really want to know what they think about Republicans, about this White

House, about this president. You want to know what they want out of this government? Do you want it straight or watered down?"

"Yes, we want to know what is really going on out there in the Southwest." He elaborated: "People in this town, and for that matter, all along the Atlantic Seaboard from Maine to the South, do not know who the Mexican Americans are. You can walk out there in front of the White House to Pennsylvania Avenue and not see any of you. This town knows only African Americans and Whites. So we, who are in government, do not worry about your concerns.

"You have been active in the civil rights movement as it affects the Chicanos. You travel and converse with leaders all over the Southwest. You do research and know what is current in the communities there. Give me three proposals on what research you will do to respond to my request."

I agreed and asked for temporary assignment to something in the Executive Office Building (EOB) across the alley from the West Wing of the White House. Outsiders considered that building as part of the "White House." Insiders knew the West Wing was the White House. Personnel working in EOB were support staff; yet, very important.

Washington rides on perceptions. I knew that news of my presence "in the "White House" would spread swiftly throughout the Spanish-speaking world; this would assist me greatly in acquiring information, opinions, thoughts, and experiences from leaders. Most important, this fact would assure that my telephone calls would be answered with celerity. Dr. George Grassmuck showed me to a third-floor office. It became my working home "in the White House."

Several days later, I returned to the West Wing to present Counselor Finch with three outlines for the proposed study. One was for a quick memo; another was for research on the literature, and a third was for a thorough compilation of research, interviews, and opinions of key persons that would require travel to gather.

He opted for a twenty- to thirty-page memo based on my experiences, telephone interviews, and knowledge of the Mexican American civil rights movement. As a safeguard for my professionalism, I pointedly announced that I was going to write factually and objectively, without reservation or worry about hurt feelings. I was already deeply aware of how Mexican Americans perceived this White House, which was based on its contrast with the unrealized expectations from Kennedy and Johnson. Also, I adamantly stated that my work should in no way be construed by him or anyone else as a bid to be considered for the position of chairman of the Cabinet Committee. I'll never forget it. He retorted happily, "Do not be concerned; that is not in the cards. We do not want a civil rights activist."

Appendix D presents the lengthy memorandum of my study: "An Overview of Spanish Speaking Affairs for White House Perspectives" Counselor Finch thanked me with a gracious letter (see Appendix B). And then, I heard nothing further. I thought that perhaps I had been too critical and harsh.

Almost a year later, my special assistant, Diana Lozano, retrieved a copy of the memo. Of it, she wrote, "I talked to Doug about several things, including the fact that we had never seen the final copy of our political report. He sent one over to us immediately. It is quite good—Doug used 85 percent of our first report to Finch and about 80 percent of our political report. The final product is an effective combination of the two, sprinkled with political pull."

"Doug" was a California lawyer (Doug Hallett) who worked in Chuck Colson's political office. We discovered that my reports and studies on issues confronting Mexican Americans were primarily used to frame and define political strategies and tactics for the presidential reelection campaign—that is, to court the vote of Spanish-speaking people.

And so, I returned to my world of reality at my office at the Civil Rights Commission. My adventure into research for the White House had ended-so I thought with relief. In April 1971 we issued the first report: "Report I: Ethnic Isolation of Mexican Americans in the Public Schools of the Southwest." My staff continued to put the finishing touches on the other reports developed from the Mexican American Education Study that I had conceptualized, designed, and directed since 1968. These would be: "Report II: The Unfinished Education," "Report III: The Excluded Student," "Report IV: Mexican American Education in Texas: A Function of Wealth," "Report V: Teachers and Students," "Report VI: Toward Quality Education for Mexican Americans," and "Methodological Appendix of Research Methods Employed in the Mexican American Education Study." (3)

Meanwhile, Washington was abuzz with the names of those campaigning for the now-coveted position of chairman. My name began to surface, even though I wasn't. And, sure enough,

Counselor Robert Finch again summoned me. In wonderment, I made the now often-repeated walk up the driveway to the front door of the West Wing. It almost seemed as if the squirrels had lost their apprehension of me.

The several minutes of processing and walking through the West Wing gate and up to the White House gave me a bit of time to reflect on my actions. They were now affecting my private and my professional lives. What did these visits to the White House represent for me and my family? Some events seemed beyond my control. I wondered these visits are harbingers of what? I had not planned, coveted, and sought any future in the jungle of the political world. Education was my field.

Mr. Finch again thanked me for my latest report. In his lawyerly manner, he went straight to his purpose for summoning me to the West Wing and offered me the position of chairman. I do not recall him reciting any whys or wherefores. It was a simple request. I reacted slowly and with dismay. I deliberated for a prolonged while, wrestling with the offer's implications for my family and myself. This would take me off the career ladder I was on and down unknown paths that might have pitfalls. It would place me into a caldron of partisan politics, of competing ethnic and racial interests, a presidential campaign, and huge expectations for achieving civil rights aspirations. It is unusual, but I cannot pinpoint the date Finch offered me the position. The truth was, I did not like the offer. I had forewarned him in February of my deep disinterest in high-level politics.

In a flash, I recalled an unhappy incident: several weeks after Nixon had won the 1968 election, three men came to my hotel room in San Antonio, Texas around 10:00 p.m. and woke me with a knock on the door. They were Richard Alatorre, a future California state senator; Phil Montez, the western field director for the US Commission on Civil Rights; and Herman Sillas, a lawyer and future administrator of the California Department of Motor Vehicles. The four of us were there to participate in the US Commission on Civil Rights hearings on discrimination against Mexican Americans.

We were also board members of the Foundation for Mexican American Studies, of the Association of Mexican American Educators, and of an informal group of twelve Chicano civil rights activists. In summary, we were the movers and shakers of the Chicano civil rights movement of the early 1960s, complete with manifestos and picketing in Southern California. By November 1967, we had added picketing in Washington DC to our list.

During the week of hearings (December 9 through 14), these three men, my cohorts, woke me to admonish me in strong, no-nonsense words that I had better not join the Nixon administration if the Republicans asked (I was the only one in our group and highly regarded in the party). They said, "If you do, we will get you, sometime, somehow, and will not forget that you betrayed us." As I write these lines, I thank God that they did forget—but then, we never again met on the field of battle. We had mutual respect; besides, we had fought for a common cause: our people, the Chicanos. We were genuine members of the Chicano *causa*, *el movimiento*. Why my compatriots, Richard, Phil, and Herman, and who were also deeply Democrat partisans choose such a moment to admonish me on political intrigues remains a mental scar. How childish and meaningless!

Finally, I responded to Finch that I would accept the position, subject to three conditions. His countenance showed his dislike for my phrasing but asked me to explain them. I told him that I needed a White House office in the Executive Office Building like the one I had already occupied for six weeks; such a thing would demonstrate the president's commitment and provide respect for the Hispanic community on a par with that for the Black community. (The president's liaison to the Black community was Bob Brown, and he had an EOB office.)

My next condition was that prior to the announcement of my position, Mr. Finch's office would receive thousands of letters of support from Chicano leaders throughout the country. This was to demonstrate beyond a shadow of a doubt that I was a nationally recognized Chicano civil rights leader, credible to my peers, who had already paid his dues. My status was well known and earned. With that type of recognition, it would be most difficult for the White House to fire me.

During the civil rights struggles of the sixties and seventies, it was common for school superintendents, mayors, governors, and so on to appoint Mexican Americans as liaisons between elected officials and the restless and surging Chicano community. But the community saw the liaisons as inherently weak and powerless, loyal only to whoever signed the paychecks.

Since an Anglo elected official selected the coordinating person, most often, someone with a Spanish surname but who was patently European with Hispanic (i.e. Spanish) features got the job. They did not like to select persons with obviously indigenous features; they did not look "American" enough to be acceptable to those in government. These suddenly promoted assistants or coordinators were variously identified as Hispanic, Spanish, Spanish-speaking, and sometimes Mexican American "leaders" and the Anglo community accepted them as such. In the Chicano community, however, they were perceived as "Gringo-appointed" leaders. Only when leaders arose from the community itself, did it support them. I learned that in politics, people do not decide to run for office; they run when the public tells them to.

Finally, Finch would have to assure me that I would have plenary authority to fire and hire personnel at the agency to accomplish its mission and my vision. He reacted quickly. "You have got to be kidding. There is no way we will meet those conditions." I was dismissed abruptly and with disdain. So, I was not the popular kid, but I was relieved that I could go on with my plan to return to California.

But, wouldn't you know it! Two weeks later, again I am summoned and again offered the chairmanship. Finch added, almost parenthetically, that two conditions were acceptable, but an office in the EOB was out of the question. (Incidentally, three years later, I was able to get that office—but it was for Fernando C. De Baca from New Mexico.) I quickly rejected the offer. This reaction seemed to provide Finch a sense of comfort. He commented, "That suits me fine. We have been concerned with your civil rights attitude, so forget it."

Feelings were surfacing and the situation was becoming uncomfortable. "I did not call you; you called me," I retorted. I remained adamant. I had come to realize that White House staffers divided people into "us" and "them." The "us" were the

White House personnel, while political appointees who "go native," captured by the interests of the agencies and of the people they serve and minister to, they saw as outsiders. (That is, the agencies captured them and made them their own.) Given the nature of these relationships, I knew that to do an effective job for the president and Spanish-speaking Americans, I would have to be one of the "us." Anything short of that would diminish the stature and power of the chairmanship over time. The chairman would, after all, deal with the president's cabinet officers—and where better than in the hallways of the White House?

The counselor was dismissive once more. Whatever the future held for both of us, matters were not going to be warm or fuzzy. But I had defined the role and function of the position.

Several weeks later, while vacationing in Williamsburg, Virginia with my family, Mr. Finch again called me to the White House urgently. He insisted on meeting as soon as possible. I was puzzled. What had happened? Was he going to accept my remaining condition? I flew to DC on the next available plane, interrupting my vacation.

From the airport, I taxied directly to the West Wing gate. The Secret Service guards there were becoming very familiar with me and processed me perfunctorily and quickly. The West Wing receptionist also knew me quite well by now. Miss Shelley, who later married Pat Buchanan, was always proper and correct, without any sign of warmth. Her words and gestures were economical; she never uttered a "hi" or "how are you." She did not ask me why I was there this time, either; she just waved me on to Mr. Finch's second-floor office.

He opened the meeting directly. There was no talk about my vacation, how my family was faring alone in Williamsburg, or otherwise. He simply stated, "We have met all three conditions. Now, will you take the chairmanship?" They had me now…I was finished. Before I could respond, he thundered, "When the president personally wants you and asks you to serve, you do not refuse." At that revelation, I was elated and humbled. At any rate, I chose that moment to define my relationship with the counselor by stating clearly and slowly, "I thought *you* had selected me for the job. I had no idea the president himself wanted me to head up the agency." Then I said, humbly and simply, "I accept." Tensions evaporated.

Courtesy Richard M. Nixon Library
Dr. George Grassmuck took this photograph to celebrate my acceptance of the presidential offer.

Years later, I received a blind copy of a May 25, 1973 letter addressed to "Dear Friend and President Richard Nixon." Among other items, Roy O. Day wrote, "You will recall I recommended this man very highly to you prior to his receiving his present appointment." (4)

In the Presidential Nixon Materials Archives, I found a significant report that attests to the discovery process preceding my selection by the president. It appears that he had asked his former law partner, Tom Bewley (a practicing attorney in Whittier), to check me out. Since I do not have a copy of Bewley's report, I must assume it was done substantially prior to Dr. George Grassmuck's memo to Bob Finch dated May18, 1971. (5) Apparently, through interviews with significant community leaders in Pico Rivera and Whittier, California since 1958, Bewley heard a highly positive consensus. His interviews appeared contemporaneous with verbal reports I received from my friends in Whittier around December 1970 and January 1971. Also, in September 2000, a request under the Freedom of Information Act showed that Alex P. Butterfield had requested an FBI full field investigation on me on June 21, 1971, and that it was completed on July 7, 1971. (6)

I should clarify why I felt so uncomfortable at the prospect of working directly for Mr. Finch. I had known of his advocacy of the prior chairman and I had the impression that he felt very bad about the summary dismissal of his protégé. But more relevant was that I had been born, raised, and educated through postgraduate school in Southern California. In every year of school and in almost every classroom, I was the only Mexican American in my class. I acquired an intense and deep understanding of European Americans: their history in Europe, their arrival in this hemisphere, and their transformation into what we Mexican Americans perceived as "*Los Americanos.*" I was a Republican activist who knew philosophically and theologically why I had chosen the party at age ten; I had registered proudly at age 21 as a knowledgeable Republican and had known Mr. Finch in the Young Republican circles of Los Angeles. As president of the first Mexican American chapter of the Young Republicans of East LA, I had many opportunities to network with other Young Republicans at the monthly meetings downtown. I entertained no illusions about who these country-club Republicans were and how they looked at us Mexican Americans. And the day I took Finch's offer, I was handing over my credibility with my Chicano community and my civil rights peers for a chance to acquire, on behalf of my fellow Chicanos, some of the good life this great country affords its citizens.

With negotiations finalized and terms agreed to, we ambled across the alley to EOB to review my future office, chatting as amiably as we could. (I remember reminiscing over incidents from Young Republicans' meetings at the Biltmore Hotel in downtown LA.) He showed me the third-floor room selected for my office. It had a window with a nice view of Pennsylvania Avenue. Why, we even discussed the color it would be painted. I was so uninitiated and naïve. Little did I realize that things would not be so easy. I did not think this was merely a ploy to get my assent. But it was. I never again saw that office.

I had entered a labyrinth of Washington machinations with my eyes open and yet did not see with understanding. My life experiences had not prepared me for the tough, competitive and the jungle-like fighting commonly wrought in Washington. From age fourteen I had lived for ten years in Catholic seminaries, preparing for the priesthood. Then, except for time as a personnel specialist at Army Headquarters, I had taught at El Rancho High School in Pico Rivera, California, and then at Whittier High School.

The US Commission on Civil Rights had recruited me with a promise of GS-14 (General Schedule (GS) is a pay classification in the Federal Government) to leave California and high school teaching for a newly created position: Chief of the Mexican American Studies Division. When Bill Taylor the USCCR Director offered the position, I had no knowledge of the meaning of a *GS*. However, when my superintendent, Mr. Holloway promoted me to assistant principal in a bidding for my services with Mr. Taylor, I soon learned the meaning of a GS. After Mr. Holloway offered the job of an assistant superintendent, Bill Taylor upped the ante to a GS 14, at that point, Mr Holloway stated that was more money than what he was making. Washington had more money. Soon after, I learned that I had been a GS 1 at one time in my life-when I was drafted into the army.

I arrived in Washington in February of 1968. I had no mentor. I knew no one other than Dr. Hank Johnson, who was of Chinese extraction. He had formerly been an educator in California and now worked at the Civil Rights Commission. I had no role models. At that time, there were only a few other Mexican Americans in DC, also recent arrivals and of rank equal to mine or higher, but they were highly partisan Democrats. I was doing a solo flight into the Land of Oz without significant others on whom I could rely for guidance or advice.

Changes came. For this new job I would have a tutor to teach me on the what and hows of high voltage Washington D.C. Big Boy's Games. Bob Finch instructed me that Dr. George Grassmuck would be my West Wing contact and would perform the necessary chores for getting me nominated and confirmed. He was a knowledgeable and genial professor on leave from some midwestern university. Days after that, he became my instructor. We met many times in Lafayette Park in front of the White House as springtime neared. The trees, bushes, and landscaping were beginning to manifest their fresh beauty.

Dr. Grassmuck spent many hours over several visits advising me on the challenges ahead and especially on how to deal with them. I became quite pensive. He was a political science professor and was going over ground that was very familiar to him. I was told to get a writer to prepare three basic speeches, which I would use over and over ad nauseam. I certainly did not understand why. But I got one, and I discovered how professional politicians did it. Later, I rarely used any of those three basic speeches. They seemed like something old, dusty, and discarded. I was very comfortable with my own speeches, since public speaking was my forte. I enjoyed speaking directly and with active and engaging eye contact. I knew where I wanted the Chicano civil rights struggle to go and how to get there.

The month of May would soon be on our schedules. I was now committed to a new job; yet, my current one at the Commission was still vibrant and demanding. We were putting finishing touches to manuscripts, tables, graphs, observations, conclusions, and recommendations in various reports.

And thus began a time in my life most difficult to characterize. My staff, the National Civil Rights Advisory Committee, and my colleagues at the Commission began to view me as "a Republican." This was in a place seething with liberals, Marxists, socialists, and highly partisan Democrats. The most common wall decorations were huge pictures of bearded ones (Che Guevara or Fidelito). I was probably the only Republican at the Commission. Prior to my engagement with the White House, I was perceived as a professional educator, sans any politics. But personal relationships were beginning to change. An air of hostility was arising. I was joining the enemy, the "intruders." And with respect to my possible and probable place of new employment, I had come to know three persons in the West Wing. Two White House personnel had taken me on lunch interviews. Dr. Grassmuck was my teacher, who continued to prepare me on what to expect and when. My trips to the West Wing became frequent and commonplace. Most White House guards knew me by my first name.

I had no authority to interface with the staff at the Cabinet Committee. In fact, some of them continued to lobby senators against me with the charge that I was a liberal, irresponsible, and a radical civil rights advocate. Their reports that I liked Chivas Regal a lot was, in my simple estimation, going a bit too far. They had hoped to derail my confirmation—even my nomination. Since one of the three conditions for my accepting the position was that the White House would allow me to back up my nomination with thousands of letters of support, I set up a campaign staffed with people with access to long distance phone lines. These informal campaigners reached out to leaders nationwide. Their diligent work produced thousands of letters, phone calls, visits, and telegrams of support. They flooded Bob Finch's office. After several months, he called me and said in a deeply exasperated voice, "Turn off the spigot. We got the message."

Time was ticking. I heard nothing and knew less. The silence caused questioning. Did they at the White House change their mind? Was I no longer the chosen one? I was in no position to call the counselor to ask: "*Hey, pinche huey, que pasa?*" And the other option of a possible job in California was obsolete. The applications for superintendents had become totally quiescent, fit only for "file number thirteen."

It was not until a year later that I discovered via memos the names of those in the White House most involved in Hispanic issues. I learned that they too were just getting organized to tackle affairs of Mexican Americans. The staffers were deciding on when to restart the engines of the Cabinet Committee. The counselor had staffed White House Personnel with his former top staffers at HEW. Frederic Malek was in charge, assisted by William Marumoto, Barbara Franklin, Al Kaupinen, and Stan Anderson. William Marumoto eventually became a key leader on Hispanic matters. He was born in Santa Ana, California, and Spanish was his second language after Japanese, the language of his parents. They had operated a small grocery store in the Mexican barrio; Orange County public schools were segregated then. In the innocence of childhood, Bill went to school with his Chicano neighbors and became a Chicano in spirit.

Sometime in late 1970, Finch took charge of all matters in the White House regarding Mexican Americans and other Spanish-speaking people. Before him, no one had been assigned clear and direct responsibility for Hispanic affairs. And, by the way, no one had volunteered. Some memos showed that tentative plans had been drafted for elimination of the Cabinet Committee prior to Mr. Finch's arrival. Buck passing had been the norm. That situation was understandable. No one at the White House but the president, his counselor, and "Bill" Marumoto knew anything about us Mexicans. Over the years, I came to know just how deeply and profoundly President Richard M. Nixon and Robert Finch knew us from their California days, starting in the early 1950s.

Mr. Leonard Garment, a New York lawyer from the firm of Mitchell and Nixon, was in charge of civil rights. However, he was concerned with Black civil rights matters only. He never evidenced any interest in the Chicano civil rights movement. He was a Jewish American with roots in New York and Europe.

The memos I read in the Nixon Archives further disclosed that my study, "An Overview of Spanish Speaking Affairs for White House Perspective," prepared for Mr. Finch in February 1971, kicked off a flurry of meetings and actions in the White House. They could be characterized as "let's do something about this, and do it immediately" memos. The memos and meeting minutes also showed that new players were getting into the arena. Questions had to be answered. Actions had to be taken.

The White House now had a preliminary plan for the inclusion of Mexican Americans, Puerto Ricans, Cubans, and other Latin Americans. Most important, they had studied the enabling legislation of Public Law 91-181, and now it was implementation time. A great deal of planning had to be staffed out. It was similar to getting ready to stage the initial performance of a drama on Broadway. The production staff knew I was not "need to know," and so I was kept in the dark. The White House disliked leaks.

The president was enforcing the law of the Cabinet Committee which called for his convening a meeting with the Cabinet to discuss how they were going to assure that federal programs reached all Mexican Americans, Puerto Rican Americans, Cuban Americans, and all other Spanish-speaking and Spanish-surnamed Americans. This would be a first: the Hispanics had arrived. The president was to appoint an advisory committee whose selection would be a very sensitive activity. These advisors to the chairman, and the chairman himself, would be sworn in, right in the Oval Office with the president. The White House press corps would have a session with the newly minted chairman, accompanied by his direct boss, Counselor Robert Finch. The new chairman would then retire to the current office of the Cabinet Committee at 1800 G Street to greet the members of his Presidential Advisory Committee. The advisors would introduce themselves for the first time in a business setting. Only the White House staff knew who they were and why they had been selected. I learned that the White House had chosen four Mexican Americans (one each from Texas, New Mexico, Arizona, and California), three Puerto Rican Americans (from New York, New Jersey and Puerto Rico), and two Cuban Americans (one from Washington, DC and the other from Florida). The environment of secrecy still bothers me. Why couldn't I, the central figure in the unfolding drama, be advised, included—anything?

Near the end of July, Dr. Grassmuck called me for a meeting. I sensed that I was beginning to fit into something yet unrevealed. The meeting had a matter-of-fact atmosphere about it. He was going to prepare me, he announced, "for an interview with the president in the Oval Office on August 5, 1971." Then I was invited to sit at a desk with a typewriter in an adjoining office. Dr. Grassmuck gave me the mundane instructions: "Write a complete script for the meeting with the president."

Incredulous, I asked, "A script?"

"Yes," he responded and added: "the script should begin with words such as, good morning, Mr. President to which he responds, 'it is a pleasure to meet you,'" and so on. The meeting, he advised, would consume but a few minutes, so the script should be rather brief.

This activity struck me as absolutely preposterous. After my tutor deflected my queries as to what this was all about, he simply reiterated the instructions: "Prepare a complete script of maybe several minutes duration, to contain a dialogue between the president and you." Then he departed. I ruminated as I typed, *Is this what dramatists do for a living?* He said. I said. Then he replied, to which I assented, etc. It became a little game but earnestly serious. I finished a one-pager. After handing it over, I was told that I would be briefed on the meeting. Sadly, I never was. I was never consulted on the program. I was never told anything, other than to show up on the appointed day and time. It was weird.

To this day, I still do not fully understand why such a brittle and artificial conversation would have to be scripted out. Years

later, during Watergate, I concluded that the voice-activated tap-
ing device had to be the reason.

I carried my copy of "the stupid script" to the interview. The
president had his copy and, thank God, he forthwith threw it
into the trash.

August 5, 1971: In the Oval
Office, President Richard
M. Nixon faced me directly
and asserted: "We gringos
have built an invisible wall of
discrimination against you
Mexicans, and you and I are
going to knock it down!

CHAPTER TWO

NIXON CONVENES FIRST CABINET MEETING ON MEXICAN AMERICAN AFFAIRS

During his 1968 presidential campaign, candidate Richard M. Nixon had made these promises on September 8 to a Mexican American audience:

It is clear that Mexican Americans have many special problems that need special attention and sympathetic study. A White House Conference to review these problems and to submit recommendations for effective and prompt action is long overdue. I shall convene such a conference shortly after taking office in January.

And on September 16, he promised:

I intend to bring to the White House Mexican American leaders from throughout the country to discuss matters of bilingual education, jobs, housing, working conditions, programs to help the disadvantaged start their own businesses and the many other problems that confront them.

Both promises were presented in a February 5, 1971 White House memo entitled : "White House Conference on Spanish Speaking Americans" and had declared the intention of convening a White House conference on Mexican American affairs. Clearly, after three years in office, Nixon had not fulfilled them. What had happened? Interviews revealed that President Nixon, within weeks of taking office, had promptly appointed Mr. Martin Castillo to be in charge of Mexican American affairs and presumably to execute on the promises. (1)

HMR Personal File
Martin Castillo, first Chairman, and Dr. Henry M. Ramirez, Chairman
(Mr. Castillo inscribed on the face of the photo warm but
now illegible words. Some ink markings disappear.)

But before the promises could be resolved, the first priority Mr. Castillo faced was to save the Interagency Committee on Mexican American Affairs. The committee's authority to function was about

to expire. President Johnson had created it through a "memorandum of understanding" (2) in the last days of his Administration to
pander to the increasingly militant voices of Mexican Americans. He
appointed David North, a political operative from the Democratic
National Committee, to run it. The memo giving life to this committee was good for only a short period.

Mr. Castillo hastened to salvage the committee. He went one better. He got a newly elected congressman (George H. W. Bush) and
another congressman who had been born and raised in his hometown of Belen, New Mexico (Edward Roybal) to push congressional
legislation through to establish a new committee. Chairman Castillo
acquired Senate-side assistance from Senator Joseph Montoya,
another compatriot from New Mexico. Chairman Castillo and
Senator Montoya got along famously; they were both Democrats.
They relished being referred to as "hermanitos"—brothers—from
New Mexico (but both enjoyed the social whirl of Washington). (3)

Congress passed the law over the fierce opposition of a
Mexican American congressman from San Antonio, Henry B.
Gonzalez (aka Henry B.). Congressman Edward Roybal, who
now lived in LA, was to confide in me the continued negative
actions of "Henry B." during my tenure. (4)

President Richard M. Nixon signed the Act of Congress into public
law on December 31, 1969. His signature established an agency called
the Cabinet Committee on Opportunities for the Spanish Speaking
People. This agency replaced the committee president Johnson organized for assisting the Mexican Americans. As of this date, Mexican
Americans were no longer the sole group of Hispanics to acquire
attention. The mainland Puerto Ricans (as distinguished from those
on the island of Puerto Rico), the Cubans, and others were lumped

together as Spanish-speakers. As far as President Nixon, Counselor Bob Finch, and I were concerned, our attention was still focused on the Mexican Americans at this time. Mainland Puerto Ricans were soon—very soon—to make their civil rights struggle publicly known.

In my Study on Perspectives presented to Bob Finch, I had recommended that the promised White House conference on Hispanic issues be replaced by high-level meetings at regional federal offices close to high-density Hispanic areas: Chicago, New York, Los Angeles, and so on. And so it was done.

A new reality had settled in. This was no longer about just the Mexican Americans. The new name of the Cabinet Committee and the proportional diversity in the Advisory Committee reflected the change. New antagonisms however, would arise later as the vying for power and position grew.

Commencing with the arrival of Counselor Finch with his staffers from Health, Education, and Welfare (HEW) at the White House in 1970, neglect of affairs of the Hispanics became a thing of the past.

President Nixon finally had his ducks in a row. He was now getting the right people to lead the charge for the Spanish speaking, something he had yearned to accomplish since day one of his presidency. In the latter part of 1970, Mr. Finch gathered a database of information on the status of efforts and programs in the federal government supporting the Spanish-speaking. He was in charge.

August 5, 1971, had arrived. The staffers had choreographed the drama of the day for optimal impact. And of course, only they knew the contents of the day's program. The only part of it made known to me was that I was going to be interviewed and be appointed chairman by the president. I was in for a big surprise.

From my office on 14th and I Streets, it was only a short walk to the West Wing to meet my family and all the "others" of that day, starting with people I had known years before. In addition to my family the "others" were standing around in the small reception office in the West Wing. As the "others" said hi, they startled and dumbfounded me with news: they were to be my Cabinet Committee Advisors and would be appointed by the president that morning! After this amazing revelation, more was yet to be unveiled: I was to see Bob Finch and his White House staff, the President's Cabinet Officers, and the White House press corps. I knew I was to meet the president. I had an appointment. Dr. Grassmuck had arranged that. The rest of the agenda had not been disclosed to me!

The Ramirez family had prepared in their Sunday best at our home in Bethesda, Maryland. They had driven to DC, arrived at the South Entrance, and parked between the EOB and the White House. My wife, Ester Gomez de Ramirez and our four kids—Mike, fourteen; Carol Ann, thirteen; Christine, eight; and Camille, seven—entered the West Wing and were engaged with introductions.

Counselor Robert Finch was our master of ceremonies. He, ably assisted by aides, was personally in charge of every detail of this historic day. The counselor escorted us, me and the advisors, to the Oval Office, sans my family. The president greeted us as we were introduced. The White House press photographers were allowed in to photograph us with the president as a group. The president himself swore us all into our new offices.

The atmosphere in the country at that time, and especially in Washington, was defined by the continuing Vietnam War. The president was under heavy pressure from his critics on the Left and on the emerging Right. He nonetheless relished this moment; this day, he would focus his full attention on the civil rights struggle of the Mexican Americans.

Mr. Finch then escorted the nine to an initial meeting with the cabinet officers in the Cabinet meeting room. I remained in the Oval Office, alone with the president. His desk was devoid of clutter. He asked me to pull my chair up close next to his desk. I felt warmly welcomed. I quickly formed a first impression: the president appeared physically trim in his dark suit, and strong, with a vibrant voice and focused, penetrating eyes. He spoke without any notes, without hesitation, and with a strong sense of confidence in his knowledge. I was very surprised at his profound experiential knowledge of Mexican American issues and personalities.

Courtesy Richard M. Nixon Library

From left to right, the just-appointed members of the Advisory Committee to the Chairman of CCOSSP were: Jorge Tristani,

Edgar Buttari, Manuel Gonzalez, Manuel Giberga, Hilda Hidalgo; and to the right of President Richard M. Nixon: Dr. Henry M. Ramirez, Ted Martinez, Ed Yturria, Eugene Marin, Ignacio Lozano

He opened with a lengthy monologue on the state of affairs for Mexican Americans. He outlined his experience with and knowledge about our civil rights struggles. He recalled his contacts with the famous Leo Carillo; with Judge Gerardo and Judge Velarde of the Whittier courts; with Danny Villanueva, the former LA Rams football player. He reminisced about the days when Mexicans were integrated into the Whittier schools. He mentioned the Mexican barrios "Jim Town," "Canta Ranas," and "Murphy Ranch." He recalled his experiences picking oranges, lighting "smudge pots" in freezing weather, and how he had come to know the people firsthand and prize their value systems, hard work, closely knit families, and their Catholic religion.

Years later in order to write this section with insights on how President Nixon had come to possess such closeness to us, I interviewed the president's brother, Eddie, several times in person and over the phone. I read his book, *The Nixons: A Family Portrait*. It was then I realized just how close he and his family really had been to the Mexican barrios. After their father failed in the citrus business in Yorba Linda, the Nixon family established a small grocery store with a gas station in front near the intersection of Santa Gertrudes and Whittier Boulevard in the unincorporated part of Los Angeles County, almost adjacent to the Orange County line. Their business catered to the nearby ranches, where Mexican families resided and worked. He picked oranges and field crops with them and attended schools in Whittier with a few. Grandchildren of Mexicans who knew the Richard Nixon who worked in the store and who remember stories of him granting credit to poor Mexicans, are still living in the Whittier area. (He is also the only US president born and raised in California—and with Mexicans!)

I am quite familiar with that area. In 1958, my wife and I purchased acreage for a new home that had been part of the Leffingwell Ranch at the intersection of Santa Gertrudes and Leffingwell Boulevard. The entire area from Murphy Ranch became the upscale "East Whittier."

As he continued his monologue, he lamented that Mexicans do not lobby for their rights. He made the usual references to the effectiveness of Blacks in this area. The crucial importance he attached to this activity quite surprised me and caught me unprepared to react or think about it. He encouraged me to make the point a priority at the Cabinet Committee and added, "They should raise as much hell as they can." At that, I went through mental gyrations. Surely he meant lobbying by the community, not by me in my role and function as a high-level presidential appointee, soon to be confirmed by the Senate.

I was beginning to sense he was not going to engage in a discussion. He was going to be the commander-in-chief. "I have assigned Bob Finch the job of riding herd on Mexican American matters in this administration," he said. "The Cabinet Committee is now Bob's responsibility." He then listed the activities the Cabinet Committee would pursue: jobs, discrimination, bilingual education, government appointments, administration of justice, and lobbying. He wanted progress reports and reports to Congress on Committee actions. He pledged full staff support and comprehensive cooperation from the cabinet.

He did not mention any other Hispanic group during our Oval Office meeting. He noted that his orientation to the needs of the Mexican Americans was derived from his California experiences and interaction with them from his early years in Yorba Linda to later times in Whittier. He and his wife, Pat, had attended Whittier High School, and he added that "in fact, it was where you also taught." Also, he noted that Pat had taught business courses there. He gave a general sense of the Mexican kids he had known at school from the barrios of "Jim Town" in West Whittier, Murphy Ranch, and "Canta Ranas" in Los Nietos. He even included "Pico Viejo."

I wondered, as he reviewed his salient contacts with the Mexican community, just how few people there were in my life who could match his personal knowledge and experience of those in my community. I knew he and Pat had honeymooned in Acapulco, Mexico. Few Southern California Anglo couples did that in those days.

He then delved into the area of discrimination. In his years as a poor, young white in Yorba Linda, he picked tomatoes, cucumbers, and oranges alongside the Mexicans. He spoke specifically of his experiences in picking oranges at a place called Murphy Ranch in East Whittier, the only large citrus ranch there. It held a Mexican colony with a company store in its midst. I knew the place very well. I was amazed to hear him reveal his work with the Mexicans from Murphy Ranch. I knew of few Anglos who had done that type of low-level, dirty, nasty labor. His discussion reflected deep awareness of the discrimination Mexican Americans endured.

Following these comments, he sat back, looked at the ceiling, placed his fingers around his jaws, and waxed eloquent: "We in the Southwest have built an invisible wall of discrimination and have kept the Mexicans away from the opportunities this great country has to offer. It is similar to the "Great Wall of China." In his monologue, he continued to compare the "a Southwest Wall of Discrimination" with the Great Wall of China. As he ended on this topic, he thundered: "It will be our job to knock down that wall of discrimination." China was also, it appeared in retrospect, very much on his mind for soon after that day, the Presidential Visit to China was announced.

It is noteworthy to recall at this time that the president's scheduler, Stephen B. Bull, kept coming into the Oval Office to remind him that he was falling far behind, that the Cabinet Officers had been waiting for quite some time (as was some ambassador as well). Dr. Grassmuck had prepared me to spend only a few pro forma minutes with the president, but we had spent what seemed almost twenty minutes—and more were yet to come.

He was enjoying our meeting. He seemed to visibly kick back, neglecting his schedule. He got into ruminating about his past campaigns in California and on how the Mexican Americans participated. In the course of reviewing names and events, he repeated a question Republicans often hear. Why are Mexican Americans Democrats? They are not liberals; they are conservative in lifestyle. He added: "I do not understand."

A year later, in 1972, then-governor Ronald Reagan spent a lot of time on the same topic during my visit to his Sacramento office. He mentioned many Spanish-surnamed Americans who fitted that mold perfectly. He spoke admiringly of Senator Ruben Ayala from San Bernardino. Governor Reagan got to know Ruben at close range and remarked, "I just do not know why Ruben is a Democrat." I tried to explain but am sure he did not follow my rationale. Reagan was a Midwesterner from a small town, and his traditions and knowledge were based on his European background. While living in California, he came into some and very limited contact with Mexican Americans, but he and they lived in two separate worlds. They knew of each other but did not know each other.

The president lurched into another topic, which he opened in an offhanded way, that made it appear that he attached only incidental interest. He lamented that all he could gather from Mexicans was 5 percent of their vote. Then he moved his chair closer and in a stronger voice rephrased the statement. This time, it sounded important to him. He repeated, "Five percent. That is all I get. I do not understand why such a low number. It is not for lack of effort. I have participated in Sixteenth of September East LA parades, ridden on horses for Cinco de Mayo parades, worn sombreros and sarapes, attended fiestas eating tacos, enchiladas, and tamales. This time, I want fifteen percent of the Mexican vote. I want to do a good job on civil rights for the Mexican Americans. I want to help you do a good job, so that we can get to that goal." He asked me what I thought about that and if I thought the target of 15 percent was feasible.

I, in my eagerness to impress and please, assured him that we could achieve it. And, lest I appear too effusive, I modestly suggested the goal should not be 15 but 25 percent! Mexican Americans are basically conservative and are responsive to those who reach out to them with respect and understanding. They would indeed respond to presidential initiatives and efforts that were authentically substantial and transformative.

He smiled and gave forth a hearty belly laugh. He sat back on his large, comfortable black leather executive chair, twirled around, and pulled forward close to me. He pontificated, "You are a Latin teacher with no political experience, and you tell me 'twenty-five percent!' You do not know what you are talking about. I am the politician. How will we get twenty-five?"

At that, I reached into my shirt pocket, withdrew a neat, crisp three-by-five card, and gave it to him. He read it intently. Typed on it were five sentences that represented my vision for the new job:

1. Appoint one hundred Hispanics to supergrade positions.

2. Count Spanish-surnamed Americans by employment and contract/grant participation.

3. Adopt and enforce a systematic program to assure federal employment of Spanish-surnamed Americans.

4. Hold high-level government meetings at federal regional centers to promote these goals at the local level.

5. Include us in White House activities to create a national awareness of the conditions of Mexican Americans.

(I wish I had made a copy of that card the morning before departing from my office. I never got it back, so I have to paraphrase.)

I proudly reiterated that the president would get 25 percent of the Mexican American vote if he were to get these goals implemented and enforced. "Good service has its own reward," I recall stating with a great deal of conviction. I knew that Mexican Americans would be responsive to the achievement of these goals and find the president most *"simpatico."* I could tell he liked that word.

He examined the card again and pushed a button. Someone came into the Oval Office. The president handed him the card with the order "Give this to [so-and-so]." (I never got the name.) "Have him read it, tell him I want those things done." He remarked to the functionary that I had said we would get "twenty-five percent of the Mexican American vote if we take these actions," and added with some nice navy-style words (he was wont to use them in our interview and also in a later Cabinet meeting), "Well, doggone it,"—and so on—"we are going to do them."

History shows that President Nixon received over 30 percent of the Mexican American vote in the next election! The Committee to Re-elect the President gathered voluminous reports describing how Mexican Americans voted in November 1972. One of them was an exit poll done in the Boyle Heights area of East Los Angeles, and another was done in San Antonio. I have not been able to garner copies of these reports (although I did have some once), but I did read them. Among the many newspaper articles that floated about, I was able to retain one by Tony Castro from the November 13, 1972 *Washington Post:* "According to a CBS analysis, President Nixon received 49 percent of the Spanish- Speaking vote in Texas and Florida and 31 percent of the Spanish-Speaking vote nationally." (5)

The president acknowledged my work on his behalf pursuant to our discussions and planning, which continued through 1971 and culminated in victory in November 1972.

THE WHITE HOUSE

WASHINGTON

February 1, 1973

Dear Mr. Ramirez:

As I look back to the results of November 7, I want you to know how deeply grateful I am for all that you did to help us win one of the greatest landslide victories in American political history.

Only with your help were we able to get our message across to the millions of voters who supported us.

I can assure you that over the next four years I shall do everything I possibly can to make a record which all Americans, regardless of party, will be proud of as we celebrate America's 200th Birthday in 1976.

With appreciation and best wishes,

Sincerely,

Richard Nixon

Honorable Henry M. Ramirez
10525 Farnham Drive
Bethesda, Maryland 20014

Then he got quite close and whispered that it would be almost impossible for me to inform him of progress toward these goals because of the system of "palace guards." He advised me to use the avenue of his personal valet, Manolo Sanchez. Through Mr. Sanchez, I would be able to get information to him on how we were doing. "You know Manolo?"

"Yes", I affirmed.

"Well, then, get to him, tell him what you want me to know!"

I write here from contemporary notes, my memory refreshed by tapings acquired from The Cutting Corporation (at 4940 Hampden Lane, Bethesda, Maryland, 20614. Unfortunately, some-one deleted from the tapes conversations the president and I held. The deleted discussions were on these topics:

- The discrimination imposed by the Gringos on the Mexicans and how he and I were going to tear down that invisible wall.
- The discussion surrounding the 5 percent Mexican vote and how I could get not the 15 percent he wished for but the 25 percent I promised.
- My discussion of how our studies at the Civil Rights Commission had proven that the SES (social economic status) of parents were both cause and effect of students' good grades.
- How I was to get around his palace guard via his valet.

(The latter may have been in the tapes, but the audio is so bad, it is hard to understand.)

After that momentous (and for me, emotional) exchange, he led me into the Cabinet Room for the first meeting of the CCOSSP. He personally saw to it that I was seated to his right.

Courtesy Richard M. Nixon Library

Photograph of First Cabinet Meeting of CCOSSP

Clockwise, from left to right:

Secretary of HUD, George Romney; Secretary of Agriculture, Clifford N. Hardin; Assistant Secretary of the Treasury, Charls Walker; Counselor to the President, Robert H. Finch; Vice Chairman of the Committee and Attorney General, John Mitchell; (seated to the left were members of the Advisory Council to CCOSSP; visible are Edgar Buttari and Ted Martinez); Secretary of Labor, James D. Hodgson; Chairman of the Civil Service Commission, Robert Hampton; Director of the Office of Economic Opportunity, Phillip V. Sanchez; Special Assistant to the President, Fred Malek; Undersecretary of HEW, John Veneman; Patricia Reilly Hitt, Assistant Secretary of HEW; Chairman of CCOSSP, Dr. Henry M. Ramirez; President Richard M. Nixon; Executive Director of CCOSSP, Antonio Rodriguez; Administrator of the Small Business Administration, Thomas Kleppe; Special Assistant to the Chairman of Equal Employment Opportunity Commission, John Oldecker; Intern, Louie Cespedes; (seated by windows) Fernando E. C. de Baca, Director of Spanish Speaking Programs, Civil Service Commission; and George Grassmuck, Office of Counselor Finch.

Counselor Robert Finch opened the first-ever meeting of the Cabinet Committee on Opportunities of the Spanish Speaking People on this day of August 5, 1971.

The president asked Counselor Finch to say a few words regarding the organization and progress of the Cabinet Committee for the benefit of the members present. Finch thanked the departments for their reports on the status of their respective outreach to Spanish-speaking people. He said that the name of the game was to upgrade federal activity for the Spanish-speaking in all areas.

Then the president addressed the committee. His tone was very serious, unlike his relaxed composure just minutes before in the Oval Office: The minutes of this Cabinet Meeting are presented in the Appendix C.

I have said before around this very Cabinet table—that there has not been enough follow-through in our efforts for Spanish-speaking Americans. There has not been enough pressure from the media, from Congress, and from within Spanish-speaking communities themselves compared to the pressures exerted by other minority groups. In government, only those groups that raise hell and threaten, "You either do something or we will blow the place up", get any attention. This has been particularly true during the 60s and the early 70s. Let me be very candid about this. I am not suggesting that any group that has not had an equal chance should be disorderly. We do not suggest that individuals under any circumstances roll over and be nice guys and not complain. The political reality is that whether dealing with Congress or federal agencies, we should make an all-out effort to rectify our record.

The president then turned to me and commented that we had both started out at the bottom in the Whittier area. He reminisced about his days working in the California orchards, and he and I traded quips on who was the best orange picker. I said that I had picked a hundred boxes of oranges per day. The president said, "You can't afford to be in government!" Everyone laughed.

Now the president became quite serious, and his mood permeated the room as he continued:

What has happened here is this: Mexican Americans, Puerto Ricans, etc., are an important factor in our total economic output, and considering what they can do, they are not getting their fair shake with regard to other groups.

This is going to change. It can only change if the members of the Cabinet get off their duffs. I don't want this administration to be one that only responds to those that only tear up the place and pound fists. It just happens that in recent times we have had some very disturbing experiences in Los Angeles and other places.

I am speaking now to the Mexican American community; for when I lived in Whittier, I had very close ties with this group. They were family oriented, law abiding people. Although they did need attention, the wheel was not squeaking much. This has to change. We owe it to all groups in society to see they get an equal chance, especially those who have been law abiding people.

You have not had an effective lobby. I told Henry that you need a lobby. You should have it, but we should not wait until a lobby is set up. In terms of jobs, we must urge agencies to fill their slots with Spanish speaking people. We have to search for openings—we should go out and find good slots and fill them. We must find the applicants—they don't apply because they think it is hopeless.

The thing I want to get across to those who are non-government is that I urge all minority groups—women, blacks, Mexican Americans—to use your capabilities and improve them. We aren't providing opportunities just as a favor to you. We must keep

America competitive. We are pricing ourselves out of the world markets. Twenty-five years ago we were first in everything—today the world is totally changed. Our former enemies are now our major competitors in the free market. The players are new—Western Europe, Japan, China, the Soviet Union, and potentially Latin America and Africa.

Twenty-five years from now, whoever is sitting in this chair will be representing the second or third stronger country unless we develop all our resources. We must develop our human resources. I would like for every American in this country, whatever his background, to have an equal opportunity to develop to the fullest of his capacity. We cannot afford to have any group in this country not have an equal opportunity to develop their capabilities. The government must assume this responsibility-private business does not move as fast in developing opportunities. We must provide opportunities not presently available where there is a great need for new talent.

The Mexican American does not have that chance now. That is going to change or the people in the personnel offices in every department are going to change.

At this point in the meeting, the president became agitated and enraged at the Civil Service Commission's lack of progress in promoting and fostering the employment of Mexican Americans. He pointed out in detail how he had ordered the Commission to adopt the Sixteen-Point Program. He had been informed that the Program was on schedule, but he had been truly flabbergasted to learn that absolutely nothing had been accomplished. He raised his voice and pointed at Robert Hampton, Chairman of the Civil Service Commission, who was seated at the far end of the huge oval desk. The president read him the riot act and warned him that if the Sixteen-Point Program was not adopted forthwith, he, the president, would have to replace Hampton. Needless to say, some action took place soon after.

The president then concluded:

Don't wait until the wheel squeaks—or something is blown up in Los Angeles. Provide opportunity until there is not one scintilla of suggestion that we are not only not discriminatory but are making positive moves to rectify the situation. Everyone has a better chance in this country to get an equal break. In government, we have an ever greater opportunity.

I want Bob to follow up, and Henry too. It is the only way to work in the future. I want quarterly reports from both of you concerning the progress of each agency—and also their failures.

And the president left the room.

For people used to the strong leadership of President Nixon, these were tough words but not unusual. He had always been precise and direct in dealing with his inner staff members and advisors. This event showed that President Nixon had a deep and real concern for the problems and progress of Mexican Americans. No one can suggest that he was playing to the public or the press on that day, because there were none. The meeting was private, and there is no need for histrionics when one speaks to confidential aides and advisors. Charm belongs in the reception line. In the Cabinet Room, you tell it like it is.

Immediately after the meeting, Counselor Finch escorted me to another room. The cameras began to whirl and blink. We were on stage, facing the White House press corps! Counselor Finch did the introductions, explained what had happened that morning, and opened the briefing for questions. For this unexpected activity, I was also unprepared and uninformed. I wanted to make the sign of the cross but chose to say a little prayer and whispered to myself, "Here we go!"

The first question came in a raspy and querulous voice. Sarah McClendon of the *El Paso Times*, of great fame in media circles, asked: "Dr. Ramirez, how can you reconcile your work at the US Commission on Civil Rights on desegregation with your involvement with this administration, which is so opposed to busing for integration?" Thoughts of students being bused to the Kiwanis Club in Whittier, or the over forty miles from Zaragosa, Texas, to Pecos, quickly surfaced. Since her question had been shot out to embarrass the administration, I mentally selected the word "busing" for my response.

As I gathered my thoughts on the topic, Mr. Finch nervously tried to take over and answer as he moved to center stage, scratching his left earlobe (his mannerism when he was upset or uncomfortable). But Mrs. McClendon insisted on my answer, so I stepped forward. I noted that as an educator for over eleven years at Whittier, I had seen students who lived far from school bused for field trips to debates at the Lions and Kiwanis Clubs. I implied that the concept of "busing" carried no opprobrium in and of itself. This wasn't enough for her. She insisted that I discuss busing for the purpose of integration, so I did.

I referred to the study on Mexican Americans I had just done at the Commission, wherein I had discovered that in the geographic area served by the *El Paso Times* (which, I noted, was her employer), the Anglo students from the town of Pecos were bused forty-five miles to the "new" schools of Zaragoza, Texas, while the Chicano students of Zaragoza were bused to the "poor" schools in Pecos. I said that apparently, all of the "powers that were" in that area had been happy with that kind of "busing," since the *El Paso Times* had never bothered to expose or object to the injustice and its obvious discrimination and segregation. And, for that matter, the *El Paso Times*, which serves a predominantly Chicano town, usually did not carry stories on weddings of Chicanos in their society section. I added vehemently that this was the type of discrimination this administration was going to war against.

At that, Mr. Finch scratched even harder. He finally elbowed me offstage and ended the press briefing then and there. The press corps itself did not file a single story on my first White House press conference, but the happenings of August 5, 1971, received extensive national and international newspaper coverage. We have no documentation of TV or radio coverage.

That day, I exited the West Wing to join my wife and children, who slowly made their way toward the car between the Old Executive Building (EOB) and the West Wing. On his way from the EOB to the West Wing, the president noticed them and broke off from the group he was with. He greeted my family very warmly, especially the children. He apologized for running late and complimented our little daughters on their beautiful dresses. Of course, everyone was thrilled that he would take the time for such a considerate gesture. My family was involved in the day's hectic events, much to their delight.

PART II:

WHAT NIXON GOT DONE

> Now it
> came to pass in those days
> that a decree went forth
> from Caesar Augustus
> that a census of the whole
> world should be taken.
> —*Luke 2:1–2*

CHAPTER THREE

NIXON ORDERS CENSUS BUREAU IN 1970: "COUNT THE MEXICAN AMERICANS"

In the Bible, the Romans conducted their census in the "year 0." Such an initiative exemplifies the essence of government: the Romans were known for efficiency and organizational skill. In their language, Latin, *census* meant "tax." Their census produced income. The physical vastness of the Roman Empire required immense resources.

Likewise, a census was performed during the formative years of the thirteen colonies. The organizers of the post revolutionary government had to pay off war debts. In 1790, federal marshals traveled the highways and byways on horseback to count human beings and their assessable resources.

Counting human beings was easy. Their "values" were determined by skin color. Each European White person was counted as "one;" each Negro as three-fifths of one, and each Original

American as zero. The theology of the European leaders of the Protestant Church had not yet defined them as human beings possessing souls. The Latin for the word for "black" is *niger* or *negro*. In the 1600s, Latin was still a second language for most educated Europeans; it was still read, written, and spoken. John Locke got his ideas for democracy from writings in Latin. As the European settlers expanded westward, they continued to take a census every ten years, visually enumerating Blacks and the Europeans. In 1848, a treaty added an ethnic group to the population: Mexicans. This recently conquered ethnic group, however, was not counted until the 1930 Census.

In 1846, President James K. Polk, had ordered the invasion of Mexico. One of his prime campaign promises had been to do this to get more slave land. (1) And so, he waged war on the States' defenseless southern neighbor. Mexico had had no standing army and had not attacked neighbors for three hundred years. (2)

As European settlers from Northern Europe had named the British colonies in North America "New England," so also the Spanish Europeans assigned the name "Nueva España" to the land from Oregon to Costa Rica centuries before. Nueva España had relied militarily for military protector on the Spanish Crown. And, just as the colonies had transformed themselves by means of revolution into an independent nation, the United States of America, so also did Nueva España transform itself into a new nation through revolution in Mexico in 1823, born through the Treaty of Cordoba. But unlike the United States, Nueva España remained militarily unarmed; it was weak, disorganized, and defenseless.

President Polk exercised European behavioral tradition and took half of the Mexican territory. He and his cohorts invoked a mythological Providence to justify their aggressive "Manifest Destiny." History reflects that President Polk used dictatorial methods to get his way and to start an unjust, unprovoked war with the Mexicans. He conspired with a certain Lieutenant Gillespie and other military personnel in Texas, New Mexico, California, and Mexico City, planning for military actions and initiatives prior to giving Congress any information on what he was doing. (3)

Mr. Polk owned more than a hundred slaves and increased the land available for America's slave owners. He was a protégé of Andrew Jackson, also a slave owner and a son of illiterate Scotch-Irish peasant immigrants. While president, Jackson continued the practice of the early European illegal immigrants: he seized land (including what is now Florida) by killing the original inhabitants or chasing them away.

The unjustified war of land grabs ended in 1848. The colonies now stretched from sea to shining sea; Nevada, California, Arizona, Colorado, part of Utah, New Mexico, and Texas had been added. And the US Marines could belligerently and victoriously sing "From the Halls of Montezuma."

Mexicans born south of the new border were counted as belonging to the Mexican race. The Mexican American children born in the new part of the United States but of parents who themselves were born south of the newly defined border were also counted as of the Mexican race. The 1930 census (4) counted 1,422,533 of the Mexican race. The census questionnaire[iv] asked for residents' specific addresses and identification. The information gathered provided a most useful map on where Mexicans lived and thus facilitated the collection and deportation of Mexicans and Mexican American children to the "realigned" Mexico during the Great Depression: those in charge of the expulsion knew exactly where Mexicans lived and how many there were.

The Mexican government, however, objected to the use of "Mexican race" as a designation. It wanted its former citizens to be defined as members of the White race. This fact causes me to chuckle—after all, the ruling class in Mexico was descendants of illiterate European peasant conquistadores looking to gain land and riches. Evidently, they had overlooked the fact that almost all other citizens of Mexico were either Indian Mexican or Mestizo Mexican (a mixture of Indian and European). In the 1930s, the ruling, literate, and landed class there were of *sangre pura*—pure blood—and they knew it. Marriage certificates were required to identify the blood purity of each party to a conjugal contract: *sangre mesclada* (mixed blood) or *sangre pura*. Hence, the European Mexicans knew that they themselves were of the White race, even several centuries after *la Conquista*.

After that, the US Census included persons of Mexican birth or ancestry in the racial definition for White. Mexican Americans were counted in the White category, not separately. As a result, we became the "forgotten Americans," the "forgotten people," and the "invisible minority." We were Indian or Mestizo; yet, only a few of us were European White.

Meanwhile other events were occurring in the country. African Americans demanded their Civil Rights. To be counted became an absolute necessity. We, however, were not participants. We were not counted; for we did not exist!

In 1957, President Eisenhower established the US Commission on Civil Rights. It could only do research and document discrimination. It had the authority to hold public hearings and to compel testimony under subpoena. The information gathered on practices of discrimination was made public and submitted to the president and Congress. The commissioners delegated authority to their staff to perform studies, reports, testimony, and hearings on discrimination in education, housing, voting, administration of justice, employment, banking segregation, and so on against the Black population derived from erstwhile United States slaves.

The extensive and exhaustive documentation of widespread discrimination against Black Americans led to the enactment of the Civil Rights Act of 1964, which improved the government's ability to enforce civil rights. Prior to this, the Commission could only study the extent problem of discrimination. Every agency would now have staffing and resources: the newly created offices for civil rights, equal-opportunity employment, federal contract compliance, community relations service, desegregation, and voting rights. Congress increased the federal budget for enforcing civil rights.

The federal government had been gathering census data on Whites and Negroes for over two centuries—since the first census in 1790. And, because of the work of the Commission, it also had extensive data on discrimination against Negroes in every aspect of American life and in most geographic areas.

President Johnson inaugurated the Great Society. The federal budget was increased greatly to finance the War on Poverty. Funds began to flow into all kinds of local organizations newly formed to fight the poverty. Official Washington knew a lot about the conditions and positions of American Blacks. The data showed awesome disparities between them and European Americans.

Distribution of funds to very poor groups and persons became of paramount interest. Washington, however, was overlooking another very poor group: the Mexican Americans. It did not count, because it was not counted. It was, in fact, *invisible* since the Census had decided it belonged to the White race. Most of this "invisible minority" did not live in Washington or New York, the national media centers, so the organs of information did not know of their existence or have a name for the group. Some called them Latinos, Spanish, or Mexicans; still others called them Chicanos. To top it off, they lived in that far-off region called the Southwest.[v]

Fortunately, one agency had the responsibility to find out and learn about this little-known group of Americans,. In 1968, the US Commission on Civil Rights confronted the matter of determining and documenting discrimination against this now-identifiable group of people, establishing the Mexican American Studies Division. They hired me, a Chicano from California, to be its chief. The Commission's leadership had heretofore been as totally unaware of these people as had official Washington. Matters were to change. The Commission had found us. We would no longer be unknown.

The children of the 1.4 million Mexicans counted in 1930 were now veterans of foreign wars. They were US citizens. They were

Mexican Americans. Discrimination against Mexican Americans caused them to be restless. Embryonic rumblings were audible. Student walkouts had occurred in Southern California and would soon erupt in Texas and Colorado. Groups had protested against the Equal Employment Commission for excluding Mexican Americans. Chicanos had protested in November 1967, marching in front of the Shoreham Hotel in Washington. The Department of Labor was hosting a national conference on manpower training, but it had included the only minority known at the time: Black Americans. We, Chicanos, were increasing national awareness.

The Commission began looking into discrimination against Mexican Americans in the mid-1960s. It took its first steps to learn who Mexican Americans were by visiting southern Texas, from El Paso to Brownsville. The commissioners and the staff learned a great deal about systematic discrimination in education, employment, police brutality, administration of justice, and housing. (5) The trip was succeeded by extensive research and interviews. This initial exploration culminated in the weeklong 1968 Hearing in San Antonio. Mexican Americans were beginning to lose their anonymity. (6)

When I took the position of Chief of the Mexican Americans Studies Division, I left my dearly loved teaching of Julius Caesar, Cicero, Virgil, Horace, and the Greek philosophers and dramatists. I had always enjoyed associating their thoughts with the humanities and the course of European history from antiquity to the present. For my new post, I was handed a job description and told to read it carefully. I had been teaching Latin, Spanish, American Literature, humanities, and had coached baseball and tennis. Now, all of a sudden, I had the awesome responsibilities of a social scientist and a researcher expected to do national studies.

The staff director, William Taylor, instructed me to submit a plan of action for the commissioners' review. I realized that the Commission's mission was to document discrimination and denial of equal protection of the law. From my own life experience, I was very aware of how Mexican Americans were discriminated against, especially in the area of education. The task ahead was seemingly so great that I could not even guess whether I was capable of performing it. As the saying goes, "In the world of the blind, the one-eyed is king."

I conceptualized and designed research on what impinged on the education of Mexican American students from grade one to grade twelve. I was given a budget and authorized to hire staff. I quickly set out to gather personnel smarter and more knowledgeable than I. I hunted for young, smart college graduates cum laude with the background and personal understanding of the subject matter. We formulated questionnaires for superintendents, principals, and teachers on issues affecting Mexican American students. The US Government, however, had no norm for visually identifying Mexican Americans. The only time it had identified Mexicans was in 1930, and that was with a simple question: "Where were you born?"

Our first order of business was to create an **identifier**: who was a Mexican American student? We included this definition in the research methodology of the Mexican American Education Study in the instructions for determining ethnic and racial groupings. Wherever ethnic and racial data was requested, visual means of identification were suggested; individuals were not to be singled out or questioned about their racial or ethnic lineage in any way.

Our definition of the students we targeted was "persons considered in school or community to be of Mexican, Central American, Cuban, Puerto Rican, Latin American or Spanish speaking origin." We noted that this group is also often referred to as "Mexican, Spanish American, or Latin American; local usage varies greatly," and that for the purposes of the questionnaire, the terms "Mexican American and Spanish surnamed American were used interchangeably." (7)

The questionnaires were sent to educators in Arizona, California, Colorado, New Mexico, and Texas in the spring of 1969 with instructions for their return by May 9. The rate of response to was extremely high. Approximately 99 percent of the district forms and 95 percent of the school forms were returned. Arizona had a 100 percent response. The Houston Independent School District was involved in a lawsuit and did not respond. Silver City District in New Mexico did not respond. In California, only two districts failed to respond (Lucia Mar and Kingsburg). North Conejos was the only Colorado district we did not hear from.

It is highly significant that almost all of the thousands of questionnaires were returned. The study could now be characterized as a census of students in the Southwest in 1969. It was the first time in history that so many Mexican Americans—1.4 million students in grades one to twelve—were counted, albeit only a segment of the whole. The Mexican Americans Studies Division of the US Commission on Civil Rights had accomplished what no other entity in the federal government had. Mexican Americans were no longer an invisible minority! We began the "counting!"

And, for us, a gigantic turn of events would change us from being invisible.

A national election had produced a president who was from California. He knew who Mexican Americans were. He had been raised among them and had gone to school with them. He had worked as a poor Anglo with them, gathering crops in the fields and orchards. Whereas Mexican Americans were an invisible group to most European Americans living in the South, the Midwest, and of course, the Northeast from Maine to the Mason Dixon Line, they, in the Southwest were well known fellow Americans for President Nixon and to many of his Presidential Team members, which he brought to staff his Administration from California in 1969. This heralded the arrival of Anglos from California and Texas who knew us and respected us.

Beginning in the early 1950s and on into the 1960s, the California Republican Party began a serious outreach to young Mexican Americans. They were the children of the two million illiterate peasants, who fled the terror and religious persecution of the Mexican Revolution. They had fought in the Pacific and Europe in WWII. They were searching for the American Dream. They were college educated, urban, and wanted "in". On the other hand, their parents generally had been born into a society lacking in any legacy or practice of democracy.

As an aspiring politician, Robert Finch tirelessly raced up and down California, chartering Young Republican Clubs. I formed one in East LA whose membership was Mexican American. Stu

Spencer, a nationally known pioneer campaign manager, and Denny Carpenter, the party chairman, trained and hired young men like David Gonzales to host hospitality rooms at conferences and conventions of Mexican Americans. Stu Spencer was placed in charge of these outreach activities. He knew us by the name only we used within our cohesive ethnic group: "Chicanos." Stu had been brought up in East LA and even spent several hours in my home in 1959, trying to recruit me for a seat in the California legislature.

President Nixon appointed his very close friend and ally, Robert W. Finch, as secretary of Health, Education and Welfare (HEW).. For the first time in US history, Finch, with the assistance of Leon Panetta (from Salinas, California and a young Republican) as the director of the Office of Civil Rights of HEW and Lou Butler (from San Francisco) as deputy secretary of HEW recruited and appointed a host of Mexican Americans to key positions at HEW in 1969. These included Dr. Juan Ramos, director of the Institute for Mental Health for Hispanics; Dr. Arturo Raya, Director of Health for Hispanics; Donald K. Morales, Director of Migrant Education; Armando Rodriguez, Director of Programs for the Spanish Speaking at Office of Education; Frank Cancino, deputy director of the Office of Civil Rights; and very numerous other Mexican American staffers and interns from the Southwest.

There was at that time in Washington an entity which had gotten a great deal of attention in the Mexican American circles. Lyndon Johnson had established a paper interagency committee named The Interagency Committee on Mexican American Affairs to placate restless Mexican Americans in a last-minute campaign gambit. Mexican Americans were expected to address their grievances at the doors of this group of government agencies.. The organization had no budget to pay its Chairman. It paid only the staff director and his meager staff. The Chairmen, Vincente Ximenes, was an employee of the government.

Nixon had brought to Washington a feisty criminal trial lawyer, a former jet fighter pilot and trainer of German fighter pilots, Martin G. Castillo; and put him in charge of overseeing Mexican American Affairs. Castillo was given the title of Chairman at above mentioned agency. He, too, was made a government employee at the US Commission on Civil Rights with the title, Deputy Director.

Martin Castillo brought a large group of young Mexican American lawyers, primarily from California, to work with him in Washington. It could be said gently (and truthfully) that there were a horde of young, very educated, and aggressive Mexican Americans in the hallways of Washington's bureaucracy. These young people were, but for several exceptions, all registered Democrats. Nixon and Finch did not mind. They wanted to change Washington to include us. And these Chicano ex-GIs would be the change agents.

Before the arrival in 1969 of these young Mexicans, the Office of Civil Rights at HEW had focused only on discrimination against Black Americans. Secretary Finch and his team expanded the focus to include discrimination against Mexican Americans in education. But their efforts were blocked by a simple problem: HEW Office of Civil Rights had data only for Black American students. To correct the problem, the staff visited me at the Mexican American Studies Division to acquire our **identifier** for counting Mexican American students. They formulated their own questionnaire with it so that discrimination against Mexican American students could also be examined nationally. (8)

Another event in the struggle to count Mexican Americans took place. In 1969, the Commissioners decided to evaluate how well the federal government was enforcing the provisions of the Civil Rights Act of 1964 over its first five years. An up-and-coming recent hire out of Yale Law School, Jeff Miller, was appointed to research and study this highly significant field. He in turn hired a dozen staff who would insert the project in every major department of the US government.

I was asked to review and consider changes to the proposed questionnaires for Mr. Miller's research. I found his methodology for counting Mexican Americans missing. The proposed survey would tabulate comparisons of Blacks and Whites only. His questionnaires presented only three columns for identifying people: African American, Anglo Americans, and "other." Mexican Americans still did not exist for the purposes of this historic study of how far elimination of discrimination had advanced over the five years. I became troubled over the exclusion. I complained over and over concerning this omission, but he adamantly refused to make my recommended changes.

I brought to his attention that my, Mexican American Studies Division asking educators in the Southwest to count Mexican American students for the first time. I added that the Office of Civil Rights at HEW had expanded this inquiry to Spanish-surnamed students nationwide. I showed him evidence that the respective agencies in Washington had previously counted only

Blacks and Whites and that his vast study of the US Government had not caught up with the times. Jeff Miller and the Commission management still did not realize that the new president would want Mexican Americans to be counted—and to count!

With the new Administration, I felt I was no longer alone. I had allies. Commissioner Hector Garcia, a highly partisan Democrat, was replaced by a new commissioner, Manuel Ruiz, an outstanding and renowned California attorney. He was one of the few attorneys that could practice law in both the United States and Mexico. He was one of the founders of the Mexican American Political Association (MAPA) and a Chicano activist. Another ally was Dr. Stephen Horn, the former chief of staff for California senator Thomas Kuchel. Dr. Horn had just recently been appointed vice chairman of the Commission. For the first time, it had three Republican commissioners.

These new commissioners and the deputy director, Attorney Marty Castillo, compelled Mr. Miller to include us in his methodology. The first of several studies of civil rights enforcement efforts also counted us. (9) But it was not easy for the invisible minority to emerge into official Washington. Mr. Castillo and I celebrated the feat of getting counted in federal civil rights enforcement data,

But, across town, at the Department of Commerce, there awaited us the biggest hurdle and battle in getting us counted. The Bureau of the Census was the fortress to be scaled. My research showed that the Bureau had already finalized their 1970 census forms. Of course, the Bureau officials as usual had no plans to count Mexican Americans. Nothing new, there! They had not counted us in 40 years, so why start now?

Little did they know to what extent matters had changed. There was a new president, and he knew and liked Mexican Americans. I energized my new allies and urged Marty Castillo to take the leadership on getting us counted. I urged now was the time for action! That only presidential action would change the plans at the Bureau. With the advent of Civil Rights advances, with billions being spent on a War on Poverty, with still being invisible, we could no longer wait for becoming participants in the national community.

Marty well understood that in Washington streets and offices, only Blacks and Whites existed. He got on his Charger and went into action to get the president to order the Census Bureau to count us. I have interviewed Castillo about this twice over the years. His memory of how he got the president to act is razor sharp. Some names he vividly recalls are those of Ginger Savell, former personal secretary of Senator Kuchel and his chief of staff, Dr. Steve Horn, and especially Robert Finch.

History now can record: President Nixon ended the practice of neglect. In 1969, although the Census Bureau had already printed questionnaires for the 1970 Census, the president, nonetheless ordered the Bureau to count us. It replied that it was too late and that it would be done in 1980. Nixon found their *no* unacceptable. The Secretary of Department of Commerce, Maurice Stans ordered the Bureau to discard its questionnaires and to print new ones that included a question on origin or descent. It presented six choices: Mexican, Puerto Rican, Cuban, Central or South American, other Spanish, No, and None of These.

Nixon ended the applicability to Mexican Americans of the axiom "if you are not counted, you do not count."

CHAPTER FOUR

NIXON EMPOWERS FINCH AND RAMIREZ TO REACH OUT TO MEXICAN AMERICANS VIA REGIONAL CONFERENCES

When I had suggested to President Nixon that he could get 25 percent of the Mexican American vote, he asked "How?" with his hands thrust up and his eyes lifted in search of an answer. The five action items on the index card I handed him synthesized my visions of what I would do as chairman of the Cabinet Committee on Opportunities for the Spanish Speaking People, if he so ordered it. My unique blend of experiences, studies, and travel gave me a foundation for conceptualizing objectives and methodologies for transformational activities—in this case, transforming the nation to include Spanish-speaking People in its mainstream. It could be done, but only if he ordered, "Do it."

It had been my habit to prepare for job interviews by writing out what I would do on the new job. William Taylor, executive director of the US Commission on Civil Rights, had asked me early in 1968 what I proposed to do as the chief of its Mexican American Studies Division. I answered, "I know how the schools in Southern California discriminate against Chicanos. We need to document whether or not that situation also exists in the rest of the Southwest and make recommendations to Congress and the president on how to change that with the laws available." (1)

In the same vein, when I designed a plan for fundamental changes to the way a high school was managed in 1964, the school principal, Seabron Nolin asked me how I was going to help students improve their education. In anticipation of that query, I had written out a detailed plan during the summer prior to the incoming school year. The plan called for an initial activity of starting a novel club, to be named New Horizons. For its student membership, I reviewed the files of students, predominantly Mexicans. I selected a hundred underachieving but high-potential students for an extracurricular effort to improve their academic outcomes. The vision I had outlined over the summer was to measure the student's progress in the five outcomes of education before and after the program. I planned to speak to community groups to explain my plan to improve our school and the lives of its clients. (2)

And now, at a most critical moment in my life, I was going to be interviewed by the president of the United States. Thank God, I was ready. "Tell Haldeman we are going to do that!"

The fourth item on the index card I had handed the president was that we should hold high-level government meetings at federal regional councils to promote our goals at the local level. Now was the opportune moment for accomplishing changes close to where the people lived. The president had given us marching orders and authority through his counselor. How much closer could we get to real power? President Nixon had verbalized his own visions in our private meeting and then at the first meeting of our committee. He had clearly pronounced on the outcomes he wanted from his cabinet officers, his counselor, and me.

I was inspired with deep awe. In moments of solitude after our inaugural meetings, I analyzed their significance and profound implications, mentally and emotionally processing my observations of the president himself, analyzing the emergence of this new American group and how the president had ordered his staff to assure equal opportunities for these no longer forgotten and invisible Mexican Americans. The president had placed the power of the incumbency at our disposal. We were to use it with profound prudence and with energetic firmness within a government that was just now discovering the existence of a new group crying out for justice, recognition, and inclusion in the res publica. We had now become official emissaries of President Richard Nixon's vision to include Mexican Americans and other Latinos in the mainstream of American life.

During these first-time interactions in the Oval Office and in the Cabinet Room, I formed impressions, perceptions, and judgments of the man, Richard M. Nixon. He was highly intelligent, very knowledgeable, warm, and kind. He was an aggressive fighter for what he held to be in the best interests of the country. I was surprised to find out how experienced, knowledgeable, and familiar he was with matters Mexican American. He recounted the names of the barrios around Whittier: Jim Town, Canta Ranas, Pico Viejo, and Murphy Ranch, where he had picked oranges as a youth. He commented on names and community happenings. He listed at length the discriminations against Mexicans in Southern California in housing, education, and employment, sometimes based on religion or color. He emphasized his appreciation of Mexican Americans' religion and their values of honesty, hard work, and dedication to family. As a lawyer, he especially appreciated that they were paragons of law-abiding citizens.

Though I had spent years in Whittier, I had not met Mr. Richard Nixon before my move to Washington. However, Mr. and Mrs. Carlos Ramirez and I had spoken of him as early as 1947 and 1948. Mr. Ramirez owned a landscaping business and got to know the Nixon brothers while contracting at Don Nixon's Whittier Boulevard restaurant. Carlos knew about Don's brother, Richard, and about his work picking oranges. Some of Carlos' Mexican employees had worked in the same East Whittier orange groves. Carlos and his wife were descended from what we called "*los Californianos*"—offspring of the Spaniards and the native inhabitants (who were called *Gabrielenos*, after the Mission San Gabriel; their forefathers had been Christianized by Franciscan Friars at that mission in the 1770s). Carlos would chuckle and smile as he related his experiences with Don, Richard, and the Nixon family: "They had been very poor and were hard working, as they struggled to get ahead. We, chile-pickers, got along great with them."

I formulated my own conviction that Nixon was not the person portrayed by those in control of disseminating the media's imagery and to hundreds of millions of listeners, viewers, and readers.

Prior to this day, I knew *of* Nixon but did not know him. I had not formed an assessment of his personality myself. Yes, I had read what Walter Lippman, a former close associate of President

Woodrow Wilson, had written. I was quite familiar with the vicious rants about him by James (Scottie) Reston, the Presbyterian and a recent immigrant from Scotland. Walter Cronkite and many others fulminated against him. I was deeply aware of the antagonistic writings and opinions of communists, their fellow travelers, and socialists. It was the time of Whittaker Chambers' "despoilers." The powerful, pro-Alger Hiss apologists and defenders defamed the man constantly. Robert Estabrook vented poisonous opinions against that great man, Senator Joe McCarthy, who was blowing the whistle on the communist conspiracy on the editorial page of the *Washington Post*. (3) Their opinions were pure straw for me. They were vacuous, vicious, and militant secularists.

Since this awesome day, I have come to another conviction. Most in the mass media do not accept the objective existence of the truth. Their definition of "objectivity" is quite truthfully either incoherent or nonexistent. Like good Cartesian disciples, if they think something is true, it must be. When first I learned about Descartes' *cogito, ergo sum* ("I think, therefore I am"), I thought how intellectually fatuous he was to posit that he could think before he existed—that he could think and therefore exist.

The Nixon I read about in the fall of 1953 in the pages of Whittaker Chambers's *Witness* came alive. He was now my boss; I belonged to his official family.

It was now the historical moment when the federal government would reach out to Spanish-speaking communities, where they lived—in the Southwest, the Midwest, the Northeast, and the Southeast. The Spanish-speaking would no longer remain a neglected group.

In 1848, Mexicans residing in Arizona, California, Colorado, New Mexico, and Texas commenced life as a conquered group who had no official identity for almost the next century. They were Catholics living in a Protestant environment and Spanish speakers in an English-language world. They were Mexican Mestizos in a world of Europeans. The Treaty of Guadalupe made them US citizens; the trouble was, no one informed them of that.

In May 1969, Mexican American primary and secondary students were counted in the schools of the Southwest. In October 1969, the Office of Civil Rights, of the Department of Health, Education and Welfare, compelled all schools in the nation to count Spanish-surnamed students. In 1970, the Census Bureau counted all Mexican Americans—120 years after the War on Mexico. In 1971, the Cabinet Committee would begin the huge task of counting Mexican Americans, mainland Puerto Ricans, Cubans, and other Latinos, in all agencies and government-regulated businesses.

Mexican American students were, moreover, counted in 1969 for the first time in history. I had formulated an ethnic identifier to use in counting them from kindergarten to grade twelve in five states. The Mexican American Studies Division of the Civil Rights Commission dispatched the questionnaires to study how educational practices affected Mexican American students—of which we counted 1.2 million. Then there was the HEW questionnaire.

Statistical data concerning Mexican Americans was growing, making the unknown known. Did the mass media inform the American public that President Nixon was unveiling invisible Mexican Americans? Of course, not. They were too busy blaming him for the war in Vietnam. They were too busy denouncing him, for nothing good was to be reported about him. They mocked his smile and his gestures.

As chairman of the president's Cabinet Committee, I was soon to expand the data on Spanish-speaking people exponentially. All federal agencies would soon be required to count mainland Puerto Ricans, Cubans, Mexican Americans, and other Latinos by ethnicity and the dollar values of the contracts and grant awards they were issued. The count by ethnicity in the federal government would begin in its regional offices.

Soon, we would know how many Mexican Americans were in military uniform. How many Mexican American colonels and captains were in active service would be known. And, what is more significant, the promotion system would present those ready for promotion to general or admiral. With the advent of computers, we would very rapidly become even better known.

When I discovered that many American Blacks were being elevated to the rank of general, I asked how many Mexican American generals there were. Robert Brown, the White House liaison to the Black community had proudly boasted that during Nixon's first term, the number of African American generals and admirals had increased from two to fourteen. So when the answer to my query turned out to be "zero," I complained to the president. His response was quick: "Go make one."

I called the White House military liaison and informed him of the president's order. I told him, "We want the best full-bird colonel now serving." They found Colonel Richard Cavazos. Soon, he became the first Mexican American general. On a 1976 business trip to Mexico City, I visited my friend, Ambassador Joe

Jova. I met a one-star general in the hallway outside Joe's office. The general gave me a real genuine *abrazo*—a hug—all the while shedding wet tears on my shoulder. As I looked up quizzically, he proudly pointed to his star and said, "Thank you. I am the one they chose." He retired a four-star general. The Pentagon could promote Blacks during the president's first term because they knew the names of the African-American colonels and captains, but they didn't know those of the ranking Mexican Americans.

On May 1972, I received a memo with the Subject: Spanish Speaking Medal of Honor Winners from a Tony McDonald, a White House staffer. The Veteran Affairs Administration had compiled a list of twenty-six Medal of Honor recipients. They were listed by their Spanish Surnames. Eleven had been in World War II, seven were from the Korean War, and there were eight in Vietnam. What a discovery! People in government were taking an interest on our previously unknown, ultrabrave participation in patriotism. If place of residence defines ethnic origin, then five were Puerto Rican and the other twenty-one Mexican American. (3) Eleven of them died from 1943 to 1945; it is highly probable that they were born in Mexico and were illegal aliens. Who today celebrates them?

Before 1970, only Black Americans could prove discrimination with census results that showed disparities in every field of life. The Spanish-speaking, who did not exist in the data, could not.

No one had data on the disparities in our lives. The civil rights laws of 1964 were meant for Blacks.

Robert H. Finch wrote a highly significant memo dated October 17, 1970, with the subject line "Administration Programs for

Spanish Speaking Peoples." The memo read: "Simple operations are now operative for gathering information on the administration's progress for the Spanish speaking." To me, it appears to have been the very first effort by a very highly placed White House official to take action to benefit Spanish speakers in the United States. Such memoranda to get information for White Papers apparently were sent out via the Cabinet Committee to its member agencies.

Finch's memo elicited some interesting information. One particular memorandum shows how much in the dark official Washington was in 1968:

> *US Department of Labor, Manpower Administration, February 5, 1971*
> *Subject: A Program for Spanish-Speaking Americans.*
> *TO: Dr. Bette J. Soldwedel, Associate Director, Job Corps,*
> *Office of Program Development*
> Background: *In February 1968 at the request of Ambassador Telles, and Mr. Califano, Executive Office of the President, Mr. Shriver, Director, OEO, and Dr. Murphy, Associate Director, Job Corps, the Ford Foundation made this writer available for one month to evaluate the role the Job Corps was then playing in serving the needs of the Spanish-speaking enrollees. The findings were that little if any effort was being made* to shape or conduct the program *to serve this group.* (4)

In the last year of Lyndon Johnson's administration, a consultant paid by the private sector to evaluate the federal government's efforts found that "little if any effort was being made."

Seven years after the passage of the 1964 Civil Rights Act, Washington had not considered that it also protected Spanish-speaking people, but things were beginning to change. In

May 1970, Robert Finch issued the landmark "May 25th Memorandum," (5) which required that there be no discrimination on the basis of national origin. The Supreme Court upheld it unanimously on January 21, 1974. The definition of discrimination was written by Leon Panetta, director of HEW's Office of Civil Rights, ably assisted by Martin Gerry, who had been a lawyer at Nixon and Mitchell law firm; Frank Cancino, the first Chicano graduate of Stanford Law School; and many Chicano educators.

In October 1968, the US Commission on Civil Rights formed a large team of civil rights lawyers, social scientists, and consultants who traveled along the Mexico-Texas border to learn about discrimination and denial of equal rights to Mexican Americans. I was there to study the area of education. Interviews and discussions with leading citizens in San Antonio, El Paso, Laredo, Brownsville, and Corpus Christi provided evidence of widespread institutional discrimination. The team's work culminated in the weeklong hearings in San Antonio that were documented in the Commission's thirteen-hundred page report. (6) We discovered that in the denial of rights and opportunities, the European Americans in Texas had no problem identifying Mexican Americans.

At the US Commission on Civil Rights and the Texas hearings, I realized the importance of counting by race and national origin for transforming a society. I grasped how government could include us with fairness as long as we made certain that we were counted. Documentation could demonstrate discrimination or open opportunities. Statistics were needed in law courts. The only way we could advance the civil rights of Mexican Americans was to determine exactly to what extent they participated in society. In a few short years, the country would be aware of the disparities between Mexican Americans and others in access to employment, education, the military, housing, and business.

The concepts and the methodologies for achieving inclusion on a par with other Americans were absolutely novel and anomalous to the hundreds in government and the White House with whom I and my staff worked. As I interfaced with them, they gave me the distinct impression that they still viewed us through the lens of Hollywood stereotypes. Hollywood had invented a cast of Mexican characters who demonstrated the ineptitude of low-life inferiors through decrepit clothing, poor diction, and an ugly, swarthy appearance. The characters were unshaven, ugly, toothless, pork-bellied, mustached, and illiterate. They were brigands, peasants, sex-driven Latin lovers, or dictators who salivated involuntarily. They were poorly armed, awkward gunmen who rode to battle on reluctant mules and burros. And, oh yes, they could not shoot straight. Only European Americans like John Wayne could take out two of 'em with one bullet.

Nonetheless, I was firmly entrenched in my vision of a transformed country that included us. The president had spoken, and party loyalty demanded adherence to his policy. He bellowed out that it would be our job, his and mine, to destroy the invisible wall of discrimination the European Americans had erected in the Southwest against the Mexican Americans. I was buoyed. Only the president could fire me as I went about this arduous task. But I already knew the personal sacrifices demanded from a visionary from my efforts to transform the educational system at Whittier Union High School District. It is all uphill, with few plateaus. I've often felt that Ravel's "Bolero" would be a good soundtrack for my crusades.

To transform the federal government's approach to these new groups of Spanish-speaking people, I asked my staff to design two projects. "Project Blue" was for federal headquarters in Washington, and "Project Alpha" was for the government's regional offices. The task ahead seemed insurmountable. The president had asked me how long I thought it would take to make the needed changes. I had replied, "A generation."

The concurrent implementation of the projects called for a simple first step: count. Counting people is a simple chore; it becomes difficult when criteria are added. Counting babies up to a year old is easy, but you can't count Mexican Americans unless you grew up with them in places like Mexico, New Mexico, Texas, or California. For those from northern Vermont, for example, the chore is almost impossible, especially if they rely on Hollywood stereotypes.

This entire matter of who was a Spanish-speaking person, a Spanish-surnamed American, a Chicano, Mexican American, mainland Puerto Rican, Cuban, Latino, Latin American, Central American, Hispano, or Hispanic was a puzzle. It seemed prudent to accept that reasonable people would encounter handicaps in counting. Most government counters did not know we came in four basic groupings: European, Indian, Mulatto, and Mestizo. Most Mexican Americans were Mestizos; Puerto Ricans were primarily European with a sprinkling of Black and Mulatto (with a very few Jibaros), and Cubans were European with only some Black and Mulatto. We simplified the task by counting Spanish surnames.

My vision was to have the entire federal government and all the functions it regulated (train and airplane travel, banks, and so on) would count participation by, outcomes for, and anything pertaining to the Spanish speaking. We had a whole lot of catching up to do. The drapes had been opened by President Nixon, and now America would begin to know us.

Counselor Bob Finch gathered a high-level team to plan and implement visitations to six regional councils. Mrs. Pat Hitt, the coordinator of all the regional councils, was very close to her mentors, Finch and Nixon. She had been born in Whittier and her husband had been in the small circle that launched Nixon's political career. She was an awesome center of power and influence. In Washington circles, mere titles do not reveal the real power that those connected to the source can exercise where or when needed. Assistant Secretary Patricia Hitt was connected.

Besides myself, the team included top-level representatives of Cabinet Committee members and staff from the Office of Management and Budget (OMB). This was first-time-ever serious business. We selected visits to regional councils close to Spanish-speaking populations in New York, Atlanta, Chicago, Dallas, Denver, and San Francisco.

In the Oval Office, I had stressed the fact that the US Government tends to assume the habits and character of the regions in which it functions. So, to reach out to Cubans, mainland Puerto Ricans, and Mexican Americans, we had to visit them where they lived. Changes had to be made at the local level. A user-friendly government reaches out and does not make people come to Washington for relief.

We were elated that the president had in the very early days of his Administration appointed a Mexican American, Mr. Hilary

Sandoval, an El Paso businessman, to be the Administrator of the SBA. It was an outstanding first-ever. No Mexican American in history had ever received such an honor. President Nixon had established a new paradigm. His administration was to include us. Mr. Sandoval showed no hesitation in removing SBA district directors whom he discovered discriminating against Mexican Americans. In fact, the first to be removed on the spot was the district director of Midland Odessa, who refused to make loans to Mexican Americans. (7)

This type of behavior was also rather common at all government levels in Texas. It was open, public, and overt. One has to laugh upon learning that San Antonio, Houston, and Corpus Christi high schools each had three sports leagues: one for Blacks, one for Browns, and one for Whites. It was colorful. It seems that the slave-owning, hacienda-living mentality eroded slowly.

Now was the time for decision making and action. I was no longer an outsider, I was now a doer! This White House was now in reelection mode. My every action would be evaluated against its impact on reelection, whereas I weighed my own achievements and accomplishments against how much they advanced *la causa*—the betterment of living conditions for Spanish-speaking people. The first presidential cabinet meeting on opportunities for the Spanish-speaking was of profound and historic significance. The president was taking actions.

Nonetheless, his staff was still unaware of the affairs of the Spanish Speaking People. The truth is that they were no different in their modalities toward us from those operative under

Kennedy or Johnson I knew from my conversations in my office with Marty Castillo just how ill-informed he found the White House staffers to be. An October 17, 1960 memo I uncovered at the Nixon Materials Section of the National Archives in Adelphi, Maryland confirmed the level of low information. It was written by a Midwesterner, Professor George Grassmuck, for Finch's signature and addressed to the White House Special Assistant on Black Affairs, John R. Brown III. Mr. John Brown was responsible for Black Americans, yet he was receiving memos on programs for the Spanish Speaking! The contents exposed the regressive mentality in the White House before the president vehemently made known that he wanted Mexicans to share in the good of this country and before I presented my five visions.

One big obstacle had to be removed so that the regional conferences could be planned and implementation started. I decided to remove the obstacle of the troublesome notion of a White House Conference by replacing it with Regional Conferences. Dr. George Grassmuck, Tony Rodriguez, the executive director of CCOSS, and I met on August 18, 1971. They quickly agreed that the regional conferences would take the place of the White House conference that Nixon had promised in his first presidential election campaign. (8)

Planning for the first regional council meetings for the Spanish speaking soon gained top priority. In the early days of my tenure as chairman, I reviewed and explored the essential need to acquire ethnic data. I reminded my staff that Washington DC only knew us as members of the White race. The White House, Congress, the press, the think tanks, and the foundations did not know us as Mexican Americans. I counseled them that we were embarking on a whole new voyage. We were going to compel the bureaucracy to count us! The president ordered counting to be done by ethnicity, not color, under our authority. I warned my staff that assistant secretaries would raise hell and charge them with using heavy-handed tactics, but I told them to proceed and not to worry. They would be backed up and supported. The assistant secretaries did raise hell, but my staff got the job done.

I instructed my staff to prepare questionnaires that asked for an ethnic and racial count of all employees in each agency, as well as an account of all contracts awarded by race and ethnicity. They also had to develop action plans with timetables, goals, and targets to assure that the new ethnic group would get jobs and federal resources on parity with others. Quarterly reports would also be required. I called this effort Project Blue.

When the president's representatives visited, each regional director was to make a presentation of findings and timetables and in preparation to kick off the visitations and reports, the regional council directors were instructed to:

1.   Communicate effectively the president's genuine concern to federal officials and regional community leaders.

2.   They had to develop action plans with goals and timetables to assure Spanish speakers' participation in each region's employment programs, contract compliance, and procurement.

3.   Acquisition of discretionary monies for funding of interagency programs with high visibility and high impact on Spanish-speaking communities.

4.   Data collection, retrieval and analysis for a comprehensive assessment of delivery of services to Spanish-speaking Americans.

5. Task forces were established in all of the Cabinet Committee member agencies, all linked to the Cabinet Committee staff, which provided direction and guidance to task force efforts. (9)

Project Alpha was the most comprehensive effort ever initiated at the local level to assess what was being done for the Spanish speaking. With the development of task forces, timetables, goals, and targets, we anticipated that we would very significantly influence the federal government to assist the Spanish-speaking over the next five years.

President Nixon had ordered the establishment of the regional councils to bring the federal government closer to the people. By September 30, 1969, the realignment of the field operations of the principal federal agencies concerned with social and economic progress into ten regions was complete. This realignment and relocation of Washington decision making to the local level profoundly benefited US citizens.

Things were changing, big-time. The president named his close friend and political ally from his very first campaign, Patricia Reilly Hitt, to coordinate all ten regional offices. She had been serving as assistant secretary for community and field services at HEW. He had already assigned his dear friend, Robert Finch, former lieutenant governor of California and former HEW secretary, as counselor in charge of all matters affecting the Spanish speaking. He was particularly instrumental in reorienting the regional offices to count and include the Spanish-speaking. Finch brought even more presidential empowerment to the regional thrust. It was a heady time. He added clout to the presidential team with

Frank Carlucci, deputy director of OMB. Frank organized and directed the regional directors to advance the president's special emphasis on the program for the Spanish speaking.

Mr. Carlucci issued memoranda to the respective chairmen of the targeted federal regional councils, charging them to comply with the "implementation of the regional Spanish speaking programs." (10) The individual agencies responded with proposals of projects for funding and reported how they had utilized advice from representatives of the diverse Spanish speaking communities from the states served by the regional offices in drafting final plans of action.(11)

The regional directors met with Counselor Finch, assistant secretaries, and the Cabinet Committee chairman to report on their progress toward the goals and objectives set by the president. It was rewarding to observe that their data on contracts and personnel included Spanish-surnamed Americans as well: in 1971, we were counted at the regional and local level for the first time. For the first time in history, the federal government was truly focusing on this new and emerging group of Americans, the Spanish speaking. The regional offices could now use demographic data on Spanish-surnamed populations in the states they served by analyzing the results from the 1970 census. The agencies would also now know where this new group lived and how many there were, so they could now deliver programs where needed.

The first regional conference meeting took place in Chicago on October 14 and 15, 1971. I could have selected San Francisco, Dallas, Denver, Atlanta, or New York, but my first choice was the unknown Midwest. My motive was to address Mexican Americans living in the Midwest—who were not only invisible but unknown. Hardly anyone knew they existed. They had not even undergone the experience of being forgotten! But over one million Spanish-surnamed Americans lived in Illinois, Indiana, Michigan, Minnesota, Ohio, and Wisconsin. These states were served by Region V offices. Mexican Americans lived in rural, urban, and suburban places. They were scattered. However, vibrant, vocal, and voting mainland Puerto Ricans lived in northern Chicago. I knew about them from Senator Charles Percy.

The best known Spanish-speaking group was that of migrant workers, and most came from Texas. A few had settled out of the migrant stream. But after the 1910 Mexican Revolution, some Mexicans settled down in the Midwest, especially in the industrial areas along the Great Lakes. I knew about them. Since childhood, I had heard stories of families that became separated and about whom little was known. The old-timers would say, without explaining, "They went to Chicago." Years later, I was to learn that the word "Chicago" signified the entire Midwest.

In the wake of the Mexican Revolution, there was disorder, lawlessness, and bloody religious persecution. The innocent and hapless Mexicans suffered under classic Marxist doctrine of achieving Communist objectives by means of a bloody revolution coupled with the destruction of the Catholic Church and murder of its adherents. Young families fled their very primitive and rural living conditions, primarily from the states of Guanajuato, Michoacan, Zacatecas, Aguascalientes, Durango, Jalisco, and Queretaro in central Mexico. Battles were fought here because the area hosted the railroads and rich farmlands, which were all needed for troops and horses. Only a single railroad provided transport from it to the northern border at El Paso, Texas.

Recruiters of labor were busy attracting these exiles to the flourishing citrus industry in California and to the thriving Great Lakes. In Topeka, Kansas, families separated as some members chose the Midwest over the West. Lawyer José Rojas Garcidueñas, who had grown up with my parents in Salamanca in Guanajuato, was an eyewitness of the town's refugee exodus. In *Salamanca: Recuerdos de mi Tierra Guanajuatense*, he wrote, "The poor refugees went to California or the Midwest. The middle class and professionals fled to San Antonio, Texas, or similar places in the U.S. or Mexico City. The well-off and landed class went to Europe." (12)

The poor refugees tended to be indigent, illiterate, landless mestizo peasants. The railroads and empty freight cars provided an escape to the North. The refugees went to "the land of the free," away from the European-inspired bloody revolution that lasted until 1930. The rails started in Guadalajara, Jalisco on the west; Morelia, Michoacan on the south; and Celaya, Queretaro on the east. All met in Salamanca, Guanajuato, and from there the tracks went north through Aquascalientes, Zacatecas, Durango, and Chihuahua to terminate at Juarez. As the locomotives stopped to replenish water, the very young married couples with several children hopped onto the empty freight cars for their journey *al Norte*. From there, a border crossing in the desert lands to the United States was no big deal. At the time, the Treasury Department was in charge, and it had hired very few agents; crossing was barely regulated. After 1924, the Department of Labor took over (13) after immigration laws were first enacted, aimed primarily at controlling the numbers of swarthy Mediterranean immigrants into ports of entry on the eastern coasts.

By 1971, we were dealing with the children of the Mexican Revolution refugees. They were born in the generation of World War I and served in World War II. They were educated, married, Mexican American veterans, and they demanded inclusion in the American Dream. Whereas their refugee parents has been born into and raised in a feudal society—that is, in haciendas or ranchos each about five miles away from the next hacienda or small town, these war veterans were returning to school on the GI Bill, getting educated to live in a capitalist society.

Since I had no personal knowledge of who was who among the Hispanic leadership in the Midwest, I hired Roy Fuentes, a longtime resident there, as I planned for the Chicago regional conference. Roy was a Michigan educator involved in the civil rights movement in the Midwest; he knew the Mexican American leaders and community organizations personally. He became our ambassador to and from the Midwest. We were preparing to deliver services to the mainland Puerto Ricans who lived primarily in northern Chicago and to the Mexican American communities scattered throughout the Midwest.

In early September 1971, member agencies of CCOSSP dispatched trained personnel to Chicago to teach community organizations how to apply for government grants and how to deal with the federal regulations of contracts and grants. .

Prior to our trip, we issued a press release: "Committee Chairman and White House Officials to Meet in Chicago with

Spanish Speaking Community Leaders from Six States." It was sub-titled: "Washington Delegation to Present Demands of Community Leaders to Regional Directors of 7 Federal Agencies," while one of its statements noted: "Mr. Ramirez emphasized that he and Counselor Finch arranged the trip, at the request of the president, to discuss the problems of the federal government toward alleviating and eliminating the problems of the Spanish speaking." (14)

The Chicago regional conference was highly successful. Due to the diligent work of the government grant and contract specialists who reached out for the first time and showed community groups how to apply for education, training, housing, and health grants (and more), about seventy-five million dollars were awarded to Spanish-speaking organizations, which had never participated in government programs before.

This event also showed me how the media worked concerning President Nixon. In this case, the president was bringing the federal government to the Spanish speaking in a six-state area. The president's first-string team was bringing the power of his incumbency to a media town owned and operated under the iron rule of a big-boss Democrat: Mayor Richard J. Daley. While the Spanish-language media handled their job in a very positive and informative manner, the English media manifested their traditionally liberal, biased, pro-Democrat side. They looked for angles and phraseology to present prejudiced misinformation to their public. I did a half-hour interview on Spanish language TV's *Oiga Amigo*, which went very well.

On the October 14, 1971, *ABC Eyewitness News* at 10:00 p.m., Fahey Flynn reported:

A fact-finding committee from the US Department of Health, Education, and Welfare visited a settlement house in a Chicago Spanish-speaking community this afternoon...but there was some reported reluctance to permit news coverage. Frank Agraz reports: 'Casa Atslan was one of the spots toured today by presidential counselor Robert Finch, Dr. Henry Valmedes, chairman of the cabinet committee on opportunities for the Spanish speaking; and recently appointed HEW regional director, Richard Friedman. Even though press releases heralded the visit to Chicago, there was an unexplained hesitancy to allow Channel Seven News to film the official sight-seeing trip. Director of Casa Atzlan, Molly Cabildo—while happy to show off her three-story, brightly painted building—never got around to asking why the group was there—and no one told her. The tour and some meetings tonight with Latin American community leaders was described by a news release as the first in a series of conferences in seven cities to acquaint the federal government with the problems of the nation's fifteen million Spanish speaking residents. It would appear that the government wants to do its homework on the nation's second largest minority in private. If only everybody would leave them alone.'(15)

Let me clarify. Mr. Flynn, a professionally trained wordsmith, had a copy of our press release in his hands and could not read the name "Ramirez" correctly. He pronounces it "*Valmedes.*" Then he identifies the community leaders as "Latin American." He worked in Chicago. Did he not know that they were Mexican Americans and mainland Puerto Ricans? And, of course, for a liberal, it is de rigeur to finish his report not with a fact but with an editorial opinion.

At that time, meetings with "the community" were latent with anger, hostility, intemperance, and impatience. It was also the era of unrest prompted by the Communist Party and its fellow travelers.

In addition, the unmet needs and lingering hopes arising from the 1964 civil rights laws caused protestations at many events.

Our conference was held by Republicans in the front yard of Richard Daley's political hacienda. On the evening of the first day, the delegation held a "community meeting" in the La Salle Hotel. Mainland Puerto Ricans and Mexican Americans were invited. The event became an unhappy interaction.

Years later I found an unread memo in my files concerning this regional conference from a Richard H. Naber, technical assistance coordinator, to Richard E. Friedman, regional director, dated September 30, 1971. The subject line read: "Recent Visit of Dr. Gil Chavez, Chief, Office of Spanish-Speaking Americans, OE, Washington D.C." The memo describes a two-and-a-half-day series of community meetings in Chicago conducted by Dr. Chavez starting on September 21, 1971. Some organizations represented were: the Brown Berets, the Raza Unida Coalition, Mexican-American Teachers, the Spanish Action Committee, United Latins, and ASPIRA. The meetings focused on question-and-answer sessions and the airing of grievances.(16)

This sounds pretty nice and innocent—government presenting itself to hear from its citizens—except that Dr. Chavez's office in HEW was supposed to be coordinating efforts with the rest of Patricia Hitt's team. This section of the federal government was a bastion of Democrats spearheaded by Dr. Armando Rodriguez, assistant commissioner. He had received his political appointment from Vice President Hubert Humphrey in the closing days of the Lyndon Johnson presidency. One can only speculate on the relationship between Dr. Gil Chavez's actions, his well-known closeness to Mayor Daley's Democrats, and the behavior of representatives of the organizations named above. That meeting reflected partisan priorities rather than concerns for the suffering Spanish-speaking people. Nonetheless, the benefits and outcomes of this regional conference would in time manifest themselves in profound systemic improvements.

The newspapers in the six-state region reported on the conference in a straightforward manner without stinging or emotional verbs, adjectives, and adverbs. The Puerto Rican paper, *El Puertorriqueno*, was the exception with their negative, anti-Mexican, and evil-spirited verbiage. Their headline was "President Nixon Hunts for Votes." What an informative headline. In a democracy, the number one job of a politician is to get votes. The reiteration of that basic reality does not provide information or political education to a population that is hungry for it. What a loss to the people for the arrogant satisfaction of Mayor Daley's buddies. (17)

The newspaper *El Informador*, catering to the Mexican Americans, wrote a lengthy, comprehensive, and informative story (here, I translate from the Spanish): "Eleven agencies of the federal government convene for the purpose of executing the orders of president Nixon relative to Spanish-speaking Americans." Its publisher, Charlie Gomez, was not a puppet of Mayor Daley. (18)

On the other hand, the *Chicago Sun-Times* did an extensive report. Their reporter discovered the most important and salient aspect of the regional conference—that it was a stormy session of US officials and Latins. The English-speaking newspaper gave its liberal European American readership a stereotype of unruly and childish Mexican Americans and mainland Puerto Ricans. Media work of this genre showed they did not know who we were. My understanding of the English-language media was growing rapidly.

The trip to the information-gathering bowels of Chicago taught me that I was not going to get much fair and objective treatment from the media in my efforts to educate and inform Spanish-surnamed Americans on the federal government's new Nixon-era interest in knocking down walls of discrimination. On the contrary. They would follow the example of Sarah McClendon. They would bear false witness. They would play the game of advocating for their side of the story: liberalism as defined by Nietzsche. Upon my return to Washington, I started a monthly newsletter named *Hoy* under the direction of its editor, E. B. Duarte from Brownsville, Texas. A list of twenty thousand received monthly copies. The list included congressmen, senators, key government officials, Washington movers and shakers, and leading community figures in the Spanish-speaking world. *Hoy* presented the administration's achievements, not promises, for the Spanish-speaking in simple, declarative sentences without colorful or emotion-laden adverbs and adjectives.

The federal agencies serving the six states of Region V began to collect data on employment and contract awards under the category of Spanish-speaking people. Mainland Puerto Ricans and Mexican Americans would no longer be uncounted and unknown. No longer would the Region V Latinos vent frustrations over their conviction that Washington had ignored them.

This was the first time a president had really addressed himself directly and personally to the regional problems and conditions of Spanish-speaking peoples abiding in the Midwest and Northeast areas of the country. He did this through two close personal friends, Bob Finch and Pat Hitt, and me, his Chicano assistant.

HMR Personal File

Counselor Robert Finch, Assistant Secretary Pat Hitt, and Chairman Henry M. Ramirez receive an orientation to the procedures for the eleven regional agency directors' presentations on how they would implement the president's orders.

HMR Personal File

A small segment of the crowd of Mexican American and mainland Puerto Rican leaders at the first regional conference in
Chicago of eleven federal agencies, mobbing Counselor Finch
in this corner.

HMR Personal File

Regional Conference in New York City Dec 9, 1971

Soon after the Chicago conference, Bob Finch led the way
to New York City on behalf of the president and the Cabinet
Committee on Opportunities for Spanish Speaking People.
Here the emphasis was almost entirely on what plans the various
federal regional agencies would implement for mainland Puerto
Ricans.

Two letters demonstrate how the regional conference outreach program was being fired up in the other regions. Frank
J. Groschelle, chairman of the southeastern federal regional
council for Region IV (Atlanta, Georgia) wrote on March 22,
1972, to the Honorable Robert H. Finch: "Enclosed is a copy
of the Southeastern Federal Regional Council's Action Plan for

the Spanish Speaking People in Region IV. The Council utilized advice from representatives of the Spanish speaking community in Miami and in Tampa in drafting this final plan of action." (19)

Mr. Groschelle also reported to Mr. Frank C. Carlucci, chairman of the Undersecretaries Group for Regional Operations in the Executive Office of the President at the Office of Management and Budget: "The Southeastern Federal Regional Council is in compliance with your memorandum addressed to Regional Council Chairman, dated March 1, 1972, subject: Implementation of Regional Spanish Speaking Program. We have examined the Spanish Speaking Plan and identified the projects we are requesting to be funded. Attached, please find the individual agencies' proposals of projects for funding."[vi]

Counselor Finch personally launched the follow-up work with instructive letters for the regional directors on how they were to continue to implement programs for and counting of the Spanish-speaking people in all the regions. The next regional conference was held in New York City on December 9, 1971. This meeting was closed to the public and was conducted in the mode of a very high-level governmental conference.

In a very short time, the vision expressed by President Richard Nixon in August 1971 was being actualized. Presidents Kennedy and Johnson had talked a good game and snookered the Mexican Americans, but they did not walk the talk of their famous speeches. With President Nixon, efforts to include Mexican Americans, mainland Puerto Ricans, and other Spanish-surnamed Americans in the mainstream of American life at all levels of the federal government were bearing fruit. A popular

Mexican dictum says: "*Hechos; no dichos.*" And President Nixon complied with *hechos.*[vii]

Washington has another dictum: "Personnel are policy." The next step called for appointments of Spanish-speaking persons to decision-making positions. The first highly visible evidence of changes, in addition to the internal work of data gathering, would be well-publicized appointments of Latinos to powerful positions: the directors of six regional and district offices.

CHAPTER FIVE

NIXON ORDERS EQUAL EMPLOYMENT OPPORTUNITIES FOR THE SPANISH SPEAKING PEOPLE

As we have seen, President Nixon told me with emotion and deep urgency, man-to-man, that he wanted his cabinet officers to include Mexican Americans in the federal government. And we at the Cabinet Committee set out to accomplish that goal.

Soon after the Second World War, Congressman Richard Nixon and his cohorts started including Mexican Americans in California. Beginning in the 1950s, a visionary congressman by the name of Pat Hillings persuaded Nixon and his friend, Robert Finch, to get the Republican Party in California to begin a serious first outreach to young Mexican Americans, the urbane and sophisticated ex-GIs. Two persons exercised hands-on leadership: Stu Spencer and Robert Finch.

Finch was elected lieutenant governor on the same ticket that brought the governorship to Ronald Reagan. He had been born and raised in Phoenix, Arizona; his father was an elected Arizona legislator. Finch graduated from Occidental College in Eagle Rock, California, which lies between downtown Los Angeles and the Rose Bowl in Pasadena; he raised his family in that area. By virtue of his upbringing and early adulthood, he got to know his Mexican American contemporaries.

Stu Spencer was raised in Alhambra, California, and went to school with East Los Angeles Mexican youth. Stu knew them by the appellation "Chicanos." And, he attended colleges in their backyard: East Los Angeles Junior College and California State University, Los Angeles. Stu Spencer was one of the first, if not the first, very successful political campaign manager and consultant in California. His company enjoyed outstanding successes. He is famous for managing the presidential campaigns of Nixon in 1968 and 1972; for running the gubernatorial campaigns for Reagan, and his presidential campaign in 1980. He worked closely with Denny Carpenter, also from Southern California, who was the California Republican Party Chairman in the sixties.

Denny knew Mexicans very well. As an FBI agent, he had been posted in Mexico City for ten years and had married a Mexican woman. Chairman Carpenter trained and hired young men like David Gonzales, a former student of mine, to host hospitality rooms at the organizational conferences, meetings, and conventions of Mexican Americans. These four men reached out to the nascent, rising voices of young activist Chicanos who had returned from WWII and the Korean War and were exiting the barrios, pursuing their GI college education benefits, and entering the ranks of the middle class.

In order to grasp the national significance of this Nixon-GOP outreach to young Chicanos, one must compare the history of the Kennedy-Democrat overtures to the same set of young Chicanos. The election of Kennedy in 1960 did not bring a surge of Mexican American appointments in Washington DC to help form his government. Instead, celebrations of the election among these young ex-GIs were described as "*a gritos y sombrerasos*"—"by means of shouts and hat-tossings." The Mexican Americans who had been deeply involved in the "Viva Kennedy Clubs" of his presidential campaign stood around in circles afterward asking each other, "Now what?" They learned the answer: Nothing happened.

The Kennedy group and its New York media followers focused their attention and efforts instead on Mexican Americans working in the rural and farm areas, achieving the very laudable goal of unionization with Cesar Chavez. The tragic November 1963 death of President Kennedy caused the elevation of Lyndon Johnson to the presidency. His incumbency to complete Kennedy's term saw huge change, with the enactment of civil rights laws in 1964. These laws improved the lot of the Blacks almost immediately, and eventually, after the passage of many years, that of Mexican Americans, who in the meantime were relegated to the back pews to pray and hope in silence.

Lyndon Johnson won election to his own first term as president. Again, President Johnson provided scant leadership in recognizing the young, restless, and demanding Chicanos out west. The Mexican Americans in Colorado under Corky Gonzales were beginning to act out. In New Mexico, Reyes Tijerina was challenging land grants and ownership. Mexican Americans in Texas had organized with the aim of teaching English and also to combat discrimination against Mexican ex-GIs under the American GI Forum.

Some hopes, however, were actually realized in the closing days of Johnson's presidency, starting in California. The Chicanos there organized a plan to confront the newly established Equal Employment Opportunities Commission (EEOC) at its March 1966 hearings in Albuquerque, New Mexico. Twelve Chicanos, who had been meeting every other Saturday at Swalley's Restaurant on Olympic Boulevard in East LA to discuss how to advance the civil rights of Chicanos, designed a walkout. Phil Montez, their leader, was at that time the western states field representative for the US Commission on Civil Rights; we chose him to lead the protest, while Armando Rodriguez, an educator, was selected as its spokesman.

The Mexican American protestors complained that the Equal Employment Opportunities Commission had no Mexican American member. Charles Erickson, former *Los Angeles Times* reporter and a member of the twelve, was chosen to issue information to the press so that news of the confrontation could be widely disseminated. The twelve invited members of two other organizations dedicated to the advancement of Latinos in Texas and New Mexico: the League of United Latin American Citizens (LULAC) and the Political Association of Spanish-Speaking Organizations (PASSO). With their presence, the confrontation included a wider spectrum of activist civil rights membership. The walkout shouted out to the civil rights community that a group called Chicanos wanted a place at the civil rights table. They were alerting the nation and the Democratic Party in particular.

Dr. Hector Garcia, a deeply partisan Democrat and close friend of Lyndon Johnson, worked feverishly on his White House Texas connections to get Johnson to do something. He did. On June 9, 1967, President Johnson nominated Vicente Jimenez as an EEOC commissioner, though this was well over a year after the Albuquerque walkout. Johnson also nominated his friend Garcia as a commissioner at the US Commission on Civil Rights a year later in 1968. So, as President Johnson was exiting the White House, the hopeful loyal Mexican American Democrats had achieved two appointments in the arena of civil rights but none that would be responsible for attention on jobs and money. Out of the over three thousand appointments a president usually made in those years, one who grew up in the midst of millions of Mexicans and Mexican Americans finally made two! And the Mexican Americans who were Democrats then heralded the feat. They still do today!

A year later, as his time in office was nearing its end, President Johnson approved a memo on June 9, 1967, authorizing a new organization, named the Interagency Committee on Mexican American Affairs. It was composed of the heads of five agencies: the secretary of labor, the secretary of HEW, the secretary of HUD, the secretary of agriculture, and the director of the Office of Economic Opportunity. They came together to assure that federal programs were reaching Mexican Americans and to provide the assistance they needed. At the White House ceremony creating the new agency, the president appointed Mr. Vicente Ximenes to two positions: chairman of the just-created Interagency Committee, and commissioner of the Equal Employment Opportunities Commission. Vicente Ximenes had been born and raised in the small, segregated Texas town of Floresville, where the big landowner was John Connolly. Ximenes' father had worked on that hacienda.

June 9, 1967, was a banner day. President Johnson in one day created an Interagency for Mexican Americans, swore in a new commissioner to the EEOC, and named a chairman to a cabinet-level committee. It had a small budget. And it never met. Its chairman would later lament that he could never get hold of the cabinet members of the Committee. He had to rely on contacts with lower-level bureaucrats. Events would soon demonstrate a stark contrast between President Nixon and his men as compared to the Kennedy and Johnson and theirs. The historical facts demonstrate that with Nixon, Mexican Americans progressed, whereas under Kennedy and Johnson, they remained invisible.

In the mid-to-late 1960s, Mexican American political activists themselves were ignorant of two vital facts: first, the 1964 civil rights laws only applied to Black Americans, and second, Mexican Americans did not exist, because they were not officially counted until 1970. With the unexpected election of "that Nixon guy," Democratic Mexican Americans went into shock. It became *our turn*, and we were ready.

Robert Finch gathered a crowd of California Mexican American talent and placed them in key spots at HEW. One might say that Robert Finch led an "invasion" of Mexican American talent into Washington the likes of which had never been seen before. It was another historic first. It was consistent with what the president had voiced in the Cabinet Room: "For when I lived in Whittier, I had very close ties with this group [Mexican Americans]." So also did Bob Finch, Leon Panetta, Lou Butler, Patricia Reilly Hitt, and many other California Republicans. The time for Mexican Americans to show up in Washington had come.

These young professionals were mostly Democrats. They had been brain washed by Democrat liberals in Higher Education. Yet they wanted to make a difference in advancing "La Causa". It did not take a lot of time to cure them of their political immaturity. Eventually, almost all of them, if not all, registered Republican. One exception stands out. I placed Henry Cisneros in the White House Fellows Program. He was the first Mexican American ever in that prestigious group. He refused to register Republican because he wanted to become Mayor of San Antonio, eventually.

In relating the glamorous account of the arrival from 3000 miles away of eager young lawyers, PhD's, and other professionals to high level government positions, we did not overlook the pressing need for the employment of Mexican Americans in the lower and midlevel of government. But there was an insurmountable obstacle. The enforcers of the Civil Rights Act of 1964 did not know Mexican Americans. The actions to count us started in 1968, four years later.

Moreover, the 1964 laws established a new agency in charge of minority employment, the Equal Employment Opportunities Commission (EEOC). It was responsible for overseeing and enforcing the prohibition on employment discrimination. The Fourteenth Amendment would now be enforced. But did it include us? No! Each federal agency was required to establish an office to administer the civil rights laws, and EEOC would watchdog each agency's personnel division. These offices focused on recruiting, training, and employing Blacks only.

The need for a "parallel" EEOC for Mexican Americans was evident. So, in 1970, the Cabinet Committee drafted their own wonderful, gallant initiatives to increase employment for Spanish-speaking people. But there were some speed bumps; we had only just been counted, and the analysis of the data had barely begun by the end of 1970.

To overcome some of the speed bumps at the Civil Service Commission, three people at the Cabinet Committee formulated the "Sixteen-Point Program"—Martin Castillo, executive director John Bareno, and personnel director Merci Hernandez. As best as I can reconstruct the history of this program from the evidence, Merci Hernandez had developed a guide for equal employment opportunity training while working with the US Air Force, probably in the1960s. In 1969 and 1970, Merci Hernandez and Irving Kator, assistant executive director of the Civil Service Commission (CSC) developed a list of actions for recruiting Spanish-speaking professionals for federal positions.

The executive director of the Cabinet Committee, John Bareno, wrote a history of the Sixteen-Point Program in *La Luz* magazine's December 1979 issue. (1) Mr. Bareno gave total credit to Merci Hernandez for formulating the program; justice demands full recognition of Merci's work. On September 30, 1971, chairman Martin Castillo honored him for it. Bareno described how, in 1970, the Committee capitalized on the rivalry between the president's and vice president's staffs. Len Garment, who was in charge of civil rights matters, learned that Mr. Bareno had approached the vice president himself directly. He further found out that the vice president wished to announce the program. Mr. Garment, however, took the action away from the VP's office and remanded it for action by the president himself but only after the program received further refinements. President Nixon announced it on November 5, 1970, in a press release, (2) but action to implement it remained dormant until 1971.

Almost a year later at the August 5, 1971 meeting of the Cabinet Committee, Mr. Nixon expressed deep frustration at the failure of his government to increase employment of the Spanish speaking. He clenched his fist and his facial muscles tightened as he remarked, "A year ago, I announced the Sixteen Point Program to assist Spanish-speaking citizens interested in federal employment, and you have been dragging your feet."

With the president's forceful impetus behind us, it was now time for genuine implementation. In August 1971 we set out to get the whole US government to count us, the Spanish-surnamed Americans. We revitalized efforts to increase the employment of Spanish-speaking Americans via the Sixteen-Point Program and also by ordering EEOC to include us, also in their enforcement work.

In our meetings that day, President Nixon had exhibited demeanor of a warrior who finally got what he had wanted for the downtrodden people he knew well: Mexican Americans. This was going to be his second chance to get his administration on the right track for the advancement of a people he had known since early life, who had been ignored, overlooked, and neglected. The president had proclaimed loudly and clearly that he wanted us still forgotten and ignored Mexican Americans included in mainstream American life. His goal was simple and his expectation clear: "Get it done!"

As the cabinet's boss, only he could get its officers to cooperate with me, the Committee chairman. I was at a level lower than they, but his support had a leveling effect. No other president had ever internalized experiences gained from living at close quarters with Mexican Americans. Very significantly, he added: "If any of you do not cooperate with Henry, he will be able to fire you!" This president, I realized, really gave a damn about us Chicanos.

And would you believe it? Mr. Romney, the secretary of HUD, refused to cooperate with me on assigning Mexican Americans to positions in the LA District Office and the San Francisco Regional Office. During my first visit to his HUD Office for a photo opportunity, I complained to Secretary Romney that he was not being a team player with respect to the president's instructions. Secretary Romney responded: "I know full well what Nixon said. But I am running this department and I will do what I think is best. And, further, I realize what he said about your firing any of us that do not follow his instructions." My rejoinder was simple: I would report back to the president and see to it that Romney was fired. He was, and he was replaced by Jim Lynn.

President Nixon did not use terms such as "the Latins," "the Spanish," "the Spanish people," "the Spanish speaking," or "Latin Americans" for us. He spoke as a knowledgeable Southern California native who knew that the best and most accurate term was Mexican American. He did not use condescending descriptors such as "Hispanic," "Spanish, or "mes'can" (as was common usage in Colorado). Nor did he fall for the Texas use of "Latino" while in the presence of a Mexican American but pejorative appellations outside it.

The nation's top newspapers were getting the drift that something big was happening. On August 26, 1971, the *Washington Post*'s Elsie Carper revealed: "Spanish-Speaking People's Committee Finally Implemented." (3) Scripps Howard News Service's Seth Kantor on 14 August had reported: "The Silent Minority has a Voice" (he added that the president had told the Committee, "You failed me. Do not do it again."). (4) The September 26 *Los Angeles Herald-Examiner* noted: "New Era for Spanish Speaking." (5)

And finally, the print media with the largest Mexican American readership in the country, the *Los Angeles Times*, weighed in with an in-depth story condensed from a lengthy interview granted to Mr. Frank del Olmo. Frank was at that time the most respected print reporter on Chicano and Mexican American activism. His article, "Chicano Wants Involvement, Not Separation" appeared at top right on the first page of Part II on September 13. The subtitle read: "Ramirez, Nixon Appointee seeks 'the Good Life for Mexican Americans'" Frank reported straight and factually— with only one error (which thankfully was near the end). He said that "the cabinet committee was created by Lyndon B. Johnson in 1967 as the Interagency Committee on Mexican American Affairs." No wonder academic researchers have repeated the mistake. (6) The *LA Times* had so often given my boss, President Nixon, such a rough time; this time they got it right. Their hammering typewriter hit the nail squarely on the head. Their editorial page opined: "Here in the Southwest we have a particular responsibility for the Mexican Americans and Mexican Nationals. It is a group which only recently has been listened to by the Anglo majority. It is a group only beginning to articulate effectively its goals, as well as its sense of outrage at the discrimination this people has suffered. It is a group whose patience understandably is wearing thin." (7)

The Spanish-language press in the States and abroad was quite elated, expansive, and highly favorable on our work. The Cuban papers of New York and Miami were effusive with lengthy stories. The Mexican American dailies and weeklies were skeptical but supportive. The big exception was in the papers catering to mainland Puerto Ricans, who dedicated their coverage to the noisy and unruly protest mounted in the offices of the Cabinet Committee several days after I was named chairman. (From that day on, press, radio, and TV exposure was to be an active new ingredient in my life. I became a very public figure. I lived in a glass cage until 1974, when I and my family returned to the anonymity of life in Southern California.)

Nine years after the passage of the civil rights laws, matters changed. After the famous dressing down in navy talk that Commissioner Hampton received from the president himself in the first CCOSSP meeting, the Civil Service Commission undertook a special study to evaluate progress on the Sixteen-Point Program. Now they had an object to study: they had ethnic data. As a result of the study, the agency recommended specific actions in January 1973. Federal Personnel Manual System Letter No. 713-18 said: "Each agency should appoint a Coordinator for the Sixteen-Point Program on the staff of the Director of Equal

Employment Opportunity." It was marked as high priority. In practice, agency personnel managers viewed it uncomfortably as a "me too" effort to piggyback on the hard-won advances of the Blacks. (8)

In 1970, in my role as a senior research staffer at the US Commission on Civil Rights, I had to review the methodology for the proposed study of federal enforcement of civil rights laws, so I became very familiar with what the entire federal government was doing to assure compliance. The apparatus was taking good care of the concerns of Blacks, but it bothered me that the study did not include finding out how Mexican Americans were faring. It was understandable, since we were just then being counted in the census and agencies had not been collecting data by ethnicity. The next year, as chair of the Cabinet Committee, I demanded that they do so. Neither I nor my Chicano cohorts who met at Swalley's in East Los Angeles in the mid-1960s had known that there was no way the federal government could directly assist Mexican American citizens, since it did not know we existed statistically. The local schools did; they segregated us. The local banks and real estate agents knew; they would not sell homes to us or let us buy in the "nice" areas of town. In southern Texas, where towns were divided by railroads or highways, the "Americanos" lived on one side, the "Mejicanos" on the other. The vestigial consequences of military conquest pervaded the ambiance and culture.

This bit of knowledge came in handy in the Oval Office, when Mr. Nixon asked me how we were going to assist Mexican Americans to gain employment. I suggested that the EEOC submit a plan for compelling businesses to gather data by ethnicity instead of just by race. I remarked to the president that if we could increase employment and augment promotions, now denied due to discrimination, we could improve the educational outcomes of Mexican American students. I showed him how my study at the US Commission had demonstrated for the first time that the socioeconomic level of parents is the best predictor of student performance.

A review of the impediments to employment of Spanish-surnamed Americans demonstrated that, in addition to discrimination, the mammoth speed bump had been the lack of data collection by ethnicity. Politicians assumed that the government knew who we were and how many we were, but they were ill informed. Looking back at those years, we can all accept the fact that we were unknown, that the first action was being taken to count us by our ethnicity, and that Nixon acted on his vision to include us in the American mainstream. The departments and agencies were beginning to use the definition "Spanish surnamed" for their ethnic counts. The pattern of designating us by the term "Mexican American" was receding. Real changes were being made.

An outstanding example of how the new count by ethnicity was presented is contained in the "Manpower Report of the President to the Congress of March 1973." Table after table of numbers are presented in columns like this:

Total White Total Negro Population by Spanish Origin

Total Mexican Puerto Rican Other

This represented a major improvement over the many, many years when the numbers were presented in the simplicity of two columns: Total White and Total Negro. (9)

I gave this statement before the Subcommittee of the Committee on Government Operations, House of Representatives, on July 23, 1973:

> *What the Cabinet Committee intends to ultimately accomplish is to institutionalize programs, policies, and mechanisms throughout the entire federal structure so that inclusion of the Spanish Speaking becomes an automatic function of government. By Inclusion, we mean bread and butter for the Spanish Speaking—recruitment, placement, promotion, contract compliance, procurement, and their right to acquire and receive an equitable share of government funds. (10)*

This said it all. This is what President Nixon had wanted and had instructed.

Certainly, the Kennedy brothers did not have similar experiences with Mexicans as they were growing up in Boston. Lyndon Johnson, on the other hand, grew up knowing Mexicans but within a closed society that systematically segregated them. In Texas, poor and vanilla-skinned Mexicans knew their place. Only light-skinned Mexicans, descendants of European Mexicans and/or members of the landed class, could interact on an equal footing with Texans, descendants of Europeans. Johnson's vote-getting methodologies were to throw beer and barbecue ranch parties to buy their vote, and he hoped they stayed bought.

Johnson may have wanted to assist Mexican Americans more significantly, but he was hindered by the Washington team he inherited. It was composed of Italian Americans, Jewish Americans, and German and English Americans, who knew next to nothing about the downtrodden, uncounted, and ignored Mexican Mestizos. The Kennedy and Johnson teams knew a lot about the Negroes. In fact, when Johnson established the temporary Interagency Committee on Mexican American Affairs, he assigned a European American, David North, to run it. That was the way the management of Mexicans was done in Texas. In an example of this social condition, I was astounded to learn from our Mexican American Education Study questionnaires that it was common practice in Texas high schools to see that European American students occupied all student body offices, despite the fact that Mexican Americans heavily predominated the student population (up to 90 percent). Carrizo Springs and nearby Crystal City were prime examples. The European American landowners in those school districts would not permit Mexican student body officers to "lord it over" their offspring. No way.

Texas was not alone in this. Someone in the White House once asked me to visit Patterson High School in California. Patterson was a sizeable apricot and cherry farming community between Fresno and Sacramento. The well-connected city fathers had requested the president to visit their town; I was told that I would go as his representative instead. My special assistant and I were gladly received by the mayor, the school district superintendent, and the high school principal, among others. Slowly and clearly our reason for being there was made known: we were expected to diffuse the tension filling the community and calm the volatile high school student body. The Mexican American students were protesting an unfair student body election. None of the Mexican American candidates had won any student officer position, despite the fact that they greatly outnumbered the Anglos. The school officials justified the election results by saying that so-called "citizenship grades" had disqualified the Mexican

Americans. The officials acquiesced to our suggestion, repeat the elections. More equitable results produced tranquility. Mo, my personal assistant, and I drove out of town and stopped at roadside stands to purchase large bags of succulent, large black cherries, just recently picked from surrounding orchards.

In the years from 1968 to 1971, I became acutely aware that Americans living east of the Mississippi River did not know anything about Mexican Americans. In Bethesda, where my little family was growing up free from the trouble of discrimination, people did not know that we Mexicans were supposed to be its objects. There, they knew that Blacks were objects of discrimination. Robert Finch cautioned me during our frequent meetings to be constantly aware that official Washington did not know Mexican Americans. He counseled me to be patient and understanding. Mutual acceptance and understanding would take time. He glanced out of his second-story West Wing office window and remarked, "You can look out all day long at Pennsylvania Avenue and not see a single Mexican." Mexican Americans from Texas and the mining towns of Arizona, Colorado, and New Mexico brought fresh perceptions to Washington, making it known that other Americans denied them their rights. Mexican Americans tended to view official Washington through the modality of back home: they were "those gringos" who were bearers of discriminatory action.

When we at the Civil Rights Commission needed to illustrate the first volumes of the Mexican American Education Study in 1971, Joe Mancias, a staff photojournalist, was dispatched to Southern California to photograph Mexican students. Not a single federal agency had a depository of this type of photography.

After the Census Bureau released data on the Spanish surnamed in late 1971, there was a rush to the Southwest to photograph Mexicans. With some luck, they might have taken pictures of signs that read: "No Dogs, No Mexicans Allowed!"

By 1966, the problems in Mexican American employment were becoming clear with the Chicano activists' Albuquerque walkouts. Mexican Americans were beginning to emulate the successes of the Blacks. Phil Montez, a psychologist who had been born and raised in Watts, had just recently been hired by the US Commission on Civil Rights and assigned to its Western Field Office in LA. Almost as part of his job, he became the agent for developing organizations and events to advance the awareness of civil rights in the Chicano communities. His office became a Southwestern beehive for coordinating people, organizations, and events focused on the issue of employment disparities in the federal government.

The Mexican American Civil Rights movement of the 1960s could be characterized as diffused and unfocused. LULAC promoted teaching English to recently arrived mestizo Mexicans. LULAC had been founded in the 1920s by lawyers, judges, businessmen and educated Criollo types. The GI Forum had been established to fight discrimination against Mexican American ex-GIs, especially in Texas. As Mexican American migrants from South Texas settled down in the West and Midwest, additional chapters of the GI Forum were established. In California, lawyers and activists formed the Mexican American Political Association (MAPA) to increase our participation in the political process.

Education and employment were their top priorities, but the fact that Mexican Americans were still classified as White was a big obstacle to improving the employment situation. In 1966, the University of California at Los Angeles issued its first mammoth report on its Mexican American study project but did not include information on employment of Mexican Americans. (The Project's bibliography alone was over a hundred pages long. The list of references demonstrates the disparate nomenclature for persons of Mexican background: Spanish, Spanish speaking, Spanish surnamed, Mexican, Mexican American, and Latin American.)

Fortuitously, I was able to define the observational method that I described earlier for determining the ethnicity of school children in the Southwest. The Census Bureau used a similar method but based it on self-identification. Finally, with President Nixon's direct support, the Cabinet Committee compelled the entire federal government to count all Mexican Americans, Puerto Ricans, and other Spanish and to publish the results. I saw that by being counted, we would now know the numbers describing our situation and could provide programmatic solutions for advancing people's lives. What happened? Everyone could finally analyze the disparities between how Mexican Americans, Puerto Ricans, and other groups were employed in the federal government.

On November 30, 1971, the US Civil Service Commission gathered employment data by race and ethnicity under the categories Negro, Spanish Surname, American Indian, Oriental, All Other. The president was getting results; they were published in 1972. But when the country discovered that we were 6 percent of the population and only 3 percent of the employment, all hell broke loose. The Democrats faulted the president for the disparity. Soon, with the gathering and publication of racial and ethnic data in other areas (such as housing and education), more hollers and complaints resounded. The Democrats commenced their attacks on the Sixteen-Point Program, claiming that it was a dismal failure. They did not want to acknowledge that first, simply understanding a situation, was absolutely required before action could be taken to transform it.

I had anticipated their attacks. I gave talks, speeches, and radio and television interviews where I repeated over and over what the President News Summary revealed to him personally: "Ramirez, chairman of the Cabinet Comm on Opportunities for Spanish Speaking, said his group wasn't succeeding in employing Spanish-speaking in lower-level federal jobs and pointed to midlevel bureaucrats as the cause. 'It's one thing for the president to give an order,' said Ramirez, 'and [another thing] for his secretaries, agency heads and immediate lieutenants to heed it.'" (11). Ray Hanzlik, assistant to Counselor Finch, wrote: "At a time when we are working to stress the positive accomplishments, it goes without saying that these comments were not well received around here." (12) My reaction? Live and learn. I comment here on what the president was reading about me in his early morning President's News Summary and reactions some White House Staffers were writing about me. In this case it was Finch's new assistant. Their concerns made my job more difficult.

The new data was being revealed in the midst of a presidential election campaign and was causing deep anxieties. In a July 12, 1972 memo, Alex Armendariz wrote: "Stop publication of July 1972 census report for these reasons: any statistical data which shows the Spanish speaking community is lagging behind...will be construed as the fault of the incumbent government." (13) My reaction was: *How dumb. In a few short months we go from being invisible to lagging behind?*

Senator John Tunney, a California Democrat, hurled negatives in a November 11, 1971 report by Public Advocates, Inc.: *Federal Government Employment of the Mexican American in California: A Classic Case of Government Apartheid and False Elitism.* Just the year prior, President Nixon had announced the Sixteen-Point Program for recruiting and hiring Mexican Americans in the entire country, not just California. The question was, how did Senator Tunney and the Public Advocates organization know the statistical data on Mexican Americans in California? The answer is, they did not—for it was not yet available. Chairman Robert E. Hampton of the United States Civil Service Commission reacted starkly to the report on December 29: "The report is misleading." Chairman Hampton's five-page refutation of its scurrilous attacks against the president's efforts and the Sixteen-Point Program is devastating. (14) The Democrats were firing straw bullets. In Washington, when someone is accused of "misleading," it means that person is lying.

Chairman Hampton responded on March 29, 1972, to an inquiry by Congressman Robert McClory, to wit: "I am providing the following comments regarding the statement made by Mr. Edwards concerning President Nixon's Sixteen-Point Program to assure equal employment opportunities for Spanish-surnamed persons. Contrary to Mr. Edwards' statement, the program has been taken very seriously by federal agencies. Contrary again to Congressman Edwards' statements, the Cabinet Committee on Opportunities for the Spanish Speaking is very highly regarded. There is, however, a failure on the part of some persons to recognize the progress that has been by this administration in working toward the legitimate aspirations of the Spanish-surnamed group in federal employment." (15)

It was a shame to learn just how utterly ignorant Congressman Edwards was. He was born in the Santa Clara Valley of California in 1915. He received his BA and law degree from Stanford during the Depression, had served in the navy, and worked for a year in the FBI. He was president of the Valley Title Company. While he was a student and a member of Stanford's golf team, I was on my knees picking ripe prunes and competing with yellow jackets in his neighborhood of San Jose, Santa Clara, Campbell, and the Saratoga Country Club's private golf course, where he hit the links. With my mother, my five brothers and five sisters, I lived in the apricot and prune orchards of the Santa Clara Valley, when in summers from May to September we cut apricots and picked prunes from sunup to sundown every day except Sunday, when we went to Mass in San Jose. Did Congressman Don Edwards get to know us Chicanos, seasonal migrant workers, at Stanford, at his country club, at his church, or his real estate title company during the Depression? I very much doubt it. His official comportment in Washington demonstrated that he did not. As the proceedings around Watergate developed, this congressman, in fact, used his position of power in an abusive manner to help destroy the Cabinet Committee. The only agency dedicated to assuring the American Dream for Mexican Americans. Some day, the Chicanos of San Jose, who aided his elections to Congress, will know what Don Edwards did to us.

Because of all the pressure Alex Armendariz was getting at the offices of the presidential campaign, to get top level-attention, he wrote a memo to Fred Malek. It stated: "Underrepresentation of Spanish-speaking Americans in the federal government remains a critical campaign issue. Our political opponents are convincing the Spanish-speaking leadership that employment disparities can be alleviated by the president "with one stroke of the pen," i.e. an Executive Order calling for more Spanish-speaking jobs. So he recommended an executive statement calling for aggressive recruitment of Spanish-speaking people in government." (16)

The ball commenced rolling at attempts to draft an acceptable presidential memorandum on the Sixteen-Point Program. My efforts were met with a "try again." It was not until June 17, 1974, that an acceptable draft was approved by Ann Armstrong, who had replaced Counselor Finch. I was to exit three months later. And the president was readying his resignation. (17)

The Mexican American spokesmen for the Democratic Party, and specifically Raul Izaguirre, who headed the National Council of La Raza then, did not understand that it was simply necessary to count who we were, where we lived, and how many we were. Evidently, those Mexican American Democrats were convinced that everybody in the United States knew who we were, simply because they themselves knew. They had missed the fundamental fact that first, we had to be officially counted by *ethnicity*, and that that is what President Nixon did. The Democrats could not reconcile themselves to this. They missed the boat.

On October 1976, the National Council of La Raza publicized their report "Cinco Años Despues: A Preliminary Critique of the Sixteen Point Spanish Speaking Program Five Years after Its Creation." (18) It is probably collecting dust someplace, if any copies are extant. It was a pathetic attempt to discredit the successes of the Sixteen Point Program. The National Council of La Raza had become an extension of the Democratic National Committee, the United Auto Workers union (UAW), and the American Federation of Labor and Congress of Industrial Organizations (AFL-CIO). It remains so today. These few tidbits reflect the anxiety surfacing in the country by groups seeking equal treatment as promised under the Fourteenth Amendment.

The maturity of the much-debated and maligned Sixteen-Point Program was in sight. On July 26, 1974, Roy Fuentes sent me a memo (19)listing the names, phone numbers, agencies, and addresses of over twenty full-time bilingual and Spanish-speaking program coordinators.

However, Mr. Ed Valenzuela, president of the newly formed organization National Image, Inc., announced at their 1975 convention that the number of Spanish-speaking coordinators had increased from a mere fifty to a record number of a thousand. Since I was no longer involved but very busy starting my own business in Los Angeles, the increase from the reported figure by Fuentes in 1974 to the number released by Valenzuela of a thousand, it is truly remarkable.

Mr. Manuel Oliverez, chairman and chief executive officer of an organization formed to promote Hispanic professionals and executives in the federal work force, invited me to a historic luncheon on July 12, 1995. He wrote, "You, Chairman Ramirez, are one of the pioneers and visionaries, whose leadership and consummate professionalism gave the program its direction and vitality. We, in the Hispanic community, owe you a deep debt of gratitude. Accordingly, we will be pleased if you will do us the honor of accepting our invitation to be our special guest at the luncheon commemorating 25 years of the 16 Point /HEP program." (The Carter Administration renamed the Sixteen-Point Program to the Hispanic Employment Program.)

One more revelation is needed to give credit where history demands it. In the 1920s, a Mexican family fled from the persecution in Mexico of the Catholics and their beloved Church, settling in El Paso, Texas. A son, Carlos Esparza, started at the bottom at the US Civil Service; by 1971 he had risen to its higher echelons and was stationed in Washington. He knew the Civil Service laws, rules, and regulations. Most important, he knew how to get things done the right way. He was the guy behind all of the actions described above. Others got the credit, for they had the titles and publicity. Carlos just did his job. Today he is co-owner of a multi-million-dollar corporation that serves the outsourcing needs of government agencies as well as the renamed US Civil Service Commission (the Office of Personnel and Management, or OPM).

Carlos wrote this for my book on March 5, 2009:

The death knell for the Hispanic Employment Program started under OPM director Don Devine, a Reagan ultraconservative appointee, who in early 1983 abolished the office's newsletter, La Mesa Redonda. The newsletter was the key instrument for guiding program initiatives across the federal government. The program's demise continued under the administrations of George H. W. Bush and Bill Clinton. Major blows were dealt to the program during the administration of George W. Bush when several key instruments for facilitating the hiring of Hispanics ended. They were bilingual certification and the use of crediting job-related cultural activities. Finally, the end of a court mandate

(Angel Luevano v. OPM) that had enabled speedy and nonbureau-
cratic hiring of outstanding scholars was negotiated away in 2007.
For almost 25 years this mandate had provided the most productive
avenue for bringing talented Hispanics (and other groups) into gov-
ernment. (20)

The era of employing Spanish-surnamed Americans became a success. Few realize that we had to compete with our Black brothers, who had the direct benefits of hundreds of millions of dollars and thousands of persons to implement the legal imposition of nondiscrimination in employment, public or private. We at the Cabinet Committee knew, as did the president, that the Black community was the sole beneficiary of the recent laws and new employment commission. They lived in DC and had been slaves; we were only conquered and unknown. As a result, we had to invent and implement our own employment program until we were counted and caught up with society.

CHAPTER SIX

EXECUTIVE APPOINTMENTS

One of the five visions that I presented to President Nixon in the Oval Office called for the appointment of a hundred Mexican Americans to executive positions in his administration. My concept for this vision rested on the practices of large corporations. They appoint board members to help run them, so why not bring in new "board members" to help run the federal government? We Chicanos had fought wars; now we wanted to be decision makers. Mr. Nixon vowed to include us in the decision making process and in the ranks of government workers. Since he had direct control over the assignment of high-level government executives, he made it happen. It was hugely successful. This is how we did it.

Cubans living in the United States had run a country that they had lost to whom they offhandedly called a bunch of "los Muchachos." Island Puerto Ricans had once run a country (now a commonwealth and US territory). They had their own governor, a legislature, and a judiciary. . The mainland Puerto Ricans called themselves Arawaks, Boricuas, or Neorquinos;

they sought out the assistance and services of the Cabinet Committee, not the island government. Ethnically and racially, they could be classified as European, Mulatto, and Black respectively. Chicanos ran their households, never a country. The United States was their country, and now their president wanted them to help him run it.

President Nixon had ordered a nationwide recruitment drive to bring more Mexican Americans into government decision-making positions. Mr. Nixon directed department heads to open top jobs for Spanish-speaking Americans during the now-famous August 5, 1971 first meeting of his Cabinet Committee on Opportunities for Spanish Speaking People.

Counselor Finch arrived at the West Wing in the autumn of 1970 reorganized the White House Personnel Office to achieve the recruitment of women, Blacks, and Spanish-speaking people. Fred Malek was put in charge. Barbara Franklin was given the mission of identifying women for top jobs. Al Kaupinen was to look out for other groups. And William Marumoto was given the job of recruiting the Spanish-speaking. Bob Finch had staffed White House Personnel with "his" team, and Washington would finally "get it." The executive search process to identify, recruit, and appoint Spanish-surnamed Americans to high-level executive positions became a hectic rush.

William Marumoto scheduled weekly meetings in his White House presidential personnel office to review high-level vacancies to see if he could fill them with Spanish-speaking executive candidates. Bill invited four persons to participate in the process: me; Carlos Conde from the White House Communications

Office; Tony Rodriguez, assistant to Bill Marumoto; and Alex Armendariz, a staffer on the presidential reelection committee. To promote the high-level opportunities, the Cabinet Committee paid for the following: Conde's salary, Tony Rodriguez' secretary, some travel for Counselor Finch, and most of Rodriguez's travel.

Conde was assigned to assist Herb Klein, the director of the Communication Office. He was to publicize the White House initiative: it was hugely important to inform the Spanish-speaking of presidential action to assure them that their needs were being met in employment, grants, and contracts. Tony Rodriguez worked for William Marumoto; he was an employee at the State Department on loan to the Cabinet Committee. His office was separate from mine and from the White House itself. We decided that he would be able to vet prospective high-level candidates from a private, secure location with limited access. He was assigned to a separate building (the New Executive Building). People there enjoyed the privilege of saying they worked "in the White House" and could use White House stationery. For recruiting purposes, it was impressive.

President Nixon's orders for including Mexican Americans, Puerto Ricans, and Cubans at the decision making levels of his administration began to demonstrate undreamed-of results. Per a January 7, 1972 report, the president had made twenty-six presidential and super grade appointments (1)—a mere five months after the president had verbalized his wishes. Of additional significance was the fact that already, the regional conferences were also bearing fruit. Seven Spanish-surnamed persons were for the first time in history appointed regional directors!

Monthly reports kept Robert Finch and Fred Malek informed. Barely ten months after the presidential orders for the Hispanic executive search, a June 20, 1972 report noted: "To date the president has made thirty-three presidential and supergrade appointments and it appears we will have more within a matter of weeks." (2) Remarkably, a few months later in November, the number had grown to a historic fifty-four. (3) An equally high number of appointments to boards, commissions, and advisory committees were also recorded.

Courtesy Richard M. Nixon Library

October 27, 1972 photograph of presidential appointees
in Cabinet Room with President Richard M. Nixon

Left to right, clockwise: Special Assistant to the President, William "Mo" Marumoto; Urban Mass Transportation Administrator, Carlos Villareal; EEOC Commissioner, Ray Telles; Ambassador to OAS, Joseph Jova; Deputy Staff Director, US Commission on Civil Rights, Louis Nunez; General Counsel, OEO, Bert Gallegos; White House Staff Assistant, Carlos Conde; Consultant to the White House, Antonio Rodriguez; ICC Commissioner, Rudy Montejano; Chairman CCOSSP, Dr. Henry M. Ramirez; the president; US Treasurer, Romana Banuelos; Director, OEO, Phillip Sanchez; Senator Robert Dole.

The White House's nationwide executive search caused a never-before-seen excitement in the hearts and minds of Mexican Americans, mainland Puerto Ricans, Cubans, and other Latinos. Men and women were being called and recommended, their resumes requested, and many were interviewed in the White House. For me, the experience was incomparable and unique. I was an observer of something fantastic and yet a vital participant. In the White House, five of us involved in implementing the White House executive search for Hispanics were nicknamed "the Brown Mafia" (I was called "the Godfather").

On my frequent trips around the country, I was besieged by persons with resumes or those recommending their friends. In Washington, I headed up a small group of Hispanics who met from time to time in an upstairs establishment on 14th Street with a small group of Blacks headed up by Bob Brown, special assistant to the president. There we studied a list of high-level positions the White House personnel office was working on that had been marked for "minorities." We discussed amicably which should go to Browns and which to Blacks. Our agreements also meant our candidates received our mutual support.

One US Commission on Civil Rights appointment was that of distinguished lawyer Manuel Ruiz. To the press, it was just another presidential appointment; it received very little play. (By way of contrast, when Lyndon Johnson appointed Hector Garcia, a Corpus Christi medical doctor, to the Civil Rights Commission, that one act was highly heralded in the media as of huge significance for Mexican Americans.) A Mexican Mestizo born in Mazatlan, Mexico, Ruiz had been the first Latino graduate from University of Southern California Law School in 1930 and was considered the "California dean" of Mexican American lawyers. He authored numerous works, including the seminal *Mexican American Legal Heritage in the Southwest,* and was one of the founders of MAPA. Commissioner Ruiz had been well known since the 1930s as a civil rights activist for Mexican Americans. In 1964, he was named the national Hispanic chairman of the Goldwater presidential campaign.

From my position and pay grade at the US Civil Rights Commission, I looked up to commissioners as those who moved and operated high up in thin air. I was just another anonymous bureaucrat. Yet, it disappointed me and my staff of Chicanos and Chicanas greatly that the first Mexican American commissioner, Hector Garcia, did not display interest in what the Mexican American Studies Division was doing. Precisely at that time, we at the Mexican American Studies Division were designing our vast study of educational practices in the Southwest. He never asked for any kind of report, and he never visited our beehive.

So, imagine how I reacted when I was summoned to the office of the Civil Rights Commission executive director (who was himself a lawyer), and instructed, along with another several employees, to put the touch on people who had received contracts from the Commission to pay for a going-away party for the now ex-Commissioner Dr. Hector Garcia (to be held in a large room in the Dirksen Senate Office Building). He never learned my name or of my existence, and yet I was the designer of the vast Mexican American Education Study. Nonetheless, when the Reagan White House had asked me; Henry Zuniga of El Paso, Texas; and Alex Armendariz of Washington for a list of three Mexican Americans to consider for the Presidential Medal of Honor, Henry pushed hard for the name of Dr. Garcia. Alex seconded him. Reluctantly, and for the sake of unity, I acquiesced in recognition for his dedication and work as the founder of the national GI Forum. He got it.

Dr. Garcia was an enigma. He was deeply partisan, almost to the point of being irrational. He was born into a family of land owning Criollos (Spaniards) in northern Mexico. He had been raised in a privileged society that lived by strict behavioral criteria of class differences. Due to the Revolution of 1910, the Garcia families hustled out of their lands for the nearest towns across the Rio Grande. There in Mercedes, Texas, they set up a retail business to serve the starving, naked, poor, and illiterate mestizo Mexicans fleeing from the horrors of that Mexican Revolution. Young Hector attended the University of Texas at Austin during the Depression and became a medical doctor in 1940. He encountered no discrimination. He was, after all, a European American. He looked no different from his European American classmates and university society. His only salient differences were: he spoke Spanish, had a Spanish surname, and had come from Mexico.

My source for many details of Dr. Garcia's life was Mr. Mo Garcia, who was my personal assistant and confidant during my tenure as chairman. Dr. Garcia's father and Mo's dad were brothers. In Mexico, these brothers had attended a teacher's college at a time when the philosophy of scientific positivism was sweeping Mexico, It was the French ideology that inspired the revolutions of 1910. This godless philosophy said that reason was the only worthy driving force of humanity and that the Catholic religion was a tool of human retardation. The Cartesian system of epistemology had won the day in Mexico in the brains of the rebellious intellectuals and educated classes..

Newspaper reporters were beginning to write about what Nixon was doing for filling his Administration with Mexican Americans. One reporter, One of the journalists to get it right was, Jonathan Cottin, in September 2, 1971 he wrote in the *National Journal*: *"President Nixon has ordered a nationwide recruitment drive to bring more Mexican Americans into government policy-making positions. Mr. Nixon directed department heads to open top jobs for Spanish-speaking Americans during an August 5 meeting of the Cabinet Committee on Opportunities for the Spanish Speaking People. "He used very firm language," recalled Henry M. Ramirez, committee chairman. "He put it to them."*

Mr. Cottin balanced his nice reportage on Nixon's efforts with statements from fierce opponents of any good done by him for Mexican Americans as he added: "Representative Henry B. Gonzalez, D. Texas said Mr. Nixon has 'merely continued' programs designed to help Mexican Americans started by Presidents Kennedy and Johnson. 'I don't think he's improved it,' said Gonzalez. The President has done things to get headlines,

Gonzalez said. 'But the appointments have been "political hacks" lacking "any particular knowledge ability or clout."' (4) And, my research also showed a vivid similarity between the life of this Congressman and his parents to that of Dr. Hector Garcia. They too were from Northern Mexico, educated, and landed-owners. Henry B was also a Criollo. Henry B. and Hector just could not rid themselves of their "European sense of superiority over these Mexican mestizos Nixon and I were bringing to high level government positions. Of course, they were also deeply partisan Democrats, and blindly so.

1972 was a challenging and cognitively difficult time for partisan Democratic Mexican American politicos. Their hopes and wishes had vanished under Kennedy and Johnson. President Richard M. Nixon advanced the Mexican American community with unexpected "first time evers."

CHAPTER SEVEN

NIXON ORDERS "A PIECE OF THE ACTION" FOR HISPANICS

Here again we observe the workings of the grand visions of Mr. Nixon. As we have seen, his visions caused the near-total inclusion of Spanish-surnamed Americans into the corpus of government. They became federal government executives, advisors, and employees with great opportunities for advancement. As super grade decision makers, they had the executive reins of authority. They hired people and awarded grants and contracts in substantial numbers and amounts.

Mr. Nixon, in his Quaker mentality, had the novel notion that human beings who can own and run their own business, participating in capitalism, advance the American Way more rapidly and smoothly. And, when society discriminates against the powerless, government can and must lead the way. For this reason, President Nixon put muscle and commitment into the economic empowerment of Blacks. He charged his secretary of commerce, Maurice Stans, and his administrator of the

SBA, Hilario Sandoval, to spearhead the initiative called Black Capitalism

Maurice Stans, pointed out how it was done in a speech entitled "Nixon's Economic Policy toward Minorities" at a Hackensack University forum on November 18-21, 1987.

Prior to 1969, the federal government had no program to help members of racial or ethnic minorities to start a business and to stay in business. Help was possible for an applicant only if he or she qualified for assistance within one of the statutory activities of the Small Business Administration. This approach was unavailing to the minorities, who would be in direct competition with the usually more qualified members of the white majority. (1)

Mr. Nixon's concept was first articulated in two radio talks in April 1968 under the title "Bridges to Human Dignity." He described two bridges that would move Blacks from welfare to dignity: the bridge of Black success and the bridge of Black capitalism. (2)

His vision called for three actions soon after occupying the Oval Office. Action one was to appoint Hilario Sandoval, a Mexican American businessman from El Paso, Texas, as the administrator of the Small Business Administration. Action two was to appoint Robert J. Brown as special assistant to the president on domestic affairs; his job was to liaison with the Black community. And action three was to sign an executive order to establish "Black capitalism" on March 5, 1969, just after a month in office. Mr. Nixon did not wait for Congress to argue for the usual two years for legislation to reach his desk for signature. This was Executive Order 11458: "Prescribing Arrangements for

Developing and Coordinating a National Program for Minority Business Enterprise." (3)

The president's original focus on Black capitalism expanded to include Mexican Americans. He now possessed the personnel and means for extending capitalism to both groups for the first time in US history. Blacks had been living in a capitalist society as observers but not really as involved participants. Now, matters would change, and very rapidly at that. Robert Brown would, from the first days of the Nixon administration, reach out to a very well-developed infrastructure of Black national organizations, including the National Baptist Convention (established in 1886), the National Medical Association (1895), National Business League (1900), National Bankers Association (1929), and National Newspaper Publishers Association (1942). In the area of civil rights, he maintained tight liaison with Whitney Young, president of the National Urban League, Roy Wilkins of the NAACP, Leon Sullivan of Opportunities Industrialization Centers, and Dorothy Height of the National Council of Negro Women.

With the help of General Daniel "Chappie" James, the US Air Force's senior Black general, and Nixon's resolve, Mr. Brown was able to see to it that the number of African American generals and admirals went from two to fourteen from 1969 to 1972. Their presence at the Department of Defense would assure continuing and dramatic changes in equal opportunity.

Spanish-surnamed Americans experienced capitalism in very different ways from those in Black America, but nonetheless, Mr. Nixon was equally adamant for Hispanic business development and opportunities, as I've described. Just as Mr. Robert Brown had toiled for Black economic empowerment, so also Mr. Hilary Sandoval, administrator of the SBA, worked assiduously to improve the economic advancement Spanish-surnamed Americans. He and Martin Castillo guided Mr. Ben Fernandez, a financial consultant, in his efforts to organize the National Economic Development Association (NEDA). A precocious young economist and CPA, Eddie Lucero, from Denver, Colorado, had already designed and implemented a model for helping Latinos get into business from (as they say) by their bootstraps. (4)

In August 1970, Vice President Agnew announced in LA the formation of this new national organization to promote business development among the nation's ten million Spanish-speaking citizens. (5) NEDA was funded by SBA and the Department of Commerce. It successfully served tens of thousands of citizens and helped them become entrepreneurs. NEDA developed Hispanic capitalists—business people in almost thirty urban areas. Another business initiative that Mr. Nixon started was the Office of Minority Business Enterprise in the Department of Commerce. The mission of this agency was to promote the development of minority business. It financed nonprofit organizations that in turn provided financial and managerial services to create entrepreneurs. It was a gateway to capitalism.

I had discussed with the president the need for banks owned and operated by Mexicans and other Hispanics. I visited the heads of the agencies that chartered commercial banks and savings and loans. Both of them encouraged me to get Hispanics interested in this fundamental area of capitalism. Mr. Benjamin Fernandez, chairman of NEDA, assisted people to apply for bank charters. By December 31, 1972, ten savings and loans associations had been established, as well as ten commercial banks. (6)

In 1970, a program had also been initiated to generate deposits for minority banks. The federal government receives large amounts of assets daily. For example, in LA alone, people form long lines to seek assistance from the Immigration and Naturalization Service, which therefore collects large sums of money that it must deposit somewhere. With this Nixon administration program, the deposits were made at minority banks.

The Nixon administration designed a vast injection of cash to go into poverty-stricken zones to turn its citizens into stakeholders. "Community Development Corporations" (CDCs) was the startling label given this program. The concepts driving its implementation held that people living in poverty could enjoy additional income if they were shareholders in local development corporations. One-third of the board of directors of these CDCs was elected from citizens in poverty. Consultants provided technical assistance to these new boards on how to conduct and transact business. Some of these CDCs are still functioning today and are powerhouses. For example, East LA's East Los Angeles Community Union (TELACU) is huge.

President Johnson's Office of Economic Opportunity (OEO) was his way of helping lift people out of poverty. This agency became famous for dispensing huge chunks of cash; in the process, it became a target in political speeches. Mr. Nixon appointed Donald Rumsfeld to run it, who hired Richard Cheney as his key assistant. Bringing an entrepreneurial approach to the war on poverty, they funded TELACU with millions of dollars of seed money for business ventures. They did the same for the Imperial Valley, Oakland, and Fresno, California. Other cities in the Southwest, Phoenix, Denver, Albuquerque, El Paso, and San Antonio were equally well endowed.

Finally, the most enduring legacy in Black and Brown Capitalism was inclusion in government purchases. President Nixon instituted completely new ways for the government to conduct business with Black and Brown companies. The SBA increased lending to minority firms in the hundreds of millions of dollars. It also administered the tremendously successful 8(a) program. Under this program, Nixon required every government procurement center to increase federal purchases from minority-owned and controlled companies from almost zero to hundreds of millions of dollars.

It is a historical fact. President Nixon introduced capitalism to Spanish-surnamed citizens. The Spanish-speaking people participated in it successfully and in huge numbers. It is such a shame that the Latino press derided this fantastic accomplishment. It almost appeared that Spanish-surnamed writers wore socialism on their sleeves and held capitalism in opprobrium.

The *Los Angeles Times* hired a top-rated reporter, Ruben Salazar, in the sixties. In August 1970, he covered the launching of a brand-new Nixon effort to bring capitalism to the barrio. Mr. Salazar wrote: "By the end of the day, thanks to the great coverage the vice president gets from the news media, the whole nation knew of the formation of the National Economic Development Association or

NEDA." Then, Salazar just had to write, sarcastically and satirically, "In the barrio Chicanos immediately started calling NEDA, *NADA*, which in Spanish means 'nothing.'" (7) I ask, was this statement really uttered by some human being in the barrio? Was Mr. Salazar inventing news or was he actually recording the facts? Was he venting some personal anquish against capitalism? Would he have preferred Chicanos grow up in the socialist Marxism of his birth-place-Mexico? Did he not know that in socialism, there is no Santa Claus? He had been a reporter in Saigon, where he covered a war Communists had started in South Vietnam. Was he impressed with what he observed of Marxist methodologies and ideology?

Nixon's visions were directed primarily at the socially disadvantaged and economically denied American Blacks. They benefited immediately. The reach out to Spanish-speaking people evolved more slowly and developed later. The Small Business Administration reported the following on March 1, 1972, three years after the start of Black and Brown Capitalism, to the Cabinet Committee on Opportunities for the Spanish Speaking People: the number of Spanish surnamed-owned companies in the 8(a) program was 173. Black firms numbered 1,872. The dollar amount of total contracts since inception of the program in 1969 was $16,059,870 for Spanish surnamed and $118,049,600 for Black.[viii] It is important to note that prior to the creation of NEDA, no Hispanic companies had entered into the 8(a) program. It is safe to assume that the work of NEDA and CCOSS brought Hispanic men and women into the 8(a) world of government contracts. (8)

A careful reader of this chapter should ask why I use the word "feudalism" here. I justify this with the reality that Mexican

Mestizos and/or the Indigenous had been landless, uneducated, and powerless peasants since the Spanish Conquest. They were the poor and rural folks who rode boxcars to the "*Norte*" from 1920 to 1930. They fled their little hamlets for the cities and farms of the US, the land of the free. For generations they had lived under a feudal system; its landowners with all their privileges were almost all European. They were not Chicanos; they were *gachupines, Criollos*—Spanish Mexicans.

Pedro Gonzalez's *Geografia Local del Estado de Guanajuato* opened avenues for understanding the isolation a feudal economy imposes on the downtrodden. (9) It is a study of the geographic description of every locality in the state of Guanajuato drawn from the Mexican census of 1900. Its synthesis of thoughts, opinions, and experiences helped me gain insights into this issue and as to how it related specifically to the lives of those I knew best in Southern California.

José Rojas Garciadueñas, a well-to-do lawyer from the established families of Salamanca, Mexico, wrote a history of his beloved town since its incorporation by forty-some Spanish families in 1605. He also fled his town—not to "*El Norte*," but to Mexico City. Massaging the data in Gonzalez's book provided for each locality in Guanajuato, he listed haciendas, villages, and ranches by the number of inhabitants. Garciadueñas presented the reformatted population numbers in an appendix to *Salamanca: Recuerdos de mi Tierra Guanajuatense.* The appendix names towns and ranches surrounding Salamanca; the distance from its center to the outlying haciendas and ranchos is over twenty miles. Today, that area is called a *municipio* (a county). Haciendas were two to three leagues apart. For the Indigenous and Mestizos, walking was the only means for getting around.

1900 Census by population for Poblaciones, Congregaciones, Haciendas, and Ranchos (from *Geografia Local Del Estado De Guanajuato*, 1904)

Total: 39,200 Urban 15,600 Suburban 1,755 Rural 22,000	
Poblaciones:	Salamanca…13,583 Inhabitants Valtierrilla…2,016
Congregaciones:	Cardenas, 678. Canada de Ortega, 453. Mexicanos, 624.
Inhabitants:	1,755
Haciendas:	Aguilares, 246. Ancon, 414. San Andres, 112. San Antonio, 123. San Bernardo, 329. Cal, 236. Cerrogordo, 451. Cruces, 44. Santo Domingo, 227. Dolores, 11. Dona Rosa, 161. Fuerte, 261. Guadalupe, 309. Mancera, 108. Mendoza, 606. Molinito, 97. San Rafael, 341. Sardinas, 84. Sotelo, 288. Tinaja, 235. Temascatio, 541. Uruetaro, 422.
Inhabitants	5686
Ranchos:	Ranchos: Adjuntas, 246. Alfaro, 34. San Antonio Bachachan, 35. Arguello, 40. Baul, 65. Barron, 265. Buenavista, 260. Cabana, 82. Cajon, 131. Calabozo, 121. Callejones, 100. Cayetano, 90. Capilla, 445. Caracol, 212. Casasnuevas, 153. Santa Catarina, 72. Santa Catarina de Pena, 176. Santa Catarina de Razos, 97. Cenizos, 331. Cerroblanco, 166. Cipres, 176. Comaleros, 258. Compania, 95. Cuadril de Lozano, 23. Cruz Blanca, 42. Crucitas, 169. Charca, 123. Chavez, 120. Damianes, 23. Divisadora, 321. Dos Rios, 177.

Duros, 60. Esperanza, 30. Estaca, 177. Estancia, 175. Fonseca, 23. Granados, 181. Guadalupe de Mendoza, 87. Guitarrera, 38. Hacienda Viega, 11. Hernandez, 75. San Isidro de la Hilacha, 242. San Isidro Puerto de Valle, 290. Isla, 68. Jerico, 32. San Joaquin, 19. Joya de Villafana, 700. Joya de Cortes, 113. San Juan, 90. San Juan de los Delgado, 110. San Juan de Razo, 99. San Juan Temascatio, 144. San Juanito, 24. Labor, 225. Lobos, 218. Locos, 397. Lo de Rayas, 66. Loma de Flores, 763. Loma de Granados, 82. Lomapelada, 312. Don Lucas, 255. Luz, 19. Magdalena, 100. Magueyal, 28. Mancerita, 132. Maranon, 121. Marigomez, 244. Mesa de San Isidro, 131. Mirandas, 473. Ordena, 723. Oteros, 81. Palma, 182. Paloalto, 66. Paloblanco, 150. Pena, 59. Perico de Cornejo, 32. Perico de Razos, 146. Perico de San Isidro, 19. Perico de Vasquez, 104. Pirules, 18. Potrerillos, 420. Prieto, 160. Puerto de Valle, 104. Puertos, 58. Purisima de Oteros, 44. San Rafael, 192. Ranchonuevo de Cerrogordo, 38. Ranchonuevo de Sotelo, 298. Ranchoseco, 66. Ranero, 71. Razos de Ancon, 319. Razos de Molinito, 74. Refugio, 65. Rodeo, 158. Rodriguez, 19. Salitrera, 146. Sanchez, 46. Santiaguillo de Flores, 153. Santiaguillo de Garcia, 177. Sauz, 192. Los Soto, 105. Tecolote, 20. Tenita, 111. Tepamal, 49. Terrero, 132. Tupe, 68. Ulapa, 43. Valencia, 160. Valtierra, 242. Vasquez, 114. San Vicente, 192. Virgen, 35. Vistahermosa, 8. Xoconoxtle, 284. Xoconoxtle de Cardenas, 90. Zapote de Mendoza, 221. Zapote de Negrete, 261. Zapotillo, 97. Total number of Ranchos are 120, inhabitants: 16,160

An economist might analyze these categories to study the characteristics and lifestyle of this population. The roads were surfaced by earth; transport was by horse, burro, or mule attached to cart, buggy, and carriage, or on foot. Both before and after the arrival of beasts of burden, human beings were porters. The landed class provided education for their offspring only, while members of religious congregations taught religion. Our economist, aided by an anthropologist, could study the culture's language, military, business, capital development, banks, currency, and so on. They might want to also diagnose just how a very small group of Spanish Mexicans could control so much land and so many landless Mestizos and Indigenous. What laws controlled the use of arms? How was foot traffic between ranchos and haciendas controlled? Were the indigenous people allowed in Salamanca after sundown? And, ever so important, how did a few male European Mexicans cause the birth of a new ethnic group—the Mestizos?

Our researchers would no doubt conclude that the Salamanca of 1900 was a feudal society with a rigid caste system. It had landless, illiterate peasants scratching out a living, and on the other hand, Criollo landowners who probably lived in the town with comforts and armed protection.

From 1910-1930, the first ever massive migration of almost two million, a veritable Diaspora, from Interior Mexico into the United States fled precisely from these ranchos and haciendas that this Salamancan sample characterizes. Central Mexico provided railroad transportation to "*El Norte* for its fleeing *campesinos* (peasants). Why did almost two million young Mexicans rush from abodes in rural and often mountainous lands into the States? Why is there scant writing about these events? Why have not the hundreds of Chicano college professors done research in answer to these haunting questions and published their findings? The Chicanos of the Southwest and the Midwest did not arrive in huge numbers borne on yielding parachutes or Pullman railroad cars.

I have nonscientific but empirical knowledge of the migration's causes. Since I was seven or eight, my propensity for asking questions often focused on the reasons my relatives came from Mexico. My understanding grew in 1951, when I spent over a month living with uncles and aunts scattered in Central Mexico. After 1974, I started a business that involved extensive travel to Mexico, Central America, and Latin America. I became a devoted reader of "Guia Roja" graphic maps. With small circles, they show the location of ranches and haciendas of years past that are now towns. This empirical knowledge, correlated with the findings of Jean Meyer, have convinced me that the Christian Wars of 1926 and 1929 were a direct cause of the huge exodus from the ranch lands of Central Mexico. For his exhaustive account of the war between Catholic peasants and the Jacobin-Masonry-Marxists out to destroy the Catholic Church in Mexico, (10) Meyer interviewed thousands of war participants. He read an untold number of letters, documents, and publications. He took thousands of photographs.

These peasants, whose descendants now live in the United States, knew nothing about capitalism. They arrived in California to pick crops in the twenties. They worked in the sugar beet fields of Colorado and Kansas. They found themselves in Chicago and scattered around the Great Lakes. They were the country's migrant workers. They became the parents of the Chicanos for whose commonwealth I struggled and toiled; their young men went off to war in Europe, the Pacific, and some even into India. These were the restive young World War II vets for whom President Nixon made capitalism a new reality.

CHAPTER EIGHT

WHITE HOUSE SUNDAY SERVICE

In the continuing effort to expose the lives and times of Mexican Americans to national awareness, as part of my vision number five, I had recommended in my study, "An Overview of Spanish Speaking Affairs for White House Perspective," that our inclusion in a White House Sunday service would be just what the doctor ordered.

Sometime in the spring of 1971, the office of Counselor Robert Finch appears to have initiated action to determine whether Bishop Patrick Flores or Archbishop Madeiros should be included in a proposal to hold services in the White House. My conjecture is based on an internal note authored by a "gg" for review by his boss, John Bareno, who was then the executive director of the Cabinet Committee. I verified via a phone call in February 2009 to Mr. G. G. Garcia, who had worked at the Cabinet Committee at that time, that he, in fact, was the author of the memo. It reads:

July 6, 1971—Telephone call from Carlos Villareal. Just returned from a trip to Texas. While there, he talked to Bishop Patrick Flores. Bishop Flores seemed very pleased that Villareal would take the time and trouble to visit him.

The Bishop expects to spend much of the summer visiting migrant workers wherever they may be—in the fields. He believes that the Church must be concerned about those who are not well off.

Bishop Flores expects to visit Washington in the Fall. When he does, he would like to meet with a group of the Spanish Speaking members of the Nixon Administration. He will probably be here in November, and hopes that a gathering can be held at that time.

Villareal hopes this can be arranged, and that Bob Finch can be a part of the gathering.

Meanwhile, it seems advisable to go ahead with the proposal that Bishop Madeiros of Boston be proposed to hold services in the White House on a Sunday.

gg (1)

Mr. Carlos Villareal was the administrator of the Mass Urban Administration at the Department of Transportation. He was from Brownsville, Texas and a close friend of Archbishop Humberto Madeiros of Boston, who had been bishop of Brownsville from 1966 to 1970. Bishop Patrick Flores was the first Mexican American bishop in the United States, ordained in May 1970; he served as assistant bishop to Archbishop Furey of the San Antonio Archdiocese.

In the study for and discussions with Robert Finch, I had advocated for the selection of Bishop Patrick Flores, precisely because he was the first Mexican American bishop. Archbishop Madeiros was a Portuguese American; that he spoke fluent Spanish was only incidental for the purpose of including the culture of the Mexican Americans via a Sunday service.

In the Oval Office, President Nixon said that he believed Mexican Americans were so law abiding and family oriented because of their Catholicism. He lauded the leadership that James Cardinal McIntyre exercised over his Spanish-speaking flock. It was precisely at that moment that I revisited with him the fifth point on my three-by-five card. He nodded in agreement.

Sometime in October 1971, a young attorney by name of Doug Hallett visited me in my office. He identified himself as a staffer for Chuck Colson, who was at that time a senior White House assistant. He assured me that his visit would take only a few minutes. He related that he had been assigned to review the study I had authored for Bob Finch. He added that he had reformatted it for distribution to White House staff on a "need to know," and said that he had put my recommendations for action into proposals for the executive branch. One of them was my recommendation for the Sunday service. He asked me what I would recommend now that I was the chairman. I responded that I would have to discuss the matter with my boss, Robert Finch. His reaction was fast and firm. "From here on," he remarked, "you tell Chuck through me what you want to do. And, Finch, you tell him what you've done." As if to clarify the new White House lines of power, he related, "Chuck has breakfast with 'the Old Man' almost every day." I understood. I now had a new White House boss. One was for relating history; the new one was for making it.

In view of the new realities, I strongly advised that a White House Sunday service with hundreds of Spanish-speaking guests was a must. Hallett's reaction was a quick "you will hear from me very soon." And I did.

By November 3, 1971, there was hustle and bustle. A date for a White House Sunday service was selected, and Archbishop Madeiros would be officiating. I was told to develop a list of five hundred key names of Spanish-speaking leaders. They would each receive a memento containing a picture of the new US Treasurer, Mrs. Romana Banuelos, seated next to a smiling, relaxed President Nixon in the Oval Office—and a one-dollar bill autographed by her. (A little sidebar: the ink on the signed dollar bills faded with time!) Invitations flew out, causing a flurry of phone calls and travel plans from California, New York, Texas, Miami, and elsewhere. Parties and receptions to accompany the festivities in the White House were arranged.

On Sunday, November 14, 1971, President Richard M. Nixon and his wife joined the invited congregation to the first White House Sunday service for the Spanish-speaking people. Former President Lyndon B. Johnson and his wife also attended. Mr. Johnson stood next to President Nixon on the reception line. The Supreme Court justices attended, as did the Joint Chiefs of Staff, members of the diplomatic corps (especially from Latin America), and Spanish-speaking members of Congress. All three branches of government participated in the religious services celebrated by Archbishop Humberto Madeiros. It was truly awesome and historical for the White House to host so many Mexican Americans, Puerto Ricans, and Cubans. It was an exciting first. We wanted to share our euphoria with the world. (2)

Courtesy Richard M. Nixon Library

Here, President Richard M. Nixon was telling Archbishop Madeiros
something. My wife, Ester, is there; our daughter, Carol, to
her left; and Michael is barely visible at Ester's right. Former
President Lyndon Johnson was happy to join the service.

Alas. We looked for newspaper accounts that would breath-
lessly inform the American public of this humongous event. The
women and men who report White House activities, however,
deemed this one to be a nonevent. I had assumed innocently
that it would, almost *ipso facto*, serve to inform the American
public and develop awareness of the national presence of the
Spanish speaking. What a surprise it was to read the newspaper
coverage the following Monday. The *Philadelphia Inquirer* led
with a photograph of President Johnson, Archbishop Humberto
Madeiros, and President Nixon, partially cropped, with the

caption: "After-Church Discussion is Held in White House." The AP report focused on the Johnsons as it recounted:

Former President and Mrs. Lyndon B. Johnson came back to the White House Sunday as guests of President and Mrs. Nixon for worship services and joined in the reception line afterward. They shared receiving lines, the two presidents and the archbishop in the State Dining Room, while Mrs. Nixon and Mrs. Johnson shook hands in the newly refurbished Red Room. Among the 300 guests were a number of Spanish-speaking representatives, who were on hand for a meeting on Monday of an advisory council of the Cabinet Committee on Opportunities for the Spanish Speaking Peoples. (3)

The reporter who wrote this to inform the English-reading public was either stupid or malicious. Five hundred Spanish-speaking leaders were invited, and most were able to attend. The number of Spanish speaking was considerably higher than three hundred. The writer made a rather startling and key observation about a questionable detail: "among the 300, were a number who were going to attend a meeting on Monday." For the sake of clarity and accuracy, the reporter could have given a more accurate count of the service or reception attendees. The number was between four hundred and almost five hundred.

It is so interesting how biases and prejudices can be nuanced with a few neatly placed words. I can use the declarative mood to state beyond a shadow of doubt that writing of this type characterized the mean-spirited persons that "reported" what they wanted to "narrate" about the Nixon era. This type of retelling reality reminded me of the epic narratives of Homer and Virgil. The AP reporter, for whatever undecipherable reason, just did not get it. I find it amazing that the reporter apparently did not learn that this was a historical first—that is, that there were so many Mexican Americans, Cuban Americans, and Puerto Ricans at a White House Sunday service. And to top it all off, one wire service filed their story on Saturday the 14th, as if it were an event contemporary with the Sunday service! My outlook—that human beings used pencils, paper pads, and tape recorders to faithfully record an event—was becoming more and more cynical. The twisting of reality was the norm.

On the other hand, compare how the most respected Spanish-language newspaper, *Diario las Americas* (headquartered in New York City with circulation in the United States and Latin America, covered the event with their own correspondent. I translate his lead paragraph:

> *The very presence of the Catholic Archbishop of Boston, Monsignor Humberto S. Madeiros, as well as that of the Hispanic crowd to the Mass officiated by the distinguished prelate, in the chapel of the White House, represent a moral triumph for the Hispanic American population of the United States.*

The story covered forty column inches. (4)

Archbishop Madeiros stated at the end of Mass that his being the first Spanish-speaking prelate to officiate at a White House religious service constituted for him "a very high honor, and that he saw with deep satisfaction the presence of so many Spanish-speaking persons at the service." The tone and tenor of this article reflects honest and authentic reportage. What a difference!

Of particular interest is the manner in which the largest, but not most respected, Spanish-language newspaper handled the

story. *La Opinion* of Los Angeles serves the most heavily populated Spanish-speaking area in the United States. It tends toward
left of center; its pages are peppered with official Mexican government press releases. And, for world news, it relies heavily on
translated United Press International (UPI) handouts. It presented the White House religious event with a photo and ten
column inches commencing on page one. The caption on the
photo of Mr. Johnston, Archbishop Madeiros, and President
Nixon reads: "EN LA CASA BLANCA" and the story headline is
"Mr. Johnson, on a visit in the White House." The continuation
column on page two is headed: "Mr. Johnson."[ix]

Why did a newspaper like *La Opinion* obfuscate the reality of
the event? Well over fifty Mexican American leaders just from
Southern California, its area of circulation, traveled to Washington
for the White House service. I know how many leaders were there,
because I reviewed the list of invitees and saw them at the White
House. Yet, *La Opinion* wrote: "About a hundred Spanish-speaking
persons showed up among the other invited guests. The Spanish-
speaking guests were really there for a Monday meeting of an advisory council." The writer does not declare that "among the other
guests" were the Supreme Court, members of Congress, the chiefs
of the military, and the diplomatic corps. The Sunday service was
not for the controversial ex-President Johnson. It was the first time
Mass had been celebrated in Spanish in the White House Chapel.
The event celebrated national cultural inclusion. (5)

An interesting sidebar to this account of how *La Opinion*
handled its reportage of such a singularly significant event for
a predominantly Catholic group occurred after I returned to
private life. Its owner and publisher, Ignacio Lozano, had been

one of my presidential advisors to the Cabinet Committee, and around 1978, we had lunch at my request. I figured that it was time for him to explain the growing left-wing orientation of his paper. He explained that his daughter was now in charge, and as a young person she had some idealistic notions. The paper was daily carrying wire releases that cast favorable light on the "Sandinistas" in Nicaragua. I said to him, "You and I know they are Communists working with the Russians and the Castro Cubans. Why not describe them accurately for what they are— Communists, instead of the phrases your paper uses—'left of center'?"

He blithely responded, "We do not know if they are Communists. We do know, however, that they are left of center." That answer filled in the blanks of why the faulty reportage of the first Spanish Mass in the White House Chapel.

A further oddity in the newspaper accounts is reflected upon comparing the AP dispatch side by side with that from UPI. The AP dispatch reads, "The Johnson's were on a brief visit to Washington after stopping in Charlottesville, Va., to visit their daughter and son-in-law, Mr. and Mrs. Charles S. Robb." An examination of the UPI's sentence shows it to be a very close translation of the one in the AP story. The entire UPI story, in fact, seems to be translated from the AP story. There is one big difference, however. The AP story said there were three hundred guests, but the UPI version in *La Opinion* only mentioned a hundred! As a result, the focus on the Johnsons, as presented in the *Philadelphia Inquirer*, is the same in Spanish in *La Opinion*! The Catholic Mexican Americans in Southern California were ill served.

La Opinion ends its version by giving the impression that the "one hundred" Spanish-speaking invitees just happened to be part of the crowd at the White House Sunday service. And that among them were some representatives of national Spanish-speaking organizations who just happened to be in Washington to attend an advisory committee meeting on employment opportunities for the Spanish speaking. The last paragraph in the AP story accurately named the advisory committee as the Cabinet Committee on Opportunities for Spanish Speaking, but *La Opinion* altered it to something incorrect.

What is of additional interest is the fact that only two members of that advisory committee were absent from the Monday, November 15, 1971 meeting. One was Mr. Ignacio Lozano, the publisher and owner of *La Opinion* (the other was Mr. Manny Gonzalez of New York).

CHAPTER NINE

THE VATICAN AND PAPAL NUNCIO ARE URGED TO ELEVATE HISPANICS TO BISHOPS

To advance the national awareness of and improve the needs of Spanish-speaking people, I perceived that the Catholic Church could and should play a vital and transformational role. I did not, however, have a plan for doing anything about that. I had not discussed it with my staff. I had done no reading or research on the matter. I had not included the topic of the role of Catholic Bishops in my study for Counselor Finch in the winter of 1971.

Nonetheless, over the years I would catch myself reflecting on the uniqueness of a bishop's position. I would imagine from time to time in what ways my life would have been different if I had acceded to the wishes of my own archbishop. He wanted me to study theology in the major seminary in Burgos, Spain, and after ordination possibly to go to Rome for further studies. I did not accept the offer, precisely because of the discrimination I had endured from Spaniards. From early childhood, I had learned about the relationship between Spaniards, Mestizos, and indigenous Mexicans. It was a matter of superior to inferior. I thought it would be absolute hell to endure discrimination in the country itself that was the font of those prejudices.

The effects of discrimination were the reason I abandoned my ordination studies. I knew quite well that acts of discrimination were endemic to the nature of man. Original sin took care of that. Catholics enjoyed no immunity from that pathology. As I progressed toward the goal of ordination, there came a moment of after-dinner relaxation with a cigar in the presence of Monsignor Benny Hawkes, the chancellor of the archdiocese and the cardinal's right-hand man. We were relaxing at Saint John's Major Seminary in Camarillo, California, in the student store.

"Henry," he confided, "you know what happened to so-and-so?"

"Yes," I responded in a prudent tone.

Monsignor Hawkes continued to make his point. "They got too deeply involved as leaders of something new in East Los Angeles. They became public leaders of the Chicanos against discrimination. They forgot that they were supposed to say Mass, hear confessions—you know, be priests! With the problem of discrimination against the Mexicans, we get no problems from the Spanish priests. They do not go public. But you are a Mexican, and people will want you to be a leader in that arena. Let this be a word to the wise. Keep in mind where those two other guys are now; one in Chicago, the other in New Orleans. You will have to be a nice parish priest and not get involved." I knew then and there that I would have to work to save my soul outside, in the secular world. I abandoned my studies.

I returned home. I had lived away from it for almost ten years, save for summer vacations. The first few days were utterly devastating, disorderly, and truly traumatic. The people in my church, in my neighborhood, in my town did not know how to greet me. They had questions written all over their faces. My pastor ensconced me in his private study and scolded me vehemently in a strident voice for being so dumb as to leave a well-defined and successful career path. All my teachers, and the hierarchy, expected me to complete my studies with ordination to the priesthood. He tried mightily to get me to return to the seminary immediately. "Don't you know," he bellowed out, "you have been selected to be the first Mexican American bishop for our diocese?" But these words had no impact on me. *How did he know that?* I thought. But it made not one scintilla of a difference. My decision was definitive and irrevocable.

In March 1971, Monsignor Jack Urban, a former classmate, took me after dinner to the common room at the rectory of Saint Basil's church in LA. Timothy Cardinal Manning was watching TV there. As the news program showed the ordination to bishop that morning of another classmate, Father Juan Arzube, at the cathedral, the archbishop turned to me and said, "Doctor, that ordination was supposed to have been conferred on you. Years ago, I had selected you." I first met Timothy Manning in 1945, when he was a Monsignor and an assistant to Archbishop Cantwell. He gave me a ride to school out in West Los Angeles from downtown. I was a freshman, and he was a young priest with a very heavy Irish accent. He was what we called an "FBI"—a foreign-born Irishman. There was something memorable about that ride; it would reappear in my mind often over the years. He was a very holy man.

From my extensive studies, I knew that Jesus Christ himself had instituted bishops: his apostles. One of them, Saint James, converted the Spaniards from barbarianism to Christianity after the Crucifixion. And Saint Patrick had been an Englishman who escaped years of slavery in Ireland. He became a priest and returned to Ireland as a bishop on the orders of the pope. Saint Patrick did a lot for the Irish. He knew their language and culture. He brought them out of their barbarianism and into Christianity.

One singular and significant event occurred in November 1971. I invited two bishops to dinner at our home. They were in Washington to attend the annual meeting of the US Catholic Bishops Conference. This was something I had never done before. I had met Bishop Juan Arzube while we both attended Saint John's Major Seminary in Camarillo, California, and I had met Bishop Pat Flores on my frequent trips to San Antonio. I had no particular or pressing reason for wanting to spend a relaxing evening with two remarkable and holy men. They had, however, expressed a desire to meet with me.

Since I have no written notes of what transpired that evening, I write here over thirty-five years later from recall. I remember that Bishop Juan Arzube wanted to discuss Father Ralph Ruiz; I did not know at the time that Father Ruiz had founded the first civil rights organization of Mexican American priests, called Padres Asociados para Derechos Religiosos, Educativos, y Sociales (PADRES). I recall that Bishop Flores responded to Bishop Arzube's interest at great length. We probably discussed the emerging civil rights struggle that we called "*el Movimiento.*"

I know for sure that the bishops did not ask me why I left the seminary so late in my studies. If I had been asked, I would not have revealed to them that the embryonic Mexican American civil rights struggle had made me confront the certainty that I would be called upon to publicly define and articulate matters of discrimination against Mexican Americans. The administrators of the archdiocese were not receptive to that type of discussion in any media. Several priests I had known as fellow students who did not abide by the directions of the diocesan administrators were sent to serve in other parts of the country. Monsignor Bennie Hawkes, the chancellor of the Los Angeles Archdiocese, had personally informed me that if I were a priest, I could not be a civil rights leader for the Mexican American community, so I had to make a decision.

Prior to the conquest of the southwest under President James K. Polk, Spanish-speaking bishops had served as its "shepherds." After the American army conquered half of Mexico, German American and Irish American bishops were assigned to take over. It was now time to make some badly needed corrections. On June 16, 1972, I decided that I was uniquely situated to define a new direction for meeting the temporal and spiritual needs of Spanish speakers. They needed Spanish-speaking shepherds again.

On June 16, 1972, I issued this press release in English and Spanish: (1)

Dr. Henry M. Ramirez, director of the Presidential Committee on Opportunities for the Spanish Speaking people of President Nixon, thinks that the Catholic Church should act quickly to designate more Spanish-speaking bishops in North America. "With ten Spanish-speaking bishops, the Church could have a large impact on the life of the Catholics of the Southwest of the country," Dr. Ramirez said. He added: "A big number of the Spanish-speaking Catholics in the United States (estimated at 25 percent) live in that area. Actually, there are only two Hispanic American bishops in the American Catholic hierarchy: Juan Arzube, Auxiliary Bishop of Los Angeles, California and Patrick Flores, Auxiliary Bishop of San Antonio, Texas. Also, there is the Spanish-speaking Archbishop of Boston, Massachusetts, a native of the Azores Islands, Portugal."

Dr. Ramirez, who studied for the priesthood before embarking on careers in education and civil rights, added that the Catholic Church "has to recognize that she can play a big role in the social betterment of the Spanish Speaking, since she knows their problems and has ways for providing solutions."

Dr. Ramirez was born in Walnut, California into a family of eleven children. He spent every summer during his youth as a migrant farm worker. He relates that he and his family, from time to time, worked as peons, gathering all that fell to the ground, peaches and nuts. After he graduated from Saint John's Seminary in Camarillo, California, Dr. Ramirez received his master's degree in education in 1960 from the University of Loyola in Los Angeles. "While working as a public school teacher and administrator, I was called a militant many times by my colleagues, since I was trying to make systemic changes to the schools based on my Christian faith." Dr. Ramirez explained that he worked to involve the Spanish-speaking teachers in outreaching to the community, so that they could become more aware of the special needs of said community. Before he became director of the presidential committee, whose members include the Secretaries of Agriculture, Commerce, Labor, Treasury, Health, Education and Welfare, among others, Dr. Ramirez was in charge of the Mexican American Studies Division of the Commission on Civil Rights. As chairman of the committee, Dr. Ramirez is responsible for directing the group toward the goal of assuring that federal programs are reaching the Spanish speaking and working for their benefit.

As a Catholic, Dr. Ramirez is interested in what the Catholic Church is doing to maintain the Christian faith in the American people. While recognizing the scarcity of Spanish-speaking priests, Dr. Ramirez added that "the Catholic barrios of the Southwest do not have Masses, or sermons, or confessions, in Spanish…everything is in English."

He also added that: "Bishop Patrick Flores, a personal friend, was reprimanded by his superior, Archbishop Furey, a German American, solely for giving a sermon in Spanish when he was a parish priest." Bishop Flores, upon being questioned, confirmed this story in San Antonio, Texas, adding that similar incidents had "occurred many times because some priests believed that preaching in Spanish was prejudicial to their congregations."

"Catholic schools," he said, "give many Spanish-speaking persons an integral quality education. Otherwise, they would have to attend public schools without receiving a Christian education."

Dr. Ramirez, who has three children attending Catholic schools, praises their work.

The chairman of the committee praised the work of the Episcopal Committee of Advisors to the agricultural workers...as mediators between the farm owners of California and the farm workers as an excellent example of outstanding work carried out by the Catholic Church.

Five months after my office distributed the above press release calling for the appointment of at least ten Spanish-speaking bishops, I was visited by Mrs. Ada Pena and Mr. Paul Sedillo at the Cabinet Committee offices in November 1972. Mrs. Pena operated a travel agency and was the wife of Mr. Edwardo Pena, a high-ranking employee at the Equal Employment Opportunity Commission and also a member of the Catholic University's board of regents. She was a very active Roman Catholic and also very involved in the national affairs of the League of United Latin American Citizens. Mr. Sedillo was the national director of Spanish-speaking affairs at the US Conference of Catholic Bishops in Washington.

The purpose of their visit was to discuss the effects of my press release and the need for the elevation of Spanish-speaking bishops of Mexican, Puerto Rican, and Cuban ethnicity. They listed a series of reasons for the need of spiritual care leadership, with concomitant effects on daily living. The rationale made abundant sense. Mr. Sedillo explained that his experience at the headquarters of the US Conference of Catholic Bishops had convinced him that the European American bishops and the Catholic hierarchy were naive of the country's growing number of Spanish-speaking Catholics. He added that they lacked experience and knowledge of the linguistic and cultural characteristics and temporal issues affecting Spanish-speaking people.

Sedillo was careful and cautious in his references to these dedicated and holy men. In response to my question of why they had presented the matter to my office, they responded with excellent justification. The government of the Church is monarchical; parish priests had no leverage on these matters, and lay people had even less. The pope appoints bishops: the leadership of the hierarchy in respective nations submits its list of prospects to the pope's representative (called the nuncio, or colloquially, the ambassador). The nuncio (also called the apostolic or papal nuncio), after consultation with the hierarchy of the respective nations, makes a final selection of candidates, which he then sends to the pope. Nuncios are vested with both political and ecclesiastical powers. At the time, the papal nuncio in the United States was Archbishop Luigi Raimondi. As of Pena's and Sedillo's visit to me, the Archbishop Raimondi had only approved of one Chicano bishop: Pat Flores. I committed to a course of action that would take me to visit the papal nuncio. But first, I conferred with Henry Kissinger, the secretary of state, and noted his approval.

That month, Mrs. Ada Pena and I visited the Nunciature (the official name for the embassy of the Holy See, the sovereign government of the Vatican) on Massachusetts Avenue. I approached the meeting from the perspective that I, the highest-ranking Mexican

American appointee of a sovereign nation, was conferring with the delegate of the sovereign of the Holy See. This was a feat no lay-man, parish priest, or bishop without protocol could do.

We were escorted to the study of the Most Reverend Luigi Raimondi. He was very generous with his time as he very patiently and attentively listened to my presentation of why the Spanish-speaking people needed bicultural and bilingual shepherds. We both explored the issue of why there were only two bishops in the Southwest—one a Mexican American, the other an Ecuadorian American—and both auxiliaries. We delved into comparing how the Church had rapidly established an indigenous hierarchy in Africa, but in the United States, the European American bish-ops seemed reluctant to submit recommendations of Spanish-speaking priests for elevation to bishops. The matter of the large loss of souls to the Protestant organized religions was covered.

I quickly deduced from the direction of the archbishop's remarks and observations that he, too, along with the rest of official Washington, had been unaware of the emergence of a formerly uncounted and unknown American population: the Mexican Americans.

The visit ended with proper formalities but with some clearly stated disagreements. At my strong suggestion that he energize the American hierarchy to submit names of Mexican, Cuban, and Puerto Rican American priests from which he would select ten for sending on to the pope, he balked and replied that the Holy Spirit would add Spanish-speaking bishops in due time. At that pontifical elaboration of the workings of the Holy Spirit, I quickly expressed my admiration for the efficacy of its actions in Africa. The Church in Africa was by and large already administered by Black cardinals, archbishops, and bishops! I insinuated that here in the States, Irish and German American bishops were impeding the work of the Holy Spirit in areas populated by Catholic Chicanos. I gracefully but firmly stated that I would send a White House cable to His Holiness reporting on the meeting and its inconsequential outcome. He assured me that he, too, would dispatch a cable with his version.

On March 5, 1973, Archbishop Luigi Raimondi was recalled to Rome and replaced by Archbishop Jean Jadot. An interesting sidebar is the fact that the archbishop did not invite me to his going-away party at the Nunciature but did invite the other and now-famous Chicano appointees of President Nixon.

Several days after Archbishop Jadot's arrival, his office called ours with an urgent message to meet as soon as possible. His invitation was warm and generous; he asked me to bring my wife and family. We met at the Nunciature on November 15, 1973, where we were given a tour of the nuncio's residence. We visited the lovely chapel, and then he and I proceeded to his study. His first words were that he had called me to meet with him because the pope had told him, "Make sure you speak with Dr. Ramirez and inform him that the Holy See will proceed to elevate Spanish-speaking bishops as soon as possible." His Excellency stated that the pope was aware of my correspondence. I was elated!

Then he topped it off. He asked for names of my former seminary classmates who should be considered for elevation. I recommended Father Henry Gomez of LA and Fathers

Gilbert Padilla and Francisco (Paco) Long, both from Tucson, Arizona. I recommended that Auxiliary Bishop Patrick Flores of San Antonio be promoted to ordinary (a bishop completely in charge of his own diocese). Some other former classmates I strongly recommended not be considered for promotion, since they were lacking in sensitivity toward Chicanos. They were already on the fast track—monsignors working in the Chancery Offices in Arizona and in California—but none of them did become bishops.

On November 14, 1973, I sent this cable:

TO: His Holiness, Pope Paul VI

On behalf of distinguished Spanish speaking Catholic laymen in the United States we want to inform you of the cordial and productive conference we had recently with His Excellency Archbishop Jadot. The meeting with the Apostolic Delegate was held in his office in Washington D.C. We discussed areas of mutual interest, stressing the need for enhancing the presence of the Spanish speaking and Spanish surnamed in the American Catholic Church. We were most heartened by his Excellency's response to the creation of a climate in which the needs of the Spanish speaking could be realized, particularly the appointment of more indigenous clergy to the positions of Bishops and including the Spanish speaking laity in appropriate Church matters. We look forward to continuing this fruitful dialogue for the good of the Church and its members.

Respectfully yours,

Henry M. Ramirez

Chairman (3)

In his seven years as apostolic delegate, Archbishop Jadot was responsible for the appointments of Father Gilbert Chavez of San Diego, California, who was ordained auxiliary bishop of San Diego, California, on June 21, 1974. On July 25, 1974, Robert Sanchez was ordained Archbishop of Santa Fe, New Mexico. In 1973, Archbishop Aponte was elevated to cardinal of Puerto Rico. Bishop Patrick Flores was promoted to ordinary of the Diocese of El Paso and later yet, to archbishop of the Diocese of San Antonio.

Upon the ordination of Robert Sanchez to archbishop of Santa Fe, John Dart wrote an article in the Sunday edition of the *Los Angeles Times* with this heading: "SPANISH-SPEAKING BISHOPS GAINING IN U.S." Dart explained: "It was becoming embarrassingly clear to the Catholic Church five years ago that Spanish-speaking Catholics had grown to 25% of the U.S. membership but not one bishop had a Hispanic background. The most typical American bishop called Ireland his home or his ancestors' home." (2)

Commentators could have noted that prior to the 1970 census; no one in this country knew how many Mexican Americans there were. The White House did not; certainly Congress did not. And those responsible for forming public awareness and opinions did not know. In the context of a national "know-nothing" about Mexican Americans, the religion writer of the well-known liberal paper could have written more objectively and less sarcastically. No one was embarrassed; there was no reason for embarrassment. There was, however, reason for elation. The Church was beginning to go in the right direction. The German American and Irish American bishops, under the guidance of the papal nuncio, would now begin to recognize these formerly uncounted Catholics. And, most important, the European Catholic Church that had been transplanted to the United States was now going to merge with the Spanish-speaking Catholic Church that was started in this hemisphere in Anahuac in 1531 with the apparitions of the Mother of God, Our Lady of Guadalupe.

This papal nuncio was not in the mold of previous nuncios. He immediately let the New York, Chicago, Saint Louis, and Philadelphia cardinals know that he would not follow in the footsteps of his two predecessors. The pope was very much aware of the fact that previous apostolic delegates had been pawns in the hands of the powerful kingmaker American cardinals. The *National Catholic Reporter* noted in 2008 that Archbishop Jadot opened the doors of the hierarchy to the elevation of Spanish-speaking clergy to the rank of bishop. He was an outsider and successfully changed the progression and promotion of only Europeans.

The Vatican had acted.

CHAPTER TEN

NIXON WANTS AMNESTY FOR THE UNDOCUMENTED

Sometime after the presidential inauguration of 1973, perhaps in March, I was in my office doing uneventful chores when the private phone line rang. It received calls only from my wife and the White House. My reaction was happy when my wife called but nerve-wracked with urgency when it was the White House. The caller calmly informed me: "This is the White House operator. Hold the line for Counselor Finch, soon he will be on the line."

Then, with a soft and gravelly voice, he identified himself: "This is Bob Finch." After I acknowledged him, he proceeded in a monotone: "I am on Air Force One, seated next to the president." A vivid picture formed immediately in my imagination of the two of them pensively reclining in aisle seats. I was so excited that, contrary to my routine procedure of logging every phone call daily (even if only cryptically), I wrote nothing and recorded the conversation only mentally. What a shame! Nonetheless, the balance of the conversation remains engraved in the tracks of my memory.

Mr. Finch continued, "We just left San Clemente on our way to San Francisco. The president was ruminating over his successful reelection and was expressing his joy over the huge Mexican American vote he received." (Just days before, I had received a signed and framed personal thank-you letter dated February 1, 1973, from the president for my help getting him reelected.) (See Chapter two). "And, he was recalling your Oval Office meeting of August 1971 and specifically the spirited discussion both of you had over the Mexican American vote. So he told me, call Henry for three highly significant suggestions, recommendations, or ideas he can think of that I, the president, can and should do to demonstrate my appreciation and gratitude to the Mexican Americans for their outstanding and historical, first-time ever vote of almost 30 percent! He wants to do something of such proportion and magnitude that he will be remembered by the Mexican Americans in a manner akin to their affection and remembrance for President Roosevelt."

"How much time do I have?" I asked.

"Take a few moments," Counselor Finch replied. A fleeting thought raced: *Pressure cooker time.* I put all of my brain cells to work at hyperactive speed. My intellect's tires spun and screeched as they tried to get a grip of the asphalt. I imposed a tranquil and controlled tenor of voice and let my mind browse over some community needs that I quickly ranked on a scale of importance based on my own life experience.

To this day, I know not why, but my very first thoughts raced to a garage on Ninth Street in Pomona, California. While the president listened, I reminisced of my vivid recollection of trips to my old bachelor uncle Elias's garage, where I and my brother, Chalo, went for our monthly haircuts. I recalled for the president my uncle's constant lament that, though financially able, he could not visit his hometown, Salamanca, Mexico, because of his lack of official papers: "*Pero, yo no tengo papeles.*" When he had entered this country at El Paso in 1923, *papeles* were not required. Now that he was retired from the Kaiser Steel Mill in Fontana, California and had the money to travel but could not leave the country to visit his birthplace and teenage home. I always pitied him, mentally shrugging my shoulders (being only thirteen years old, that's all I could do).

However, my dad, Pascual, Elias's older brother, had traveled several times to Mexico, visiting family, cousins, and pals in diverse cities. As a result, he enjoyed a constant stream of correspondence with people in Mexico. The 1910 Revolution and the 1926–30 *Cristiada* war had emptied and scattered the population of Salamanca. My father would regale uncle Elias and their other brothers, Rosendo and Alfonso, in detail on his visits "back home." My father was lucky: he had a "border pass."

My recollections simply tumbled out as I remarked that situations similar to that of my uncle Elias were commonplace and could easily number in the hundreds of thousands. Since I worked at the rectory of Sacred Heart Catholic Church from 1944 to 1953 filling out forms for baptisms, Holy Communions, Confirmations, marriages, funerals, and such for thousands of families from all the nearby towns, I came to know personally hundreds who also lamented their shattered aspirations: "*No tengo papeles.*" The expression was replete with unfulfilled long-ings, haunted by fleeting memories of youth and dreams and hopes vanishing with the advancing years. I wondered how we could ameliorate that state of affairs.

Bob Finch snapped at that and stopped me. He said, "The presi-dent likes that issue. He does not need to hear about any other ideas. He wants you to flesh it out. Get consultants to advise you. Get it staffed out. Get your congressional relations staffer to start working on it. At the University of Connecticut there is an expert that can help you."

I was stunned! And the next statement from Bob Finch made me sit up straight: "The president wants to give them amnesty! Get moving! And that's an order. Give us some paperwork as soon as possible." And just like that, the phone conversation ended.

Then there was Watergate, propelled by the black cloud of a Congress that had been in control of the country for my lifetime. The majority party had exercised its power in all three branches for all practical purposes since the early 1930s. The Democrats, the *Washington Post*, and others were now busy stirring up the pot later to be called the Watergate break-in. I learned about how John Dean, counsel to the president, had foiled the FBI from checking his office files several days after June 17, 1972, the day of the break-in at the Democratic Party's campaign offices. The presidency was clearly becoming endangered. I proceeded, how-ever, to do what I had been ordered to do.

I immediately summoned my close and trusted staff to share with them the phone call from Air Force One: my personal secretary, Mrs. Mercedes Flores; my speechwriter and personal assistant, Mo Garcia; my spokesman and chief of information E. B. Duarte; and my chief of congressional relations, Robert Brochtrup. (For this book, I interviewed Mercedes, Mo, and E. B. all separately and in detail about this event. Since I had no paperwork on it, I needed to get their memories. It was remarkable; they all remembered what I had shared in my office.)

The phone call defined a novel and entirely unexpected direction for me, the chairman of the Cabinet Committee. I had no experience with the issue of immigration. In fact, in February of 1973 my cup was already overflowing; I had no interest in this area. The election result of almost 30 percent of the Mexican American vote for a Republican set the hair of the Democrats on end. They were going to come after me. They would be looking for blood. It was haunting and horrible for them. How could they lose 30 percent of the Mexican vote?

The migration of my parents, siblings, relatives, and friends was history: prior to my birth. It was a constant and perplexing subject of their conversation that yielded few (and troubling) answers to the questions of why, how, where, when, and who. It was not until years later, when I read the four volumes of *La Cristiada* by Jean Meyer (1) that my curiosity about the immigrations in the 1920s was partly satiated. By then, I had traveled extensively in Mexico, conferred with hundreds, and read many books on the subject. I learned that Mexico censored and controlled information and knowledge through its very secret police system created to work just like the secret police in Communist countries. It was called the *Direccion Federal de Seguridad* and a font of invisible tyranny. President Fox dismantled it immediately upon taking power in 2001.

Since the phone call, I was to add another dimension to the mission of the Cabinet Committee, which was viewed with new awe and respect and had a good reputation for getting things done. We would now focus on the people *sin papeles*. I did what I always did when faced with a new challenge: I took time out to acquire intelligence on this new-to-me issue: immigration, migration, illegal aliens, undocumented workers, those of no legal status, "guest workers."

I began with my own life and connections to people *sin papeles*, retreating for a time to research, read, consult, and recall events and pertinent experiences. My parents had a separate garage and small barn with electricity, gas, and running water on an acre of very tillable and rich, loamy soil at 1235 West Grand Avenue in Pomona, California. Purchased in 1939, this property had another feature: it was a block away from La Iglesia del Sagrado Corazon (Church of the Sacred Heart), which in the early 1930s my father had petitioned Bishop Cantwell to build. In 1939, my life became meaningful and significant.

I began to introspect about everything. Prior to 1939, our family with its eleven boys and girls had lived at 105 North Gordon Street. My father had been an employee of the Southern Pacific Railroad Corporation; as a railroad maintenance worker, he had toiled in the areas of Long Beach, La Puente, Walnut, Spadra, and Pomona, California. A Mr. Ahern, the area superintendent, was in charge of the railroad work in all of those towns. He and his wife were very devout Irish Catholics from the Old Sod; they made arrangements for my parents to occupy their roomy "executive house" (something the railroad provided for its area superintendents) rent free from 1929 to 1939. What a blessing! The house was quite roomy and had all utilities.

Mr. Ahern had a little side business. In the barrio we called Celaya, he owned a spiffy white house with a separate building in the front yard that faced the corner of Hamilton and Monterey avenues. It was a little grocery store catering to the barrio's Chicanos. Our grandmother, her widowed daughter with her daughter, her three sons, and the son of a recently deceased son lived in that barrio. It was their little Salamanca.

We had to move in 1939 because the city of Pomona was realigning the track of the Union Pacific Railroad Corporation to widen First Street. Up to now, the tracks had occupied half of the street. It happened that the house on Gordon Street had been built between the tracks of both railroad companies, only about forty feet away from either. Somehow we became immune to the sounds of steam locomotives and grinding iron wheels pulling a hundred freight cars and a caboose.

My memories of the years between 1934 and 1939 are vivid, rich, and pleasant. Downtown Pomona was but a few feet from our house. Its streets and stores were my recreational backyard. I made friends with the shopkeepers and was intrigued with their work. I asked zillions of questions, as the curious young are wont to do. One acquaintance in particular directly connected to my life in Washington. At a young age, I came to know the publisher of the local newspaper, the *Progress Bulletin*. His name was Roy O. Day. As of May 23, 1973, he was still writing personal, confidential letters to his "Dear Friend and President Richard M. Nixon" on my behalf.

My parents were most contented and involved at our new home at 1235 West Grand. My father, despite an inoperable knee injury, made sure we worked every square inch of its land. We raised hogs, pigeons, rabbits, chickens, and goats—for cheese, milk, meat, eggs, and cash. We harvested chiles, tomatoes, and sundry vegetables and fruits for canning, consumption, and sale. (Land ownership? For the first time in my father's life, he owned land! In Mexico, poor people could not own land.)

We were at church frequently. My father was the choirmaster and president of the local Mexican Nocturnal Adoration Society. I was the perpetual altar boy and after age fifteen, the clerical assistant at the rectory. I filled out forms and distributed bulletins door-to-door to Mexicans in two barrios (Celaya and Silao) and to houses in between. I got to know the names and faces of the churchgoing Catholics, the fallen-aways, some of the converts to Protestantism, the few retail businesspeople, and the handful of educated and privileged offspring of former landowners in Mexico (*gachupines*: Spaniards), and finally a few rabidly anti-Catholic Jacobin Masons.

In 1941, the Second World War started. Chicano boys were drafted. Their parents hustled to Los Angeles to confer with the Mexican consul to seek exemption from military service. Their sons were born in Mexico and were Mexican citizens. They were aliens. But whether they were legal or not didn't matter. They had been working in the citrus groves picking lemons, grapefruit, and oranges, and now they were going into the army.

In 1942, a bilateral agreement between Mexico and the United States brought other Mexicans to pick the citrus. We began to see them at Sacred Heart Church, at fiestas, celebrations, dances, and shopping in downtown Pomona. Their hats, shoes, and clothing made them stand out. I remembered that they were neither immigrants nor migrants. They were contract laborers working for a specific, limited time. Upon contract termination, they returned to Mexico. And, very often, they returned for another contract. They were called *braceros* ("arms"); the agreement was called the Bracero Program. The program lasted until 1964.

However, in the late forties and early fifties, I began to notice the presence of former braceros at Sacred Heart Church. They had moved into the barrios and were joining organizations in the church. And they were asking for forms to be filled out at the rectory: they had to prove with church documents that they had been baptized, made their First Communion, and received Confirmation. If they wanted to marry, they also had to prove with a letter from their church in Mexico that they had not been wed. It was my job to help them out.

The United States had become addicted to the cheap, bountifully available Mexican labor. And, as it is so often stated, laws frequently have unintended consequences. Just as the Teutonic peoples of the Dark Ages, the 400s to the 800s, learned via the excellent Roman highways that winters in Spain, the Riviera, and the Po River Valley were highly desirable, migrated thereto, and remained, the four-million-plus Mexicans of the Bracero Program learned that the winters in California and Texas were nice—but that the dollar was even nicer.

In the early 1960s they began to return to the States with their families, *sin papeles.*

But from their days as Braceros, they knew the owners of the horse stables, the flower ranches, the cattle ranches, and so on personally. These owners were only too willing to fill out Department of Labor forms affirming that they had found healthy and reliable workers for their job vacancies. The Department routinely approved these requests, forwarding them on to the Department of Justice, Immigration and Naturalization Service for the issuance of "green cards." As a result, millions became legal. The illegal migrants became immigrants. The semi permanent became permanent.

Vast numbers of prospective workers "sin papeles" continued to cross rivers to get to the States; in 1954, the Immigration and Naturalization Service implemented a program called "Operation Wetback" to catch hundreds of thousands every year. Yet, the numbers kept increasing. In the Oval Office, President Nixon had asked my opinion on what we could do to curtail the illegal flow. I responded that if in twenty-five years, Mexico might finally get tired of its dictatorial and socialistic government and move toward capitalism, industry and a reformed judicial system; this might supply the jobs that would keep people in the country. His throw-away response was, "Let us see in twenty-five years." Twenty-five years from then, it was 1996. Amazingly, that's when the socialist, Marxist government of Mexico was ushered out of power.

After several months of soul-searching and research, I realized that my parents had immigrated during the first serious exodus from Mexico between 1910 and 1930, motivated by the 1910 Revolution and the Cristiada war. Nothing had ever before caused people from Central Mexico to leave the only world they knew, to move to a strange land with a different language, a different religion, and different attitudes—and worst of all, a country that had, in the memory of their grandparents, invaded theirs.

The Bracero Program, the second wave departure (albeit intended as temporary) was also occasioned by war. The braceros were here to replace the sons of the first wave who had been sent to war. The motivation for these moves was now economic—a pure and simple bid to improve standard of living. The pattern of migration showed that the relatives of the Bracero workers also wanted the good life the US dollar could provide—not only in their poor hovels in Mexico but even more so in the United States itself. The contractually regulated flow of human labor became a torrent, with or without legal papers. Awareness, personal knowledge, and quick, convenient means of transport and communications caused a new surge of illegal aliens. The world got much smaller.

To discover the extent of illegal immigration, research would have to be done. There would be dialogue between my congressional liaison and congressional staffers. The Office of Information would have to be prepared to handle requests for information arising from our increased activities regarding the immigration situation and our efforts to develop conditions for presidential amnesty. I conferred by phone with the consultants from Connecticut, yet my appointment logs do not record meeting with them in Washington. I am unable to recall any specific actions I took to advance their work or even if they were given a personal services contract by the executive director. It was a murky, chaotic, and disorderly time. The president and his inner staff were implementing policy directions for the next four years; political personnel in all agencies were transient; many were replaced with new faces trying to get their bearings.

I personally visited with the executive director of the House Appropriations Committee to present my ideas for counting illegal immigrants. I suggested that in the near future, the matter would become nationally troubling. I asked him to add fifty thousand dollars to the Department of Justice budget for designing and field testing a protocol. I later was informed that such a contract was duly awarded to Century, Inc.—a company owned by Mr. David North, the former Johnson-appointed executive director of the Interagency Committee on Mexican American Affairs. I was also informed when he completed the contract.

Sometime in the summer of 1973, I returned to the Rayburn House Building to ask Chairman George Mahon for one and a half million dollars for the Immigration and Naturalization Service (INS) budget. (The executive director of the House Appropriations Committee was sitting beside him.) The money became available on July 1, 1974, to be deployed according to the protocol designed and tested by Century, Inc.

Meanwhile, Robert Brochtrup, my congressional liaison, quietly held one-on-one conversations with congressmen who represented populations with 10 percent Spanish surnamed or more. They discussed the Air Force One phone call and the Cabinet Committee's preliminary efforts to come up with recommendations and suggestions for actions leading to amnesty. But we were overwhelmed by the black cloud of the Watergate break-in created by a corrupt Democratic Congress.

President Nixon had not forgotten the matter of the phone call after eight months. For, in November 1973, into my office strode an imposing figure with a firm gait in proper, dark business attire. My secretary introduced General Leonard Chapman, former Commandant of the US Marine Corps. She departed, closing the door behind her.

General Chapman had come unannounced but on the specific instructions of President Nixon.

He was to work with me on regularizing the status of so many Mexicans who still lacked proper documentation, even a simple border pass, after being in the States for a long time. Again I was startled. The president had not forgotten. The highly imposing general declared that president had appointed him commissioner of the Immigration and Naturalization Service and had instructed him to work with me on immigrant amnesty. "Where do you suggest we start?" I thought *this is marvelous! I, an ex-army corporal, working with a retired four-star general on the president's instructions! Can this get any better?* And with Watergate swirling, the President still remembers!

In answer, I confessed that I still did not have a firm grip on how to comply with the president's request for "some paperwork." I had responded to the Democrats' Watergate investigations, subpoenas, documents, and harassments, done a search of the current status of immigration, and searched for ways to identify the size of the problem by counting the number of illegal aliens. I had started congressional contacts. I should probably have simplified the fleshing out of a report by addressing our efforts at people in situations akin to my uncle's. But reality dictates that when the concept of amnesty is discussed with respect to immigration, the task is no longer simple.

I had sought the pulse of American reportage on illegal immigration as reflected in newspapers between 1971 and 1973 and reviewed with the general my search of the literature gathered through a daily newspaper clipping service. We had found only a few articles; immigration was not a big issue on the minds of Americans. I found an interesting April 1972 editorial in the *News-Examiner* of Connersville, Indiana: "Mexico has decided to dry up the 'wetback' problem." The story ended, "Finally, in co-operation with U.S. authorities Mexico is tracking down and arresting "coyotes"—the recruiters responsible for the wetback traffic. The Mexican Justice Department has already jailed 200 of these animals." (2) It was a real puff job. The entire article could have been prepared by some public relations firm. The American public was not yet aware of the growing lines of humans walking out of Mexico and into *El Norte*, seeking the American Dream of prosperity.

But a sign of things to come showed up in Chicago. The Immigration and Naturalization Service district director denied Monday that his agents use harassment tactics on Mexican Americans in their search for illegal aliens. (3)

I related to General Chapman my efforts to educate myself on the current state of affairs and attempts to crystallize opinions on what we could do about this potentially vast, growing problem. We could take any possible presidential actions now, looking toward congressional legislation of amnesty for longtime residents who had demonstrated that they were solid citizens. I suggested that the general invite me to address his district directors when he introduced himself as head of their agency, so I could outline my recommendations for them (and I did). I told the general how we planned to count illegal aliens. He learned about the fifty-thousand-dollar questionnaire and the $1.5 million to implement the actual field count. We remained in touch over the months.

Toward the very last days of my tenure at CCOSS (definitely after the new fiscal year started in July 1974), the INS received its money from Congress. I got General Chapman (now known as "Chappie") and Joe Reyes, owner of an 8a firm, to have lunch at the swanky Sans Souci Restaurant close to the White House. We discussed how INS could award Reyes a contract to count illegal aliens.

A year later, I was in my office at 3600 Wilshire Boulevard in LA. E. B. Duarte, then a special assistant to Chappie at INS, called me with the news that Reyes had just secured that contract. I have tried without success to learn its findings. (4) Mr. Leonel Castillo of Houston, who was appointed commissioner of the INS in 1977, terminated the Reyes contract on the advice of his staffer Arnold Flores. I have not been able to learn how much work Joe Reyes was able to perform, but it is a fact that no illegal aliens were counted for the record. What a shame! (5)

The issue of illegals had been thrust on me; as a Mexican American leader, I was expected to know something, but I lacked hard intelligence and research on the problem. Yet, I had to come up with some solutions. In the beginning of 1974, I formed these notions, opinions, and solutions: The children of the first big wave of Mexican refugees from persecutions in the 1920s, of which I was one myself, were no longer the labor pool for picking agricultural products; we had been replaced by the Braceros. Their children, in turn, were now the agricultural, manufacturing, construction, and service business labor pool. They were the new illegals and were coming in huge numbers, especially from southern Mexico (its "Appalachia"). Their physical appearance and behaviors were quite different from those of prior waves of Mexicans. They were more Indian, more indigenous.

After "the phone call," I was under the gun to come up with something significant for the president to sign and do. The migration problem kept cropping up; matters were beginning to boil under the surface. On a trip to a conference in San Diego, I spoke with Frank Saldana, a reporter for the *San Diego Evening Tribune*. He got some of my thoughts in print: "Exploitation of illegal aliens could be stopped if the current work force could be stabilized, a federal official says. 'It would stop the turnstile approach to the problem created by the needs of employers,' said Henry M. Ramirez." (6)

As I had opined to General Chapman, the migration from Mexico of illegals did grow and become a highly publicized international issue. Six months later, General Chapman himself was featured in a July 23, 1974 *Seattle Daily Times* article: "Flow of Illegal Aliens: a Gusher." (7) And in the *San Diego Union*, General Chapman elaborated on the severity of the problem with detailed specifics, estimating the number of illegal aliens at six to seven million. (8) A *New York Times* headline of July 23, 1974, was: "Chavez Seeks a Halt to Nation's 'Worst' Influx of Illegal Aliens." In Fresno, California, Cesar Chaves, president of the United Farm Workers of America, demanded that the Border Patrol crack down on illegal alien workers. (9) I was to learn years later that the Democrat National Committee, together with George Meany, president of the AFL-CIO, were utterly opposed to any amnesty, in concert with their new Mexican American ally, the National Council of La Raza, headed up by Raul Izaguirre.

On March 6, 1974, Pat Flores, a reporter for the *San Antonio Express-News* interviewed me. He wrote: "Ramirez said his committee will propose amnesty for countless illegal aliens in the U.S. 'Those illegal aliens who have been here for years, established roots, and are law abiding, should receive amnesty from deportation,' he said. Ramirez said support for this recommendation 'has been well received' in Congress." (10) This interview shows we were trying to get the amnesty proposal to become a reality while the dark clouds of Watergate crowded the skies.

The two months of June and July 1974 mark a change in reportage from previous quiescence. After the phone call, I had to become aware of this exploding issue. The drumbeat began in Mexico, which protested the ill treatment of its workers in the States, demanding improvements and denouncing the wholesale hunt for undocumented workers. (11) On the US side, editorials appeared complaining of "More Illegal Entry." One opened with, "The illegal, alien invasion continues unabated [...]." (12)

Finally, a very nasty article appeared in a Spanish-language Chicago newspaper, *El Nacional.* The article read: "Ramirez

Acquires Entry for 32,000 Cubans. Dirty, Traitor: Henry Ramirez. "He is working on getting parole for the immigration from Spain of refugees from Fidel Castro's Cuba." (13) Some Mexicans journalists in Chicago disliked what I had done on behalf of Cubans who fled to their ancestral mother land, Spain, and discovered they would be much better off, in the US. I worked with my Presidential Advisor, Manuel Giberga and the Attorney General, member of the Cabinet Committee to get parole status for these Cubans. Perhaps, just maybe?, some Mexican reporters were fashioned by the Chicago opinion-makers a la Saul Alinsky and hard-line leftists and as a consequence had a strong dislike for Cubans who fled Fidel Castro's island paradise?

"The phone call from Air Force One in early 1973" opened a Pandora's box of ethnic emotions, legal issues, and international tensions in the 1974's.

I was on my way out of Washington D.C. and into the private sector seeking anonymity and a tranquil life for my family back home in California. Immigration would become someone else's hot potato.

Somehow or other, these and other efforts culminated in the enactment of the Simpson-Mazzoli Act in 1986, granting amnesty to more than three hundred thousand illegal alien Irish and about two million Mexicans. It would be a nice touch to give Nixon some credit for starting the ball rolling. It does take years for ideas to grow and become actualized.

CHAPTER ELEVEN

NIXON FACILITATES AWARENESS AND OFFICIAL RECOGNITION OF THE FORMERLY INVISIBLE PEOPLE WITH "NATIONAL HISPANIC HERITAGE WEEK"

And now, I come to the fifth of the visions on my three-by-five card. I suggested that the White House should include Mexican Americans in its cultural activities to improve official recognition and national awareness of their existence and conditions. I pointed out that Washington and its region, unlike the Southwest, did not know Mexican Americans. This is why I wrote a fifty-page essay on what Mexican Americans should expect from the administration. As mentioned earlier, it was titled, *An Overview of Spanish Speaking Affairs for White House Perspectives*.

The first concern my *study* reviewed was the need for official recognition of the Spanish speaking and it suggested that they be identified by ethnicity in all government data tabulations. It also suggested the following actions; the Administration invite Spanish speaking community leaders to a White House Sunday service; the White House hold a meeting with members of Congress to discuss issues relevant to Spanish-speaking communities. And that we recognize the issues of farm labor.

Sometime later, I was able to acquire a copy of my study. It had been altered substantially. One copy was a fifty-two-page document marked "CONFIDENTIAL." It was a total conversion of my study into a political strategy and tactical report Some one at the White House political shop had inserted a line after each area of concern that suggested a presidential action to approve or disapprove. These were actions the president might take. In retrospect, the realization that my study on Mexican Americans achieved presidential oversight is deeply impressive and gratifying for this former migrant worker.

Upon reviewing the chronology of White House activities with regard to Mexican Americans initially, and later on with respect to mainland Puerto Ricans and Cubans, I realized that the mid-1970 arrival of Robert Finch in the West Wing had caused the initiation of the White House's outreach to this new group, the Spanish speaking. In August 1971, Washington did not really know what we Mexican Americans looked like. There were only a few of us around. This state of affairs was very soon to change, permanently. (1)

To find pictures of Mexicans, Washington DC and the states east of the Mississippi had to look at *National Geographic Magazine.* Hollywood had stereotyped us. This problem of recognition on the Atlantic Seaboard was truly unlike the issues in Pecos, Texas in July 1951. I and several seminarians were motoring to Mexico City from LA. We had departed from Albuquerque that morning, arriving in

Pecos well past lunchtime famished and thirsty. As we approached the city limits, still out in very, very hot country among open cotton farms, we were so happy to read a sign advertising "The Best Hamburgers" at a roadside restaurant. Its vast parking area was surfaced with gravel. It obviously catered to motorists and truckers.

We got out of the car and quickly made for the entrance. But just as quickly, a glance at a sign posted at the steps made me come to a halt! Discrimination in California was subtle and oblique, but here, it was the "Texan way"—open, overt, and in your face, as I will show. My mind raced back to my 1938 and 1939 seasonal migrant days in San Jose. While cutting apricots in open-air sheds and on our knees picking prunes lodged on clod-cluttered earth, I had met European Americans from Texas, Arkansas, and Oklahoma. We called them Okies. My mother did not permit us children to associate with them. She admonished us in Spanish that they were barbarian-like and somehow pagan, odd and unacceptably different.

Now I had come face to face with living history. The scrawled sign read: "No Mesi cans, No Dogs, No Niggers." With great celerity, my mind told me, *European Americans in Pecos probably know what Mexicans look like. They will not hesitate to recognize me as the genuine article: a Mexican.* And then they would have to deny me service, a greasy hamburger, and a Coke.

They did identify me but not my classmates (who had names like 'Bob Hempfling'); my cohorts left as hungry and thirsty as I did. I quickly assured them that this was an opportunity to offer our mortification for the suffering souls in purgatory. Maybe we got one or two souls an early release." We resumed our journey toward Laredo. Had we taken a photograph of that scandalous sign, this chapter would be better illustrated. But we scurried out of there in such haste that the brand-new, black four-door Buick sedan with four portholes left tire marks and a billowing cloud of dust raised by screeching wheels.

I ruminated on that emotional event. If I had attempted to purchase food, I would simply have interfered with the social norms and behaviors of the descendants of recent slave owners. These European Americans possessed certainty of their White "superiority." The European American residents of Pecos, Texas were still abiding by the vestigial effects of the Invasion of this former part of Mexico by President Polk's minions barely a hundred years earlier. As a professional researcher and civil rights government official, I was to document in 1969 that the trustees of the Pecos school system bused children so that Whites could go to new facilities almost fifty miles away in Zaragoza, while the Zaragozan Mexicans were brought in to the old buildings in Pecos.

In 1968, I interviewed an El Paso elementary school principal for the Mexican American study. I was amused to hear her solemn, yet delicate statement: "My job is so demanding. It is so difficult to bring these little 'mes'can' kids up to our superior culture." My grimace, with upraised eyebrows, might have been a little too clinical. Her pronunciation was quite different from the mid-American version I had been drilled on at Saint John's Major Seminary. My speech tutor also instructed Hollywood actors. On my many trips to Texas, I did acquire some Texas-English patois and pronunciations (such as "awl" for oil). I heard that there was a dictionary of the Texan English dialect but never found one.

The world of superior and inferior cultures with it consequences in acts of discrimination was by this time in my life no longer a source of annoyance or surprise. I became schooled on human interactions and relationships derived from the world of class differences almost from the moment of arrival at the age of reason. Experiences, spoken words, and gesticulations could very well be recaptured in an essay on that topic. The US Army Research Institute in 1974 termed that behavior, "dapping.". As a teacher, I vigorously battled a disorder that impeded student achievement, and that was "the negative self-image" that so penetrated the psyche of Mexican mestizos.

In 1971, creating national awareness of who we were was a must. Recent political history and its personalities had taught us nothing about this national need. John F. Kennedy had not developed a strategy to include Mexican Americans in American society. Bobby Kennedy, with his Viva Kennedy Clubs, had not even promised to count us! The Kennedys did make the unionization efforts of Cesar Chavez, a rural leader of a few Mexicans working in the vineyards around Fresno, CA, a national concern. Lyndon Johnson's memory was jogged in the last days of his presidency as he recalled his elementary school teaching days in a Mexican American school in Cotulla, South Texas; he decided that he had to do something. Sadly, I add that the VIPs of the emerging world of Mexican Americans did not write about our great need to become known by being counted, either. The Dr. Hector Garcias, our academics, Mexican American union bosses, elected representatives, Congressmen (like Don Edwards and "Little Joe" Montoya) did not point to this deficiency.

People can rightly state that the Civil Rights Act of 1964 profoundly diminished discrimination and credit President Johnson for it, but the law was enacted to benefit Black America. We had to struggle to be included, because at first, we were not seen as included. We were on the verge of making our presence known nationally. Jeffrey Miller, at the USCCR, was assigned to study the enforcement of civil rights. He designed methods to measure how much discrimination had diminished by 1971—but only with respect to Black Americans. Given the limits of his methodology, I was able to convince the six commissioners that they approve of Mr. Miller's work only if it included the impact on the Spanish speaking as well. The struggle to assure incorporation of Mexican Americans and other Latinos into civil rights efforts continues even today.

I understood that as late as the early seventies, few people in official Washington knew who we were. We needed national awareness. Barely a month after President Nixon appointed me chairman of his Cabinet Committee, I wrote this memo, a step toward developing this national awareness.

September 3, 1971
MEMORANDUM FOR COUNSELOR FINCH
FROM: HENRY M. RAMIREZ, Acting Chairman of the Cabinet Committee
    On Opportunity for the Spanish Speaking
SUBJECT: Proposed Action by the President to Commemorate Mexico's Independence Day of September 16, 1971
1. At my direction, Mr. Clayton Willis, our Public Affairs Director, has discussed the attached proposal with Mr. George T. Bell, Jr., Special Assistant to the President. Mr. Bell has told Mr. Willis that he fully endorses this proposal. However, he indicated that it will be difficult to have the President issue a formal statement on the occasion of Mexico's Independence because such messages would go directly to the President of

Mexico who would then release it himself. Mr. Bell will be in the U.S. Virgin Islands until Wednesday, September 8, 1971.

Proposed Action to Be Taken

However, I see no reason why we cannot go ahead and have the five-member Mexican American delegation and the Ambassador of Mexico visit the President in his Oval Office on September 16th which would be a fine opportunity for photographs and for the Spanish speaking people to see once again this Administration's interest in them.

The pictures and the meeting would reinforce the President's declared policy of boosting the importance of Spanish speaking people in America. It would make the Mexican American people feel that the President really does care about them, a point which must be very clearly demonstrated between now and November of 1972. I would appreciate your considerable persuasive powers behind this proposal which could be of great value to the Spanish speaking people and to the Administration.

(Perhaps some graduate student may discover this "attached proposal" in the archives; I no longer have it in my personal files with my copy of this memo.) (2)

With respect to this matter, Congress had already acted three years before. The Ninetieth Congress approved Public Law 90-498 on September 17, 1968, authorizing the president to issue an annual proclamation designating the week including September 15 and 16 as "National Hispanic Heritage Week" and called upon the people of the United States, especially the educational community, to observe it with appropriate ceremonies and activities. But President Johnson did not proclaim it.

In August 1973, two years after I submitted my memorandum to Bob Finch, the White House took action. I submitted a list of two hundred potential recipients to receive copies of the first presidential proclamation of National Hispanic Heritage Week. (3) President Nixon signed it in September 1973. This singular act caused spectacular advances in awareness of Hispanic people in the United States.

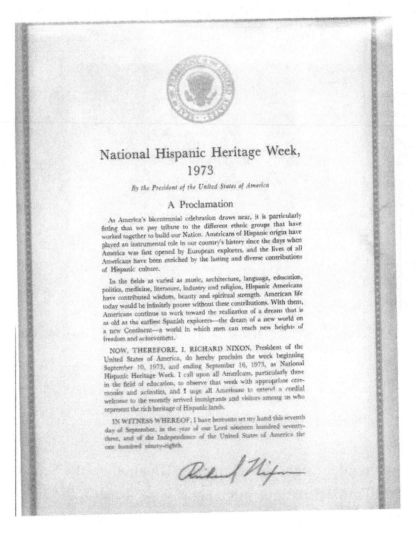

National Hispanic Heritage Week, 1973

By the President of the United States of America

A Proclamation

As America's bicentennial celebration draws near, it is particularly fitting that we pay tribute to the different ethnic groups that have worked together to build our Nation. Americans of Hispanic origin have played an instrumental role in our country's history since the days when America was first opened by European explorers, and the lives of all Americans have been enriched by the lasting and diverse contributions of Hispanic culture.

In the fields as varied as music, architecture, language, education, politics, medicine, literature, industry and religion, Hispanic Americans have contributed wisdom, beauty and spiritual strength. American life today would be infinitely poorer without these contributions. With them, Americans continue to work toward the realization of a dream that is as old as the earliest Spanish explorers—the dream of a new world on a new Continent—a world in which men can reach new heights of freedom and achievement.

NOW, THEREFORE, I, RICHARD NIXON, President of the United States of America, do hereby proclaim the week beginning September 10, 1973, and ending September 16, 1973, as National Hispanic Heritage Week. I call upon all Americans, particularly those in the field of education, to observe that week with appropriate ceremonies and activities, and I urge all Americans to extend a cordial welcome to the recently arrived immigrants and visitors among us who represent the rich heritage of Hispanic lands.

IN WITNESS WHEREOF, I have hereunto set my hand this seventh day of September, in the year of our Lord nineteen hundred seventy-three, and of the Independence of the United States of America the one hundred ninety-eighth.

Courtesy Richard M. Nixon Library
President Richard M. Nixon signed this
proclamation in September 1973 (4)

President Reagan changed Hispanic Week to Hispanic Month. on August 17, 1988. (6) The concern over the national void of awareness of Mexican American matters had now been shredded. Their inheritance, culture, lifestyle, history, and arts were to be known and appreciated. President Nixon is to be credited for this accomplishment and would have signed the second proclamation in September 1974, but sadly, he departed a few days before from the frenzied Democrats. President Ford signed it.

Courtesy Richard M. Nixon Library

Vice President Agnew read the proclamation on the September 16, 1973. From left to right: Joseph Juarez, chairman of the American GI Forum; Pete Villa, president of LULAC; Phillip Sanchez, ambassador to Honduras; Manual Lujan, congressman (R, New Mexico); Dr. Henry M. Ramirez, chairman of CCOSSP; Jose Juan de Olloqui, Mexican ambassador to the US; and Vice President Agnew. (5)

This action of Congress brings thoughts both negative and positive. Congress acted admirably, but what took it so long to become aware?

While I reached out to advance the nation's awareness, the White House Communications Office had to join us in the effort. I was delighted to know that Counselor Finch and the communications director, Herb Klein, accepted my assignment of Carlos Conde to the Communications Office. Fluent in Spanish, Mr. Conde was instrumental in delivering information to the media in Spanish and English—another first!

The other member agencies of the Cabinet Committee also soon began to issue information to Spanish-language publications. To assure equal protections, provisions for Spanish language communications were legislatively mandated where necessary (as, for example, in the Voting Rights Law of 1982). And, since taxes are a fact of life for every citizen, the Treasury Department quickly issued "how-to" brochures in Spanish. (7)

I knew that I would be the definer and articulator of our efforts to inform these new Americans, especially on what the federal government was doing to reach out to them, and to assure them of their equal opportunities. Our information newsletter, *Hoy*, performed remarkably well. (8) My knowledge of European classics and humanities, coupled with my experiences with ethnic universality in Catholic school education, equipped me to weigh, understand, and perceive other points of view and opinions. The experience of being the only Mexican American student in all of my classes endowed me richly with a catholicity of cross-cultural understanding. By the time that President Nixon appointed me to be in charge of matters of the Spanish Speaking people, I was acutely aware of the sociopolitical effects of race, ethnicity, and land and business ownership.

I commissioned a study on the value structures of Mexican Americans, Puerto Ricans, and Cubans. When I was in charge of processing personnel paperwork for the army at Fort Irwin, I observed that Puerto Rican enlisted men tended to come from the rural farmlands of Puerto Rico. I volunteered to teach night classes to help them improve their test scores. From my work at the USCCR, I learned that mainland Puerto Ricans living in Bridgeport, Delaware, and Manhattan also came from poor families with rural roots. And finally, in Washington, Chicago, and New York, I found that light-skinned Puerto Ricans were college educated, with social and business roots in the urban areas of the island, and tended to be of European descent. Only the rural and poor tended to be *jibaros* and *mulatos*. Mainland Puerto Ricans perceived that their future was in the States; they had no loyalty to the island government. Island Puerto Ricans were still fighting battles for statehood, commonwealth status, or total independence.

Cubans were basically concerned with their lost country but were beginning to see no other alternatives than to become US citizens. My conversations with hundreds of exiled Cubans told me they wanted no part of any politics that appeared even slightly leftist. They were very attuned to the political world. For centuries, the administration of the New World Spanish Colonies had been funneled out of Havana. A few Cuban immigrants were Black or Mulattoes, but most were European with roots in Spain. They had been landowners, those who had managed the affairs of state, professionals. Had they been English speakers, their difference from European Americans would have been imperceptible.

Mexican Americans lived in the Midwest and principally in the Southwest; those in California were comfortable self-identifying as Chicanos. Mexican Americans from Colorado and New Mexico identified themselves as Hispanic due to their historic trajectory from Spain. Mexican Americans in Texas lived primarily south of what was called the Mason-Dixon line, stretching from Houston to El Paso. Those in the Midwest had been largely forgotten; awareness of their presence had reached rock bottom.

Years before, England had established its Colonies as a subordinate entity known as New England. In like manner, the Spanish crown, represented by a viceroy, ruled Nueva España (New Spain), which stretched from Costa Rica to Oregon. The original inhabitants of that part of New Spain, which became the southwestern United States after war with Mexico, were indigenous peoples. Many of their offspring became Mestizos and Catholics beginning in the 1500s. Miners from Zacatecas, Sonora, and Guanajuato arrived in Colorado, New Mexico, Arizona, and California in the 1600s. Workers from Acapulco, Mazatlan, and Guadalajara helped the Jesuit and Franciscan Missionaries build the California Missions and their facilities in the 1700s. Other workers from the interior of Mexico, who tended to horses, mules, cattle, and sheep accompanied the Spanish. They were to be known as cowboys and mule-train drivers. These were the people who came to live in the Southwest—those described by Professor Dr. Julian Zamora in his 1966 *La Raza: Forgotten Americans.* (9)

To create awareness of these forgotten peoples and have their presence felt in these United States, I traveled to the major media markets and to the military bases in Europe. Publicity for the president's actions and orders turned matters around. By 1974, the nation became aware of the role and presence of the Spanish-speaking people in our country.

What role did the legislative branch play in this? Although James Polk, the Speaker of the House of Representatives about a century earlier, had targeted Mexico for slave land, two House members now created legislation in favor of Mexican Americans and other Spanish-speaking people. George H. W. Bush, (R. TX) and Edward Roybal, (D. CA) persuaded Congress to vote for the creation of the Cabinet Committee, which happened in 1969. Bush and the new Committee's chairman, Martin Castillo, shared much in common, including service as fighter pilots. Ed Roybal and Martin Castillo's father had both been born in, Belen, New Mexico. As a registered Democrat then, Castillo supported Congressman Roybal. The blend of personalities, commonalities, and careers wrought a historic outcome. (10)

However, the new committee did not hold a single meeting for twenty months. It was supposed to be a well-behaved agency that didn't make waves. The Democrats up on "the Hill" entertained no concern. The Republicans in the White House did not know what to do with it. The little and new kid on the block agency created to assure Mexican Americans their rights and opportunities struggled like a little orphan under "benign neglect."

With a reelection campaign on the horizon, energizing the Committee became imperative; the president himself took charge and infused it with support, direction, and energy.

Once elected, officials become acutely aware of the instrument of their elevation: the vote. Before November 1972, most members of Congress did not really know who we were. But when Nixon got over 30 percent of the Spanish-speaking vote, they woke up to a new reality. They hustled to learn about us.

Success! We were on the road to becoming known and recognized. The formerly invisible, forgotten, neglected, unknown group, the Spanish speaking, would now be courted for their vote for the first time in history.

The president had produced, and now it was our turn to reciprocate, remembering that service is its own reward.

PART III

WHAT ENDED NIXON'S ACTION ON BEHALF OF SPANISH-SPEAKING PEOPLE?

CHAPTER TWELVE

END OF CCOSS AND THE ROLE OF WATERGATE

The day was Thursday, June 11, 1972. It was early: around nine o'clock. The call came on my private line in the usual fashion; the voice of my contact was urgent and nervous: "It's a Plymouth, dark green, tag number such-and-such. Be at I [Street] and 17th, southwest corner, at ten-seventeen, OK?" My FBI liaison needed to talk.

He had been my connection to that world for almost a year. He was always notified of any of my possible travel plans. Once, he warned me to change my plans for a speech in Long Beach, California to avoid an attempt on my life the FBI had uncovered. Another time, he asked me to listen for a certain name as I traveled in the Southwest, explaining that certain persons are targets of surveillance: deep-cover operatives who might threaten national security. Their handlers do not permit them to become involved in publicity-attracting actions or events. They acquire new names and new lives, melding anonymously with the woodwork.

During cocktail receptions or otherwise, I was to listen for the name of someone who had graduated from advanced training for Communist agents in Pyongyang in North Korea. The FBI had kept track of him while he was a student in the North Korean capital but had lost track of him once he entered the States: he had undergone plastic surgery. This subject, Mr. L. had left San Antonio, Texas years before for training on Marxist ideology in Mexico; the FBI had begun tracking him when he enrolled at Morelia in Michoacan. Since he did well in Morelia, his handlers had promoted him to Saltillo, Coahuila, Mexico, for advanced training on Communism. Graduating with high marks, he was dispatched to North Korea for top-of-the-line preparation. The FBI followed his training path through North Korea. (Incidentally, I was familiar with the training in Morelia. One of my many nephews trained there. Thank God, I got to him and washed his brain just in time. He is OK now.) I assured my FBI liaison officer that I might well be able to assist, since I had known the subject while he was in high school in Texas. His involvement and leadership roles in civil rights demonstrations had drawn publicity.

On another occasion, as he drove about in DC, my liaison gave me an interesting and very different assignment. Since the FBI knew that my presence at events in the Southwest drew substantial crowds and that I mixed in cocktail receptions and after-dinner speeches for small talk and photographs, he asked me to listen for the initials of two Communist groups. He added that representatives of them had moved into the Southwest to implement their objectives in Mexican American communities. I was already familiar with the initials; my close contacts in the Mexican government of President Luis Echeverria had provided me with intelligence on the bloody military actions in the state of Guerrero against the armed revolutionaries of these Marxist organizations.

For the sake of political clarity, he advised me that Cesar Chavez was not a member of the Communist Party but a very devout Catholic and daily communicant (that is, he attended Mass and received the Eucharist, daily.) My FBI contact named a few persons very, very close to Mr. Chavez, however, who were active members of the Communist Party. In my speeches at Princeton, Harvard, Yale, and other places, when students became very strident against me, I would give them a litany of my efforts to help Cesar Chavez unionize the stoop laborers from Florida to California. Negative noises and comments would cease! I would give the information I had received about the Communist penetration into the United Farm-workers Union. With that, the hecklers would depart from the lecture halls.

My naming names and retelling how I had tried to help Chavez unionize the farm workers led intriguingly to a total absence of protestors at many of my appearances. During Nixon's reelection campaign, Cesar Chavez's noisy protestors routinely showed up to heckle Mexican American Republican speakers. The United States Treasurer, Mrs. Ramona Banuelos became a favorite target.. How interesting! They never, but never, picketed or protested my appearances!

My efforts to help Cesar Chavez unionize farm workers came about in this way: Frank Fitzsimmons, president of the Teamsters Union, invited me to breakfast in the commodious dining room adjacent to his office on Capitol Avenue in Washington. He related that he and the president often had breakfast. He had discussed my efforts with the president; his executive director, Wally Shea; and one of the trustees of the Teamsters Pension Fund to figure out how the Teamsters could work with the United Farm Workers Union to unionize all of the farm workers from Florida to California. I had reached out to the two Catholic priests advising Cesar, who had adamantly opposed any cooperation with the Teamsters. As I understood it, the crux of the problem was that the Teamsters wanted to continue their control over the truckers at the secondary processing stage of agriculture, the warehouses. In Brawley, California, the United Farm Workers Union wanted to include the warehouse workers. That's where violence erupted when negotiations failed. I guess I was involved in something way over my head.

My motivation for getting involved arose from my years of hardship with my mother and siblings working in the farms of California and my studies of the papal encyclicals *Rerum Novarum* and *Quadragesimo Anno* in the Catholic seminaries.

As mentioned above on prior occasions when my FBI liaison would pick me up at different Washington D.C. places, he would drive around aimlessly, while he lead the discussions and was quite talkative and informative. This occasion was very, very different. It had a secretive air about it, like something out of the pages of Le Carre's spy novels. It was the FBI working and it was marked: "deeply confidential."

My contact drove across the Potomac River into Virginia with only small talk. He was particularly aware of all traffic about us. He kept looking in all directions. He assured me, "I will tell you what this is about." He went to an eerie, heavily forested area, looking around and trying to seem nonchalant. I marveled at his mannerisms and wondered, *what is this all about?*

We walked in silence, deep into the forest. He stopped and faced me. "I was assigned to visit John Dean several days ago. He told me, 'Come back tomorrow and I will gladly cooperate with you.' So I returned to his office as agreed. This time, his office was neat but bare, in stark contrast with the cluttered and disorderly condition of before. Dean pointed to two neatly taped boxes stacked in the corner of his office. He remained seated comfortably as he informed me: 'Those are my files. That is all I have for you.' I asked a couple of routine questions, closed my notepad, and left." Then, nervous and agitated, he proclaimed clearly and forcefully: "I am applying for a transfer to Puerto Rico. I am getting the [heck] out of this town. I will not get caught between giants. That guy, John Dean, lawyer to the president, knows what this break-in is all about. (1) When they start fighting, they hurt people like me. This break-in into the offices of Lawrence O'Brien, the chief of the Democratic Party, reaches into the offices of the White House Counsel. It will reach into the Oval Office, if the president does not excise the cancer. We already have information on that. There is one high-up person in our office that wants to take on this White House group. He and several of my bosses call them 'The Germans.' My advice to you is simple: Get out and say nothing. They are going to get this president and topple him. There is a lot of hatred out there." That there was a cloud of hatred toward Nixon was nothing new. I had observed it from many years back in Pomona, California and read about it between the lines in the left-leaning national newspaper reporters and columnists and television newsmen, and finally lived it in Washington D.C.

Since I took no notes, I do not recall the many things we talked about. The conversation about John Dean, though, is a matter of vivid, crisp memory. It frightened the beejeebers out of me. Fears for my wife, my young family, my national standing, my pride, my future ability to earn a living, all these thoughts raced about my mind. Oh, how I prayed that the president would be Machiavellian and quickly excise John Dean from his inner circle, before the Democrats used it to conduct a partisan war. Oh, how often did I long for an exit from the world stage. My FBI contact could get transferred; I was stuck. He could remain anonymous. How fortunate!

I shared the big burning secret with my wife and no one else. From that day, I conjectured, dreamed, and thought about how I, now a very public figure and in the middle of a presidential campaign, could get out of the employment of the federal government—without causing dire results for my family. In the anxiety of solitude, I came up with three plans, but they did not prove feasible. For me, June 22, 1972, marked the date of the decline of the Nixon presidency.

In the excitement of the campaign, indicators of the decline were imperceptible, seemingly nonexistent. My knowledge of the break-in and John Dean's involvement burned holes in my brain. Years later in the National Archives in College Park, Maryland on Adelphi Road, John Dean would observe me with obvious questions racing out of his eyes and forehead. He saw that I too was studying the Nixon materials. He kept looking up from his own pile of documents, but he never inquired. I surmise he could tell I wanted nothing to do with him. We surreptitiously glanced at each other across a few research tables; he more than I. I wished I could enter his mind and discover his questions about me. I thought: *He is hunting for information so he can rationalize his "innocence."*

As I write these sentences, I have reviewed documents, photos, and memos dealing with an event that could be termed the apex, the summit, the singular highlight of recognition and awareness of Mexican Americans. The official visit of President Jesus Echeverria of Mexico was the manifestation of the heights to which Mexican Americans had arrived in such a hectic, frenetic, short time. There were so many highly significant and positive historical firsts for a president of the United States. (2)

President Echeverria's visit to Washington, New York, Chicago, San Antonio, and Los Angeles took place during that fateful week of June, 16–20, 1972. It was hectic and exciting. So many Mexican American leaders attended a White House state dinner for the first time in history (3). The official count was twenty attending the dinner for the president of Mexico. (4) For the after-dinner entertainment, eighty (5) more were invited. Over a hundred Hispanics, handsome men and beautiful ladies, danced into the night. (6)

I reviewed the 1973 hearings on the presidential campaign and discovered that the White House staff had arranged to use Echeverria's visit as part of a strategy to celebrate the advance-ments of Mexican Americans. The protocol for head-of-state vis-its requires many social and business activities. A cross section of Hispanic leaders were invited to luncheons at the Department of State, (7) Mexican Embassy receptions, (8) and Mrs. Agnew's luncheon (9). Yet other Hispanic national leaders were invited to tours, embassy receptions, Kennedy Center presidential box seats, and social meets and greets on the presidential yacht, the USS *Sequoia.* Guests were also invited for Blair House dinners. (10)

My wife and I were personally invited by the president of Mexico to join him and his wife, Dona Ester, on Air Force One as the Mexican presidential party traveled to New York, Chicago, San Antonio, and Los Angeles to be feted. (As you may imagine, I could write a whole series of chapters, illustrated with films and photographs of that trip.)

As I returned to my office on June 22, 1972, after being on an emotional high, nefarious news awaited me in the person of my FBI liaison. Today he remembers nothing about that day. As I write, the name of one of those FBI bosses who so hated Nixon surfaced. Upon his death in California, the Washington Post confirmed that former FBI official, W. Mark Felt was the confidential source known as "Deep Throat." I now conjecture, could that man, Mark Felt, be the one my FBI Liaison informed me wanted to topple Nixon?

Political campaigns in this country have historically used several methods for acquiring intelligence on other parties, espionage included. When Counselor Robert Finch acknowledged my acceptance of the Cabinet Committee chairmanship, he instructed me to "sweep [my] office frequently." My expression told him that I instantly imagined myself physically sweeping or vacuuming my office. He immediately straightened me out.

In the park with Dr. Grassmuck, I received more education on the realities of big-time political spying. He set forth carefully how partisans gain information and intelligence on the "enemy." D.C. is a town infested with people who need to know: waiters and cabdrivers who get paid for tips, foreigners stationed in this, the World's Capital, reporters, and domestic politicians. Bob Finch's lessons came in handy during my tenure. The Democrats constantly purloined information from my office and my staff. Oh, how naïve I was. Most of the employees at CCOSS were Democrats. Here are just two tricky examples out of many: Dolores Huerta, the sister-in-law of Cesar Chavez, entertained my very private and confidential secretary at my favorite watering hole, the Class Reunion, when I was on the road. This tricky and sneaky action was revealed decades later. And someone purloined an analysis of my study on Hispanic values from my *locked* safe and handed it over to the Democrats.

A year later, a copy of that analysis reappeared in the July 23, 1973 hearings before the Government Operations Committee, printed on pages 27–33 of the proceedings. (11) I had given it a glancing look but had not yet perused it. On the day after the theft of the analysis, I boarded a very early-morning flight to Las Vegas. A crowd of reporters swarmed around me as I stepped away from the stairs of the plane. Reporters from the *New York Times* and the *Los Angeles Times,* among others, badgered me with queries on some controversial aspects of the analysis where the study had portrayed Puerto Rican voting behavior negatively. My response was "No comment," because I could not respond without knowing what the memo had revealed. My reaction to the break-in was, "So what else is new?" Both sides do those things. But according to the news from my FBI liaison, matters were different.

I struggled mightily with my secret knowledge. *Do I dare call John Ehrlichman? Do I remain silent and not ask questions of those who know full well what happened and are keeping themselves informed on events as they gradually unfold and become public?*

A perplexing situation occurred several days after the election. We presidential and Senate - confirmed appointees (PAS) had been convened by John Ehrlichman in the auditorium of the Executive Office Building. The president gave us all a hearty and enthusiastic talk. He thanked us and congratulated us on our work. He wished us a few days of rest and relaxation at our favorite "watering holes" before returning to the hard work of finishing his visions for the next four years. We were all instructed to submit our resignations effective on such and such a date. We were told that for some of us, it was merely perfunctory.

People were asking questions casually. I burned with anxiety to ask one myself but dared not. I endured the torment in silence. Yet, I had hoped beyond hope that Erlichman or Haldeman or both would announce their resignations due to the problems they had caused in the matter of the break-in. *That alone would save the presidency,* I thought.

Perhaps the president would accept their resignations. That is the way power protects itself. That is the way it is supposed to work. I thought that if the president himself knew what John Dean and his cohorts had done, then he would cut off the staff responsible as well as those perceived as responsible. But if he didn't know what his gremlins had done, he would perform the usual Washington reflex: protect his official family against his nasty, mean-spirited perpetual enemies. My intuition homed in on my patterns of asking myself if he knew. I answered myself, *Doggone it, he does not know what John Dean and his cohorts have done! Well then, we all are in for a rough ride, where the corrupt Democrats have subpoena power and the vicious will to destroy!*

While the hectic preparations for the inaugural festivities were underway, gnawing harbingers began to appear. My understanding boss, Counselor Robert Finch, was quietly making his preparations to return to California and resume his law practice. Did he also shelter burning secrets? Haldeman, Erlichman, and Colson, together with others, had frozen Mr. Finch out of the inner circle and access to his friend, the president. His departure left the White House with only one person with real power who understood the Mexicans—the president himself—but those who pushed Finch out made him unavailable to me.

Sometimes one asks oneself the question, *What would I have done differently, given a choice?* In the White House's request for my perfunctory resignation, I was offered three options: become ambassador to Mexico or some Latin American country, assistant secretary at HUD or HEW, or a White House aide. I answered, "Wherever the president wants me." The truth was that my team was leaving, and the new team was not attuned to the needs of Spanish-speaking people. So, duty dictated I remain at the Committee. I wish it could have been different. (12)

The inaugural activities in January 1973 were an outstanding celebration. Latinos from every part of the country and Latin America participated as never before. The festive parade down Pennsylvania Avenue even featured a mariachi band led by a *charro* from Chicago on his gleaming horse. Mr. Bernardo Cardenas, a well-to-do Chicago, Illinois, merchant had donated the band's services, along with a famous Mexican singer. The mariachi band was another first! In addition to marching, playing, and singing in the parade, they performed at parties and were feted all over town. The *Washington Post* declared that we were celebrating "Chicano Power."

But throughout all of the glitter of inaugural festivities and the exhilaration of victory, my heart remained silently troubled and unsettled, like a troubled conscience that insidiously harps at the mind of a guilty person with "something is not quite right here." The admonishment of my FBI guy—"Get out, they are going to get him"—would not leave me. On the outside, I was smiling, but on the inside?

HMR's Personal File

Mrs. Ester G. Ramirez of Claremont, CA and her husband,
Chairman Henry M. Ramirez, celebrating Chicano Power
during Presidential 1973 Inaugural Festivities

Barely two weeks after these festive celebrations, my boss,
Robert Finch, left the White House for a law firm in California.

His departure was an indicator of the decline to be of Chicano Power. He was replaced by a powerfully connected South Texan. On February 2, 1973, Anne Legendre Armstrong became a presidential counselor and my boss. She came in on a gold-plated career path; she was very wealthy and the first woman co-chair of the Republican Party, the first woman ever from either party to deliver a keynote address at a national political convention. She had been a trustee of a South Texas school board district that had offered inferior, discriminatory education to Mexican American students. (13) While doing research I discovered her White House Press Release in the pages of a contentious House Hearing devoted to my time as chairman of CCOSS.

The saga of the break-in unfolded. the Democrats would now wield naked power. The Senate established a committee on February 7, 1973, to investigate the Republican presidential campaign activities. We were to learn how a corrupt, one-party Congress can criminalize a political campaign. Of course, the campaign of the Democrats was exempt. They set about venting their abysmal hatred of Richard M. Nixon by investigating his, and only his, campaign with subpoena power. The Washington world—huge liberal law firms, think tanks, universities, theology centers, newspapers (and their top reporters, and of course, opinion makers, the columnists), liberal television and radio—opined—no, knew—that a one-sided criminal investigation of a political campaign was normal and all right, because the Democrats knew what was right. Conservatives did not exist. Orthodox Catholics were out of place.

The one super-powerful presidential assistant concerning Black affairs, Bob Brown, left the White House in February 1973 after serving for four years and two months. What did he know about the intentions of the Democrats? It is interesting that Watergate lawyers did not publicize their investigations of Blacks' campaign efforts. Since the vote totals of the Blacks showed no shift to Republicans, it became unnecessary to highlight their campaign activities. Did the lawyers ever question the Blacks and their campaign activities? I have no knowledge of it.

I never discovered in all my interactions with Counselor Armstrong what she knew or had experienced of the overt discrimination exercised routinely and systematically against Mexicans in Texas and even more openly in her region, colonial South Texas. She never discussed the matter. I assume she was blithely ignorant of the discrimination. She grew up at a time and in a place when "people just knew their place." It just seemed that I and the civil rights struggles belonged to another era or maybe just another suppressed mental department. She had been raised in the world of European culture and wealthy privilege in New Orleans. "Darkies" knew their place there.

Her moments with me were so unctuously correct that I unconsciously made bodily motions to presume comfort and understanding. In Catholic theology, we call that self-mortification. It builds stronger souls. Did she not know that I had been the chief of the Mexican American Studies Division at the Civil Rights Commission and had issued many reports documenting the horrific negation of normal and civil educational environments for children in Texas? Did she not know of the attitude of European American educators in Texas reflected in the oft-stated theme: "It is hard; but we must bring these mes'can kids up to our superior culture"?

And so, Armstrong replaced my Chicano understanding boss, Robert Finch. One of her first acts was to open the first Office of Women's Programs in the White House. She then promptly announced that Nixon was committed to appointing women to important positions. It was clear to me that women's affairs would become her number-one priority, which to me was certain evidence of the decline in the importance of the Mexican American civil rights. Her resume showed her lifetime affinity for her cause. She had been the student body president and valedictorian at her all-girl high school and had received her BA from an all-girl college; she served as a member of the Advisory Committee for American Women and Politics at Rutgers University, the Department of Defense Advisory Committee for Women in Service, and was founder of Tops 'n Texas, a statewide awards program recognizing three women annually.

The mere fact she was a European American of a French family and was also a huge landowner from South Texas gave me angst about her knowledge of and commitment to the civil rights struggle of Chicanos. I, born and raised in the open society of California, learned with deep apprehension and yes, fear, how to travel by myself in 1968 into the depths of the closed society of South Texas, where people "jest knew their place." The European Americans of South Texas knew all about "outside agitators." It was for sheer and wise self-protection that I rented unmarked government cars in San Antonio and hid my rather large United States Commission on Civil Rights government ID under the floor matting. I had personally studied, documented, and witnessed anti-Mexican American discrimination. I had directed teams of lawyers and my own Civil Rights Commission staff to interview public school officials from the state's superintendent of education down to local school officials and teachers. My staff documented thousands of hours of classroom instruction. I became a disgustingly knowledgeable expert on educational malpractice in South Texas.

As I recounted just one experience to my wife upon my return home to Bethesda, Maryland, I broke down and cried. At an elementary school in South Texas, a janitor, a Mexican American, gesticulated for me to "come." He took me to his supply room. He urged me quickly to step up on a little ladder he had leaned on the wall and told me to look out onto the playground through the transom window while the first-graders were on recess (Texas did not offer kindergarten at that time). He said no more. I could not believe my lying eyes. I rubbed them, seeking more clarity of vision and reaffirmation. But, no, what I was seeing remains seared in my memory. The first-grade teacher held with one hand a tiny little girl by both or one ankles,(my memory does not serve accurately), while with the free hand she administered a proper spanking on the spot for speaking a language—Spanish—that Texas had outlawed, in their State Constitution! A vestige of conquest. For that child, this physical punishment must have been an incomprehensible battery. These were the incipient days of her school life, and she was doing what she had done since birth and at the warm bosom of her mother who caressed her in Spanish. She was only communicating in her medium. And, in Washington D.C. several years later I inherited a boss who was a former member of the Kennedy County, Texas School Board since 1968! A trustee who was responsible for that type of legally administered physical sanction. The action of that teacher was common practice in that part of Texas.

In addition to her big job of bringing women into the mainstream of American careerism, Armstrong was assigned that of overseeing Mexican American affairs and, therefore, me. Since I had become an authority on Texas discrimination against Mexican Americans, I entered an uncomfortable but cordial relationship with her. Polite comportment was the paradigm for contact with this lady from the world of grace, gentility, and unjust discrimination. Chicanos and mainland Puerto Ricans were raising hell with me in raucous voices, yet with the counselor, I had to be on my very best behavior.

Yet, I was frequently chided by my personal assistant, Mo Garcia, and my information officer, E. B. Duarte, for my sometimes obvious lack of thoughtfulness toward this "Southern lady." Mo and E. B. had been born and raised in that part of Texas, and they would go on automatic pilot with her. On one occasion, Mo blew up at me because she had arrived at our building in one of long, black White House limousines. Her trip consisted of traveling a distance of two very short blocks away from the West Wing! How proper and fitting for a southern lady. I did not bother to run out of my tenth-floor office to the elevator to greet her as she alighted from the limousine. I dispatched Mo. I remained in my spacious office awaiting her arrival. I remained uncouth and ignorant of Southern civility toward a person ignorant of the sufferings endured by Mexican Americans at the hands of the victors at the Alamo.

I am sure that my body language and facial expressions betrayed utter discomfort when Congressman and Reverend Father Drinan, a Jesuit from Boston, questioned me in the July 1973 hearings (14) about when I had last met with Mrs. Armstrong for any length of time over the business of the Cabinet Committee. The answer was that we had not met at all as frequently as I had with Bob Finch (or, for that matter, with President Nixon). So, in a long and somewhat convoluted reply, I truthfully articulated a list of actions, meetings, and phone calls designed to satisfy the congressman and keep him away from his real intention of asking "for some length of time." So, he continued with another angle, by which I inferred he intended to find out Mrs. Armstrong's qualifications for being in charge of Mexican American affairs. What was her background in Spanish-speaking affairs prior to her appointment? "Does she speak Spanish?" He inquired. *Don't blow it; don't get into discussing South Texas society,* I alertly thought. From beginning to the end of questioning by this Congressman, I mentally fumed with sarcasm at his mean spirited attitude; he too knew nothing about us, the Chicanos. He also showed personal animus toward me, a Republican and a Mexican. He could not swallow that. I had planned to address him with: *Tu es sacerdos ad eternitatem secundum ordo Melchizedek, (You are a priest for eternity according to the order of Melchizedek), but was advised by Congressman Horton of Rochester, NY, against my verbalizing that title in a Congressional Hearing.*

There would be a new equation in the White House. Bob Brown's replacement, Stan Scott, would represent the interests of the Blacks; Anne Legendre Armstrong would represent the interests of the women. Len Garment would represent the enforcement of the civil rights laws. And, oh yes, Anne Armstrong would be a liaison to Mexican Americans, mainland Puerto Ricans, and the Cubans. Eventually, she would even claim to be a member of the Cabinet Committee. Fred Malek, Director of the Office of White House Presidential Personnel was replaced by Jerry

Jones, a wealthy Texas oil man. Dave Wimer, former employee of Bob Hope, moved from the Department of Labor to be his, Jerry Jones', assistant..

With this new arrangement, the civil rights struggles of the Chicanos were no longer the priority they had been. Unanticipated, sobering events enhanced this threatening and negative trajectory; some of them events came from the White House. My user-friendly White House edifice began to crumble. The walls around the office of White House Personnel were cracking. Staffers who had served the president for his first four years were embarking on their own career paths in November and December, when new appointees are being screened. Al Kaupinen had assigned himself to the Government Services Agency (GSA). Stan Anderson became assistant secretary at the State Department in charge of security of all embassies and facilities. Fred Malek was moving to OMB. Barbara Franklin was becoming secretary of commerce. William Marumoto, who had been key for access into the Office of White House Presidential Personnel where the "Brown Mafia" met weekly, to consider candidates for an ever-expanding list of high-level positions, had already printed fancy stationery for his new business. And Tony Rodriguez, who had been his assistant, was moving to California to start his business under the sponsorship of the SBA's 8a program. Finally, Carlos Conde, assistant to Herb Klein in the Office of Communications, was also departing for a high-level position at the Inter-American Development Bank. Chuck Colson's staff, with which I had had substantive interaction, disappeared before my eyes.

There remained one structure to which I had not been given access for implementing my Five-Point Program. I knew from my experience at the Civil Rights Commission that there existed in the White House an office named the Domestic Council. That part of the White House became quite famous when President Nixon appointed a big Democrat early in his Administration by name of Daniel Patrick Moynihan to be in charge At the Civil Rights Commission that action caused never ending speculations. The Domestic Council was in charge of executing the president's programs in the domestic agencies. On the other hand, the National Security Council, under Dr. Henry Kissinger, was responsible for the Pentagon, CIA, and so on.

As a consideration for accepting my presidential appointment, I had requested of Bob Finch that I have access to the Domestic Council for purposes of civil rights. After all, I thought, both Len Garment, the lawyer in charge of civil rights, and Bob Brown had access. In the Oval Office, I had discussed with the president my need for the same access to the Domestic Council as Bob Brown's. What I did appreciate was that Bob Finch had deep clout with one half of the White House—the Office of Management and Budget. He did not have any clout with the other half—the Domestic Council; that was John Ehrlichman's baronetcy. John had been presidential counsel; he had brought his UCLA friend, Bob Haldeman, to Nixon, who then made him chief of staff. John had also brought John Dean to be presidential counsel as he himself moved over to take charge of the Domestic Council. From those days onward, the center of power would be in their hands.

And, now as my own access was evaporating, I would try to gain access to a place of power that was new to me. I called John Ehrlichman and left a clear and succinct message: it was time for the Cabinet Committee to be afforded its long-denied access to the Domestic Council now that Bob Finch was departing. In my quest for a friendly port, it made perfect sense to carry the hopes, dreams, and aspirations of the Mexican Americans, mainland Puerto Ricans, and other Hispanics to a well-oiled organization integral to the workings of the White House.

On February 21, 1973, my secretary, Michele, took a call from Ehrlichman and took this message: "He said that the president would like you to see Anne Armstrong instead of him." What did this mean? Access denied. Whether or not the president had actually voiced the instruction, life in eternity will reveal the truth. It was common practice for Washington underlings to utter orders, instructions, or phrases and then give the impression that their boss was the author. The assistants to senators, cabinet officers, and even of the president—especially, when they knew there was no chance of being corrected or contradicted, would utilize this modality. (15)

John Ehrlichman staffed the president's inner circle with Bob Halderman and John Dean. The Mexican Americans were of deep concern to the president and to Bob Finch and his guys, but not to Ehrlichman and his guys. We did not exist for them.

The Cabinet Committee, therefore, was to continue under the auspices of the office of the new counselor to the president, Mrs. Armstrong who would report to the team of Ehrlichman. The Committee would be subjected to the "*personalismo*" of the "new kid on the block," who was inexperienced in the Chicano Revolution and new to the infighting of the White House jungle. But for a very few powerfully connected women, this White House had been the land of warrior men who knew how to deal with each other. Now we (I mean, I) would have to be deferential, proper, and very correct. In retrospect, I wish I had returned to my profession, education.

An obituary appearing in the *Washington Post* on July 31, 2008, characterized Armstrong's career with these words: "Anne Armstrong, 80, a strong willed Texas Republican who helped run a working cattle ranch, championed women's rights and served as the United States first female Ambassador to Britain died July 30." Toward the end of the obituary is: "Fluent in Spanish, she was Nixon's liaison to Hispanic Americans and was a member of a Cabinet committee on opportunities for Spanish-speaking people." (16) It is a fact that she viewed herself as the liaison to the Hispanic Americans. After all did she not replace the prior Counselor to the President who had been explicitly assigned to be in charge of all matters dealing with the Mexican Americans by the president himself? She performed that task marvelously well, so long as she was dealing with New York Puerto Ricans. She reached out to the Puerto Rican leadership in New York and in the process caused disruptions in the organization of the Cabinet Committee. She was not, however, a member of the Cabinet Committee. No wording in the enabling legislation stated that the counselor to the president, even with a cabinet ranking, was also a member of the Cabinet Committee. Was she fluent in Spanish? The writer of her obituary says so. I never heard her voice one word in her "fluent Spanish."

Since Mrs. Armstrong had no preparation, no background and no experiential knowledge of the civil rights struggles of the Chicanos, especially in South Texas, or of the very recent claim to opportunities by the mainland Puerto Ricans, or by the even more recent political involvement of the Cubans, her work led even more to our decline. She hired a very young, inexperienced person, almost a kid, who was entirely ignorant of Chicano struggles—Fred Slight—and placed him on my payroll. It was highly significant that she acted unilaterally in adding a person to the budget of CCOSS without my involvement or approval. She dealt directly with the executive director, Ray Maduro.

Maduro enjoyed delegated fiscal authority as a function of his position. His loyalties were always deeply suspect. He presumed to represent the interests of the mainland Puerto Ricans, and toward that end he exercised independent actions and behavior where and when he felt he could get away with them. His posture and comportment caused frightful tensions at the Cabinet Committee. Senator Javits and the White House had foisted him on me. I had already fired the last executive director, another Puerto Rican and favorite of Senator Javits. I did it while the senator was skiing at Christmas at his winter vacation place, San Moritz. Finch complained bitterly as he remarked: "That firing will cost us a hospital and a bridge. Javits will demand compensation." I should have used the four-page, handwritten report on legal-size paper that I had received from my FBI contacts. The report, written in Mexico City, detailed highly questionable activities of Mr. Maduro in Mexico and Latin America while he had worked as a law enforcement officer. I had exhausted my supply of silver bullets. Javits would allow my Senate confirmation only after I hired Maduro, months after my nomination. Such is the world of Washington, where senators get what they want, irrespective of the effects on the citizenry. I needed my staff imbued with loyalty in the same way a senator hired his own staff.

Anne Armstrong housed Fred someplace in the executive offices. Whereas Bob Finch immediately defined the relationship between his assistant, Dr. George Grassmuck, and me, Anne Armstrong never defined the role of my new employee, who was somehow on full-time detail in her office. Fred himself told me that he would be our liaison. But then he added another role; he began to write memos that had the effect of "overseeing" the CCOSS. Who was he? What was his resume? From where had he come? What qualified him to be a bridge between the Cabinet Committee and the White House? Questions went unanswered. He dealt directly with the executive director, from whom I had already withdrawn many management chores because of his demonstrated disloyalty and acts of espionage. Both of them set up a phone system independent of the switchboard. Essentially, they both subverted the management of the Cabinet Committee. He was no Dr. George Grassmuck!

Armstrong's unilateral and unexplained actions to "manage" the Cabinet Committee only added to the woes wrought by the intrusion of Watergate, the loss of presidential power, the loss of influence, and the rise of opposition in the halls of Congress. My Texas staffers would often comment on the arrangement she made with us, the Cabinet Committee: "She needs *un caporal* (a foreman)." A *caporal* is the management tool for running a plantation or a hacienda. On Texas ranches, a white Mexican or an Anglo American (a gringo) is in charge of the Mexican American labor.

The Chicano movement, nonetheless, had now matured. We were no longer invisible or forgotten. The "official gringo" in Washington still had no idea of the Chicano tsunami, which was unseen and unforeseen in the world of English-speaking people. They were still writing and reading memos that characterized us as Latinos fighting with each other and without leadership. Mexican Americans knew not whether they were White or Indian or Hispanic or Latin. Official Washington knew they were somehow Spanish and Spanish speaking. Mainland Puerto Ricans were finally to get their voice of disenchantment heard. And of course, other memos showed that the Cubans could not care a whit about Mexicans and Puerto Ricans. My recent archival review of memos of this type among White House staffers of the time reaffirmed my original opinions. Ignorance of the Spanish speaking still prevailed when Bob Finch left for California.

It was imperative to resuscitate my condition number three: an office in the White House. Two years earlier, Counselor Finch had confirmed that he had accepted it so that I would agree to serve on the Cabinet Committee. As I've noted, I had even selected the office's paint and furnishings, but I was never installed.

My research has permitted me to reconstruct some apparent motivations within the White House "jungle." We were all working for common ends, yet motivated with individual ambitions, goals, and objectives. I have been able to identify who kept me out of the White House contrary to the agreement Finch and I had reached in 1971. Self-enrichment, pride, avarice, and greed were the driving ingredients predicable of certain people for whom the principles of the Republican president were secondary.

Power for Chicano affairs was evanescing. We would remain absent from the Domestic Council. We would no longer have the strong sponsorship of the Office of Management and Budget.

The presence of some brown faces walking and talking in the halls of power and influence, where decisions are made, became an overriding priority, and for the Chicanos, an absolute requisite. So I restarted the effort for a "White House" position. As I rummaged through my personal papers for this chapter, a memo showed up that had been specific as to the exigency of a Mexican American in the White House at the time. I have asked the Nixon Foundation people in Yorba Linda, California to get me a copy of the original memo from the Nixon Archives located at the Library. As of this writing, I have not received a copy.

I have no recall of having read this September 2, 1971 memo or of the meeting it describes. Its author, Glen Waggoner, is unknown to me. It is directed to Henry M. Ramirez, Acting Chairman. My copy is on onionskin paper. It has no title for the author and no indication of the originating office. "The Subject is Meeting of September 1, 1971. For review, items discussed at our meeting of September 1, 1971." Attendees at this meeting were: Waggoner, Counselor Robert Finch, Henry M. Ramirez, Assistant Secretary Mrs. Hitt, and Mr. Marumoto. The memo's.

The seventh item in the memo reads as follows:, "The matter of arriving at firm dates and firm details on the office at EOB for the Chairman was discussed but mostly left unresolved. Nonetheless, it is my understanding that the Chairman is to have the office formerly occupied by Mr. Ramirez during the period of the study conducted for Mr. Finch. It is imperative that the date on moving into the office for the purpose of using White House phone inter alia be decided." How I now wish I had seen and read and acted upon this memo during those frightfully packed days as an innocent voyager ill prepared for the "big time."

Others were on same wavelength: the affairs of the Spanish speaking had to be represented by equals in the halls of the White House. In an administratively confidential memo (17) for Fred Malek and Chuck Colson on November 30, 1972, Bill (Mo) Marumoto wrote on the subject of an "Office of Special Concerns:"

The past four years has seen the emergence of the minority and special interests groups into viable forces within and outside government. Backed by large vocal constituency groups, they are gaining sophistication in federal participation. The Nixon administration has been increasingly involved in their affairs during the past four years and much of this activity has been originated, directed or decided at the White House level. These groups have included the Blacks, Spanish-speaking, women, the American Indian, and the civil rights and equal opportunity activists.

Mr. Marumoto also notes: "To strengthen the role of the White House, to overcome some of the policy mismanagement and ineffectiveness, and to speak with a single voice on policy, an umbrella office should be created."

These special concerns were soon to be organized into the "Liaison Office" under the presidency of Gerald Ford. And later, President Ronald Reagan expanded the Liaison Office under the leadership of Elizabeth Dole (later to become a US Senator), to outreach to other identifiable groups: the aged, the veterans, the Hispanics, the Blacks, small businesses, Catholics, Evangelicals, and so on.

As chairman, I had reported to Counselor Finch, to the Office of White House Presidential Personnel, to the White House

Scheduling and Advance team, to the political office of Chuck Colson, to the Office of Management and Budget, to my general counsel at the Government Services Administration, to the House of Representatives, and to the Senate. Counselor Finch tried to define White House policy directions, but as we have already seen, he was countermanded by other White House offices.

As the campaign to reelect the president marched to its conclusion, my thoughts dwelled frequently on what leadership actions I should take to assure a firm continuum for the civil rights of the Chicanos. The world about me was changing and would change even more. Our place in American society was in its infancy and very vulnerable. Our protector, President Nixon, who was enjoying his outstanding victory, was going to be fighting for his political life. This I knew. The "big secret" that the FBI Agent had confided in me had been an accurate prediction: "They are going to get him." I begin to put the pieces together.

The Spanish speaking had to have their interests represented in the White House; anyone selected would have to have an understanding Senator as a godfather. This is a fact of Washington: one needs a Senator for protection and to acquire high-level positions. That meant Senator Pete Domenici would have to make the call on who it would be. Since I had no Republican senator from California, my ticket to be a candidate was canceled. Further, I had become a controversial target for Congress and their partisan Hispanic Democrats. The 30 percent Mexican American voter turnout for President Nixon had been unforgivable. They branded me ineffectual because I had been too, too political! What utter nonsense. Washington is politics, and politics is Washington. Oh how I wished that people protesting the work of the Cabinet Committee as being too, too political, would have learned the Greek and Latin etymology of the words "policy," "police," and "politics."

The five-year authorization of CCOSS would be up for renewal in a short ten months—and in the middle of Watergate investigations. I was convinced that Congress would not allow a continued life for CCOSS for many reasons. The incumbent president for two more years would be a Republican; the temptation to use the chairman of CCOSS for another presidential campaign would be viewed as unacceptable. It was time for the Spanish-speaking to join other Americans in their quest for participation and representation. They could, for example, make their congressional representatives and senators really and truly represent them.

We had been so successful and in such a brief period of time, that other groups—Blacks, Asian Americans, Italian Americans, and more—had already submitted proposal bills for their own committees, which were already in the hands of the Government Operations Committee chairman, Chet Holifield. In a private meeting, Chet Holifield slid the pile of proposals modeled after CCOSS for me to review. Chet remarked, "How can we in Congress favor only the Hispanics?" I knew then and there that the Cabinet Committee had seen its last days. Continuation of CCOSS would cause the interests of the Spanish speaking to become a permanent fixture, making us dependent on it as American Indians had become dependent on the Bureau of Indian Affairs.

Incidentally, at that meeting, the congressman and his wife wished me the best. They were warm and charming, as they noted that they were packing for retirement. The congressman represented the area of Whittier, former Congressman Nixon's seat. He added that they and the president wanted me to run for Congress in that district, offering to help with the money and the campaign. (A certain high-level person in the White House corroborated the president's similar intention and wish.) Why did I not run? Among other reasons having to do with my personal spiritual life were Watergate and my disenchantment with the behavior of most congressmen and senators. (I had met a few wonderful, ethical, and dedicated ones. They were great, unselfish, and devoted to their fiduciary responsibilities.)

On one of my many hours on airplanes, in November 1972 I wrote a memorandum for the record, part of which reads: "As respects the Cabinet Committee, the following major work must be started: 1. Clearly focused delineation of the changes to be made; 2. Justification for major improvements or abolition of the agency." (18) Another November 1972 memo (19) by Mo Garcia marked "HMR—EYES ONLY" reads:

My travels to the Spanish speaking areas. Since you named me to this position 15 months ago—the equivalent of seven times around the world—have demonstrated to me the Spanish speaking know that no other president has done as much as you have for them. It is the work of you, the president, and of the super grades that has really brought about our inclusion and the addition of more super grades and other Spanish speaking people in high jobs, such as assistant secretaries and White House advisors, would definitely insure the entry of our people into the mainstream of American life. As the number of higher positions increases, the Cabinet Committee will become less necessary. The Committee should be phased out [emphasis mine] as super grade and higher positions reach, or surpass, the 100-mark; and before its permanence brings about *negative effects. I, therefore, suggest you phase it out while continuing to add super grades and other Spanish speaking persons to higher positions, including at least one to your White House staff.*

In response to my quest for wise and prudent ideas for advancing the interests of Spanish-speaking people, Carlos Conde wrote on White House stationery:

Henry Ramirez   As requested:
For several weeks, speculation has been increasing about the Spanish speaking role in the second Nixon administration. That attention has understandably focused on the Spanish speaking appointees, since we carried the president's message to the people in the recent election. It created further speculation when the president recently met with the Black appointees to discuss their future participation.

Carlos was claiming that our concerns also had to be discussed with the president himself. As a former highly respected Houston newspaper reporter, Carlos was beginning to catch the drift of other sniffing reporters. (20)

As I pondered ideas and opinions emerging from quickly changing events, I defined new imperatives to assure the civil rights of the now-visible Chicanos. The "Old Man" was beginning his sad, unexpected and unforeseen journey. Len Garment and Bob Brown had arranged for the Blacks to meet with the president, but the interests of Chicanos were no longer directly and personally represented in the White House. I quietly introspected and argued with myself. In the lonely solitude of leadership, I listed considerations, thoughts, and realities impinging on the civil rights revolution of Mexican Americans and Boricuas.

The realization set in that this presidency lived in jeopardy. My daily life in Washington educated me on what made it tick. We were facing a powerful and dedicated opponent: liberalism. Our time on life's Shakespearean dramatic stage was obviously diminishing. I decided to dedicate my efforts to making systemic changes begun under Projects Alpha and Blue. This work was not glamorous or publicity related. It was hard and quiet. Eventually, every agency would have to assure that the Spanish-speaking were being counted and the data analyzed. Every agency's annual reports to Congress would include a separate column with the heading "Spanish-surnamed Americans!" These actions would have to be performed irrespective of who was in the White House. The civil rights laws mandated that, and we were now included in them!

People wanted visible signs of continued commitment. They wanted new, glamorous, and powerful appointments. The real bread and butter lay in being counted and in officials being held responsible for enforcement of the civil rights laws, now that they knew we existed. (The US Navy, however, was not cooperating. Years later I was told why by Frank Gamboa, a Mexican American Annapolis graduate and former navy captain. He had received his appointment to the Naval Academy by then-Senator Richard Nixon, the first Mexican American from California to get into Annapolis. (21) Frank told me that most of the navy admirals were Southerners.)

I began to travel to army and air force military installations in the United States and Europe. My message to the generals was simple: the president wants you to identify your men by ethnicity. No more just Black and White! And, after you do that, include them in all of the opportunities assured by the civil rights laws. This proved to be an exciting and fruitful arena. In the military, everyone has a boss, and you better obey. I represented the concerns and wishes of the president. The generals held the awesome power of command. Spanish-surnamed military officers enjoyed hearing for the first time that equal opportunities also applied to them. (22 It mattered greatly in that world that while traveling as a personal representative of the president, I bore the rank of a three-star general!

People were focused on the glamour of high-level appointees and wondered if the second Nixon administration would continue that activity. I knew better. We had seen the end of the rainbow. In view of my "secret," I just had to continue my quest to build a support system to replace a formerly powerful, now-crumbling edifice. As planning and preparations were made for inaugural balls and parties, I asked Carlos Conde to set up a meeting with his political godfather: ambassador, former congressman, and new Republican National Committee chairman, George Bush.

This memo uncovers a part of Chicano history:

"ADMINISTRATIVE – CONFIDENTIAL

MEMORANDUM FOR: Dr. Henry M. Ramirez

FROM: Mo Garcia

SUBJECT: Aide-memoire on a conversation with Ambassador George Bush, Chairman-Designate of the Republican National Committee

The conversation with Ambassador George Bush was held at the headquarters of the Republican National Committee (RNC) at 2:30 p.m., Friday, 12 January 1973, and lasted forty minutes. Present were Dr. Henry M. Ramirez, Mr. Carlos Conde, Ambassador Bush's personal assistant Tom Lias, and myself.

The meeting was arranged by Conde. Dr. Ramirez wanted to manifest to the incoming RNC Chairman the growing concern and uncertainty of the Spanish-speaking people of the United States about their participation in the affairs of government and, more specifically, the federal government.

Dr. Ramirez expressed his concern and the concern of other high Spanish-speaking officials and party members about a seemingly apparent disinterest in the White House for the Spanish-speaking. He explained that he had been receiving numerous calls from all over the U.S. from people. They were showing surprise and a certain amount of alarm because no Spanish-speaking persons are being named to high government positions.

Dr. Ramirez went further. He explained that, for the first time ever, the Spanish-speaking had voted Republican in very large numbers and cited percentage figures in support of this statement. The figures ranged well over 30% generally and above 60% in certain instances. Dr. Ramirez pointed out that he has been a life-long Republican and that he is concerned that a failure to act on the part of the government could mean the loss of this valuable number of votes to the party. He also stressed that, given the good showing made in the last general election, the Republican Party could increase the percentage of Spanish-speaking supporting it.

At a later point, Ambassador Bush asked Dr. Ramirez if this support manifested so strongly for the President in the recent election, could be translated to the local level. Dr. Ramirez said that he felt that it could.

As Dr. Ramirez was still explaining the reason for his visit, Ambassador Bush asked his aide to call in Mr. Richard Thaxton, the RNC patronage man. Unfortunately, Thaxton was not in the building.

Conde followed Dr. Ramirez. He engaged in a dialogue with Ambassador Bush, who was desirous of knowing who in the White House was responsible for seeking to place the Spanish-speaking in high government jobs. Conde explained that the man directly involved was Mr. William Marumoto who works under Mr. Fred Malek. Conde explained that Marumoto was at a secondary level and, therefore unable to exert very much influence. Conde said Marumoto was doing an excellent job even though he was at a secondary level. Dr. Ramirez supported Conde's statement about Marumoto's job and the nature of his efforts. Dr. explained that these matters were really in the hands of persons like Haldeman and Ehrlichman.

At this point I interrupted, attempting to make clear to Ambassador Bush that the concern expressed was the result of the critical situation of the high appointees of the Nixon Administration. I told him Phil Sanchez was out; Carlos Villarreal was out; Mrs. Romana Banuelos was on the way out; Antonio Rodriguez was out; and Carlos Conde was out. I added that not only were they out, but that no Spanish-speaking persons had been named to high positions and that no announcements had been made that these people, out of jobs, were either being given better jobs or lateral transfers—even though the statement had been made that there was a reshuffling and that these people, or some of them, would be put in other jobs. I also explained to Ambassador Bush that every single Spanish-speaking leader in the nation, with the exception of Mr. Cesar Chavez, who is definitely committed to the Democratic Party, had called upon Dr. Ramirez when it became known and visible that the federal government was obviously doing something for the Spanish-speaking people, more than any other administration had ever done. I also explained that these leaders were now beginning to wonder about the future of the Spanish-speaking people in the federal government. I explained to him that on one hand these leaders were being subjected to questioning in their areas, and on the other were being told something like, "I told you so; they used you, and they no longer have any need for you." I expressed to the Ambassador the feeling that these leaders were beginning to lose their leadership in the face of this situation.

Ambassador Bush gave the impression of a very tough man but in a very urbane manner. Despite this reflection of toughness, it was obvious that he was very interested, frank and concerned over (1) the possibility that the Spanish-speaking might not be properly taken care of, and (2) the resulting negative effect this would have in the Republican Party. As an indication of his concern for the Mexican-Americans, Ambassador Bush was quite upset about Conde losing his job at the White House and interested in looking into the possibility of his continuing there.

At this point, Conde brought up two points about the Spanish-speaking that the President had made at a meeting with his top Spanish-speaking appointees. One was that he would continue to appoint more Spanish-speaking persons to high jobs; the other was that the Party would support Spanish-speaking candidates for political office, would help recruit them, and that he had instructed outgoing RNC Chairman Bob Dole and incoming RNC Chairman George Bush to see to it that this would happen. Dr. Ramirez reiterated Mr. Conde's remarks about the President in greater detail.

Ambassador Bush said that he did not believe there was any attempt to exclude the Spanish-speaking. He added that this is a time of great uncertainty for everyone. He noted that, with the exception of a few Cabinet positions, there have been relatively few appointments and that he knew himself, being at the State Department, that there was great uncertainty among the people there.

At this point I broke in to make the point that I understood that everybody was feeling uncertain at this time but that with the Spanish-speaking things were different because, for the first time, they had gotten something and suddenly they were seeing all of their top men losing their jobs.

Ambassador Bush said that he had met recently with Robert Haldeman and Fred Malek and expressed his interest in the Spanish-speaking. He said he had told them that he was going to meet with Dr. Ramirez. Both men seemed to show surprise and asked Ambassador Bush what the subject of the meeting was going to be. Bush said that he told the two men that he felt sure it concerned the Spanish-speaking. Both men asked Ambassador Bush to get back to them after he had spoken to Dr. Ramirez.

Bush wound up by explaining to us that he understood very clearly what was happening. He said, "I want you to know that you have an open door here and that I am sympathetic. I think we'll get things moving pretty soon."

Ambassador Bush went on to explain that he was just taking over the chairmanship and that he had left his very high position for this chairmanship because political power was now moving to the RNC from the hands of the President, who is at the end of his electoral career. He expressed his intention of improving the party position and asked Dr. Ramirez if some of the Spanish-speaking could be brought in permanently into the Party. Dr. Ramirez said that this could be done and that he had several suggestions to make along this line. Ambassador Bush expressed an interest in pursuing this matter with Dr. Ramirez at a later date.

Senator Bob Dole arrived at this point for an appointment with Ambassador Bush and we all went over to greet him. Dole commented on the good job Ramirez had done for the Spanish-speaking.

MG:mhf (15 Jan 73) (23)

Along with the smoldering and not yet visible volcano burning in the halls of power, I had lost my contacts in the White House. A new team had come to occupy key offices, and it was not concerned with the effects the Watergate burglary might have on their new positions of power and prestige. I could not find out what new philosophy and policies the new administration was implementing. Something new was in the air, but what was it? My meeting with Bush, where I thought I would get some signs or signals, left me uninformed. He excused himself by remarking that he had just arrived at the new job. Yet, in the archives I read that he had called Ehrlichman to ask what I wanted from him. And that Ehrlichman had responded, "Keep us informed as to what Ramirez wants."

In view of the unproductive meeting with Chairman George H. W. Bush, I pondered whether or not I should forthwith seek a meeting with the president himself. He had given me a way to do precisely that—by speaking to his valet. But I did not. Prudence dictated otherwise. This I knew: Someone in White House personnel had selected a very public conservative, Howie Phillips, to replace Phil Sanchez at OEO. Fred Malek now had a new deputy. Sure enough, he was a Texan. I conjectured: *Does Fred also know something, since he has selected for himself a new job?* He would be the deputy director of OMB.

The new man was Jerry Jones, a very wealthy oil man. He brought in a Dave Wimer, who had worked for Bob Hope. They bounced Carlos Villareal, an Executive Level II, out of the Department of Transportation. Mr. Villareal had been in charge of the Urban Mass Transportation Administration, performing with high merits. It bothered me deeply that these European Americans, who were in charge of White House personnel with an awesome power to affect the lives of human beings and families, could pick out cushy jobs for themselves and with a flick of a finger bounce out Mexican Americans who had worked so hard for the reelection of the president. They were, willy-nilly, dismantling one of our key five visions: the appointment of at least a hundred Spanish-surnamed executives.

I consoled myself with the knowledge that personnel changes are intrinsic to presidential elections (or any type of election). But this one was different. I had come to *do* a job, not just to get one. These new White House guys did not know or care about the Chicano civil rights struggle. They had other agendas. They called it the "growing conservative movement." I sensed its lack of concern of and for the Civil Rights struggle of the Chicanos.

While I searched for support for the Chicano Revolution, my "big secret" was being played out in the courtroom of Judge Sirica. As I rode to my office at seven in the morning in the backseat with the reading light on, I browsed the morning papers and wondered if the Democrats' court proceedings against the burglars would affect my work and reach John Dean, Haldeman, and Ehrlichman. By January 15, 1973, the burglars had pled guilty. Talk was all over town that the Senate, controlled by the Democrats, would establish a Select Committee to investigate the Republicans' presidential campaign activities. They smelled blood. They wanted to lynch Nixon.

The Democrats had a monopoly in the House and in the Senate and wanted to get even for Helen Gahagan Douglas, for Alger Hiss, for Whittaker Chamber, for Vietnam, and for Nixon's hatred of Communism. The boys in the press rooms were so joyful. And wouldn't you guess? As I write, the newspapers reveal that Judge Sirica was in secret negotiations with the Department of Justice investigators over what they had uncovered, an action entirely unacceptable in jurisprudence. But then, he was from New Jersey, as was his buddy, Congressman Rodino, chairman of the Judiciary Committee that oversaw J. Edgar Hoover's FBI.

The audible, open, and emotional hostility prevailing at this time in Washington reminded me of the vicious wrath so evident at the US Commission on Civil Rights, when Nixon won the presidency in November 1968. Expressions of hostile disgust became even more evident when he was inaugurated. Conversations in the halls of the Commission on Civil Rights formed my firm opinion that Democrats "knew" that Republicans had no right to be in charge of the White House. Washington, but for the gentle years of a harmless and peace-loving General Eisenhower, had been the realm of the all-knowing and all-caring Democrats since, it seemed to them, time immemorial.

By contrast, I marveled at the reception Senator Teddy Kennedy's staff was given on their frequent visits to kinda check into how things were coming along at the Commission. His people were provided inside information on "work in progress." At the meetings, references to the Senator were made as if people were discussing an august icon deserving of plenary adulation. I found it disgusting. I knew he was a scandalous lapsed Catholic.

A member of the General Counsel's office convened meetings at the Commission's conference room after working hours for the Students for a Democratic Society (SDS), a Communist organization. He and his SDS partners made their plans for pro-Vietnam Communist demonstrations, called "moratoriums." Jane Fonda was one of their heroines. A "Mr. F" was especially vitriolic. During our site visits to the economically depressed Texas-Mexico border, he would recite to me the benefits his philosophy could and would bring to South Texas. Hegelian dialectic and imperatives would flow from his mouth as if he were reciting enchanting poetry.

Almost all employees agreed with or verbalized sentiments that the presence of Republicans in the White House was tantamount to a political abortion. The derision and ridicule of matters and people Republican was incessant. "Republicans do not belong here [in Washington]" was a common expression.

The employees at the Commission on Civil Rights viewed it as a bastion of the Democratic Party. Liberals were at home, enjoying their comfort zone. I was often asked with a variety of attitudes, how I, a minority, could be a Republican. These poor souls had no basis for understanding in their liberal, left-wing Ivy League education and militant secularism that a knowledgeable Catholic knows that human acts of discrimination are sinful. And they categorically knew little about my philosophy, that of Saint Thomas Aquinas, and even less of my faith. They did not know Communism was diabolical. The walls of their offices were adorned with huge poster images of Che, Fidel, or Mao. I think I can conjecture why Stalin did not rate. He and Hitler were two peas in a pod.

The rumors were actualized. Early in February 1973, the US Senate established their Select Committee to investigate, and I began gloomily to sense that I was becoming an "omniscient spectator" of a Shakespearean drama. The drama with its players was unfolding before my very eyes. But, this was not fiction; it was not a live reenactment of *Macbeth*. The Washington disciples of the "Jacobins" were honing their political guillotine. The burglars had provided the excuse. I still hoped that the ulcer would be excised. In retrospect, that operation would have been easy.

To this day, as I write these words, my intellect struggles to understand and unravel how it came about that one party legally imposed its will on the other for the purpose of criminalizing its political activities. I have reconciled my mind by examining in retrospect the Washington milieu of those years. The Democrats had controlled the town almost totally since the early 1930s. The size of the government grew tremendously under the New Deal and with the wars. The think tanks and the law firms were in the hands of the Democrats. The unions had become formidable in power and size. The press lived and worked inside a bubble described by these words: positivism, socialism, communism, relativism, free sex, pornography, abortions, same-sex lifestyles, and paganism. The members of the press enjoyed being characterized by the word, progressive.

The almost total political control led to deep-seated corruption. The Democrats could get what they wanted. And they wanted to get Nixon and keep the Republican Party in the absolute minority. So they investigated its political activities and found them scandalous. Did the press object to this patently horrible unfairness? Oh, no! To this day, have voices arisen to object? Oh, no! Why? "Nixon had it coming to him," it is uttered. Have Republicans screamed of inequity? No! Nixon was the only person to be born in California, the West, in poverty, to become a Republican president! Real Republicans come from places like Ohio. He just did not seem to fit quite right. The feelings were mutual. Nixon never liked the Eastern effete elites.

And, around the corner were the new generation of Republican conservatives. They did not like the Republicanism of Nixon's West. They were enamored with the thinking of the new intellectual, Bill Buckley. These new, conservative Republicans would in years have no use for the memory and legacy of my boss. They too would disdain the Chicanos. Somehow, Chicanos were not real Americans. They did not look American: with blue eyes, blond or brunet hair, tall and European looking with names like Fisher, Faber, or Cook.

And now, the Democrats wanted to scandalize everything I had done at the Cabinet Committee. It dawned on them that Mexican Americans were no longer their obedient voters. They thought Mexicans felt that the Republicans now had tender loving care for them. That was not the case. President Nixon, born and raised amid poor Mexicans, is the only President who knew them and cared; not the Republicans or their party.

Mexican Americans were enjoying the political education of a two-party system. They broke the voting habits that once reflected a flock of sheep faithfully and innocently moving in response to a ringing bell. In Austin, Texas, I had delivered a speech in May 1972 with the title "The Chevy Mentality" to the Texas LULAC convention. The thrust was that the faithful sheep no longer had to follow the bells of Democratic politicians. The audience was composed of college- and high school-educated Mexicans and Mexican Americans. They now had a choice. It was time to do some "comparison shopping."

Mexican Americans were famously known for their propensity to purchase used Chevrolets at auto lots. In this election, they stopped buying only "Chevys"—voting a straight Democratic ticket. They voted for a person who had discovered Mexicans and *included* them in mainstream American life in huge numbers, for the first time ever. And the Democrats, via Watergate investigations, planned to recapture the lost loyalties of their up-to-now loyal, "si, señor," Mexican voters. Thinking, educated Chicanos began to view the members of both parties as indistinguishable with respect to their interests. In a country-club setting in Texas or Colorado or wherever, the European Americans were identical, as far as the Chicanos were concerned.

A day after my meeting with Ambassador George Bush, Democrats and the media let loose with a barrage of stories that can best be characterized as "the honeymoon is over." On January 13, 1973, the *San Antonio Express-News* carried this: "Congressman Henry B. Gonzalez, (D.TX) declared in a Houston, TX speech, 'Nixon Administration is rewarding its Mexican American supporters by replacing high officials of Spanish surname.' The congressman took a swipe at another San Antonian, Tony Rodriguez. 'What are we left with? Tony Rodriguez, who holds a job with no known function, other than to come out and tell the natives how lucky we are, because he has a soft job. And, we are left with Henry Ramirez and his powerless, meaningless Cabinet Committee.'" (24) Congressman Gonzalez fired off the first salvo in what was to become an incessant attack against what Nixon had achieved with the inclusion of Spanish-surnamed Americans.

A week later, he was followed by Tom Bryan of the UPI, who recounted, "The Spanish-speaking leaders who worked for President Nixon's reelection are showing signs of resentment over the removal of Latinos from top administration positions." Ben Fernandez of Los Angeles, who served as chairman of the National Hispanic Finance Committee and as cochairman to Maurice Stans on the Republican Finance Committee, was the principal source for Bryan's article. Ben Fernandez had added that "he was very distressed by the apparent attitude of the White House toward Latinos who worked for Nixon." (25)

Peggy Simpson of the Associated Press reported in her February 19, 1973 story, named LATINOS that "Leaders of the Spanish-speaking community are complaining that despite a record vote for President Nixon, Latinos are getting neither the programs nor the top-level jobs they want from the administration. The second paragraph of her account repeated Congressman Henry B's gutter comments: 'You have been used and you have been deceived and you have been lied to,' Rep. Henry B. Gonzalez, D-Texas, told one gathering of Latino leaders."

For this article, she interviewed Fred Malek, who had been chief of White House presidential personnel and as such had the responsibility of submitting nominations for top-level jobs directly to the president. At the time of the interview, however, Malek was the deputy of the Office of the Management and Budget and no longer responsible for nominations. His team was being replaced with more conservative persons who had no conception of the Chicano Revolution and were probably anti-civil rights. After all, Pat Buchanan was still energetically and influentially at work in the White House. And so, for the interview, Malek could blithely state, "When the dust all settles you'll probably find more Mexican Americans and other Spanish-speaking in high positions than you did before the election." Yet, I ask, what did Fred know about my "big secret" that had encouraged him to leave his enviable top position as director of White House personnel and seek refuge at the Office of Management and Budget?

The next day, Peggy Simpson's AP story broke in Mexico City in *El Sol de Mexico* with the title (my translation) "The Spanish-speaking people complain that Nixon did not fulfill what he had promised." It was followed with a subtitle: "He promised much so that they would vote for him, and *nothing*." On the same day, another large-circulation daily, *El Nacional*, heralded Peggy's article with: "The Latins who gave him their votes consider themselves defrauded by Nixon." (26)

On February 25, 1973 Jack Vargas of the *El Sol de Houston* writes: "As Steve Morales, from Corpus Christi, said and I quote: 'It is water under the dam, but let this be a lesson to all of us as we prepare for the District, State, and National Conventions this spring. Let us not again be used, deceived, and lied to by politicians, regardless of party affiliation." (27) Frank del Olmo, the top-rated reporter for the *Los Angeles Times*, weighed in on February 26 with a thorough airing of the rising discontent. He interviewed extensively and prepared a well-researched story presented in a professionally objective and dispassionate manner. The beginning of his report signals the direction of his research:

> For two years before the last election, the Nixon Administration made a major effort to woo the nation's Spanish-speaking voters. But since November, the small circle of Latins appointed to federal government posts as part of that effort has been surprisingly quiet, and their almost deafening silence has angered many Latin activists outside Washington. "No one anticipated the major reorganization of personnel that is going on," said Henry Ramirez, Chairman of the Cabinet Committee on Opportunities for Spanish-Speaking people. "And no one knew it would take so long as it has. I know this has raised questions and discontent among many people," he said, "but the Spanish-speaking are in no different position than other groups in the country whose representatives are being reassigned."

When del Olmo interviewed me, he said, "Tell me what you know about the burglary, which is now being named 'Watergate.'" I smiled in response, making the appropriate humble gestures. "Frank, you know I am just *Mejicano*. I do not work in the White House at those very high levels of the Haldemans and Ehrlichmans.

That is high-powered gringo land." He nodded in agreement and echoed, "Yep, you're right." I was happy. I had not lied. I did not have to tell him the truth of my "secret" with the usual warning of "this is off the record." Years later, after I was in business in Los Angeles and no longer made copy, I related to Frank what I had known about the break-in over a cup of coffee. I am convinced he never forgave me for not sharing the explosive story. (28)

On March 5, 1973, I sent a memo to Anne Armstrong with the subject "Meeting with the President." In it, I recommend "the best immediate step to assure positive and significant impact is for the President to meet with you and me to provide public reassurances that the bond between the Administration and the Spanish Speaking people continue." She did not respond! (29)

Meanwhile, Jess Perez, mayor of Orange, California, is quoted by the daily *Orange County Register* on March 11, 1973, as saying, "Nixon betrayed voters." (30)

And on March 30, 1973, the California director of LULAC, Fidel Gonzalez, Jr., presented an open letter to President Nixon in the LULAC state organ, named *Lulaction*. The letter starts with, "The Democratic administration during its entire history ignored the Mexican-American." The letter adds, "During the last two months, it appears that all your apparently sincere efforts have been undone" and "Many Mexican-Americans believe that they have been duped." Then the letter asks for a meeting with the president. (31)

Finally, a March 31, 1973 clipping from New York's *ABC de las Americas* quotes me as saying "Do not lose faith, Hispanics."

Pamela Terry was a Washington reporter for this paper; her interview of me was very fair and decent. (32)

I knew that I enjoyed the confidence of Richard M. Nixon, and that was all that mattered to me. It had given me the energy and motivation to continue to implement our five-point vision. I had received notice from a highly placed source that Haldeman did not like me because I received too much press coverage. He did not like anyone working for the president to get too much press.

What was important to me was that the president and I had already achieved the substance of the Five Points. We had made them a *systemic* function of the US government and its civil rights laws of 1964. Yes, we were losing a few high-level and very visible jobs; that is usual and customary after any presidential election. We had, however, achieved a new paradigm and defined for any future president the duty to include Spanish-speaking people in all levels of government, White House itself, included!

The "big secret" was about to manifest itself in my life. Congressman Charles Wiggins, who had called me to a lunch meeting in December 1970, again called me on January 5, 1973, to warn me in clear, yet almost whispered tones: "The House Judiciary is coming after you. Don Edwards has been assigned the job 'to get Ramirez.'" Chuck Wiggins was the ranking minority member of the Subcommittee where Edwards was the chairman. "Be aware, he has hired a Linda Chavez to head up the research and the negatives on you. Do you know her?" I replied that I did not know her. The congressman also added that she was bent on destroying the Cabinet Committee. I thought, *How can a Mexican American think that way?* I branded her with the name "La Malinche." She remained an unknown quantity until the summer of 1980.

As I prepared the strategy for getting the Mexican American vote for Governor Ronald Reagan in his bid for the presidency in 1980 at the request of his daughter, Maureen Reagan, the matter of Watergate and the hearings conducted by Congressman Don Edwards arose in the process of drafting issues. The story of Linda Chavez's involvement also came up in connection with the hearings. I learned that in 1973, Linda Chavez and my old antagonist, Jeffrey Miller, had worked together to frame a questionnaire for the CCOSS. While working in Congress, she had conspired with him while he was working at the USCCR to get information for Don Edwards' hearings, at which I would have to testify. It was stated that she had been the special assistant to Al Shanker, founder of the American Federation of Teachers (AFT). It was also revealed that her father was a Chavez from Albuquerque and her mother from Colorado. (Hence, I assumed both parents were European Americans.)

She had continued her interesting career in governmental affairs. And, after the election of Ronald Reagan, was I ever surprised to learn from some newspaper article, now lost, that quoted Pat Buchanan as saying: "Linda Chavez is a world class act!" Shortly thereafter, I discussed this article with Lyn Nofziger. Ronald Reagan was surrounded from the very start of his political life in California by Lyn Nofsiger, by Ed Meese, and by Mike Deaver. At our favorite restaurant on K Street, The Prime Rib, Lyn added to my incredulity by remarking with pride,

"We are thinking of her as the new executive director for the US Commission on Civil Rights!" And she got appointed.

In a short six years, she went from being a left-wing socialist to being one of the leaders of the "English-only" movement" and a columnist propounding the merits of the hard Right! Wow, that was quite a conversion! Behold, miracles do happen!

The hearings of Don Edwards merit a full discussion of the struggle of the Democrats to use the power of their offices and the resources of the National Democratic Committee to get people with Spanish surnames to destroy the only agency legislated to assist and assure that Chicanos were full-fledged Americans enjoying the good life of this country and protected under the civil rights laws.

The truth of Congressman Charles Wiggins' advance warnings of "they are after you" began to materialize. Sam Dash was empowered as a member of the Senate Select Committee on February 7, 1973. A couple of weeks later, phone calls assumed a strange pattern. Calls were coming from the concerned and anxious in the White House, in DC, and from out in the country. On April 5, 1973, I learned that the other Brown Mafia team members were getting lawyers and paying tons of bucks! As of April 24, 1973, I was informed that the House Government Operations Committee had ordered an audit of my agency as a prelude to a witch hunt and the hearings. A GAO Official, Gene Essner, called. My reaction was, "Happy hunting." (33)

Sam Dash had dispatched his trusty investigators to document the activities of the Republican presidential campaign.

The vengeful Senate Democrats were at work. Sam Dash's staff, which included the young lawyer Hillary Rodham, was at work digging for scandal. In late February and early March, Dash's junior Sherlock's were after Carlos Conde, Bill Marumoto, Tony Rodriguez, Alex Armendariz, and me. March had entered with ill winds. On March 22, 1973, Carlos Conde left me a phone message: "Gone to Texas." On the same day, Tony Rodriguez also leaves a message: "Call at the house, please." But two days prior, he had left me a message to call him at "NEOB 456-2813" (part of the White House). What the hyperactive newspaper reporters did not know was my "big secret" and how it was being played out by actors in what today the media business calls the Watergate Scandal. It was the power-corrupted Democrats using their monopoly to hunt for speeding tickets. The European Americans were going to find something that we, Mexican Americans, had done "illegally."

Since I found out that Senator Joseph Montoya (D-NM) was on the Senate Select Committee to investigate, I checked with my contacts in his office and learned that he was still deeply hurt about something: a couple of days after I took control of CCOSS, I fired his favorite mistress and did not even ask him. I had discovered that she was very pretty and very good at chewing gum, period. I got "Little Joe" on the phone and let him know that his investigators would find nothing on me, because unlike the treatment the Teamsters had provided him via Mexican banks, making him wealthy, I had never taken "a nickel." I could go to Confession with a clean conscience. In essence, I taunted him. I too had a beef against him. His personal secretary had informed me over breakfast that her boss, Little Joe had informed his

Senate Building next-door-neighbor, Senator Richard, that he would block any Senate confirmation of a promotions the president might want to give me. A Presidential And Senate Confirmation appointment for me was then to be out of the question. Sadly, Senator Joe Montoya was such a little man and a bribe-taker.

This little vendetta was to continue. A year later, the USCCR director, John Buggs, invited me to be the main speaker at a national conference in San Antonio to celebrate the completion of the Mexican American Educational Study. Senator Montoya refused to be seated on the same dais with me. Matters got ticklish for the Commission. Montoya threatened their budget. I made things easy for my friend, John Buggs. I attended on a different day.

Montoya's sister visited me to obtain assistance for some Catholic college in New Mexico. At dinner, she confided how her brother had become a millionaire despite knowing nothing about business and having such a low government salary all of his life. Washington does cater to an abundance of characters.

When I received notice that Sam Dash's investigators were coming to my office to question me, I called the former chairman of the Cabinet Committee, Martin Castillo, for legal advice. I told him, "You know what I have done. You were here in this seat. Do I need a lawyer?"

His quick response was, "Is there something you have done that you must confess to a priest in the confessional?"

Immediately, I retorted, "Hell, no."

Marty shot back, "Ta hell with lawyers, you do not need any." Of the five members of the Brown Mafia, I was the only one not to hire legal counsel. Years later when Colonel Ollie North hired me as a consultant to his new company, I remarked to him: I have never met you and you do not know me. Why are you hiring me? He responded: "Everyone in the intelligence community knows who you are. You are one of the few who never retained legal counsel during Watergate. You are clean."

As I wrote notes summarizing the questions I would probably be asked, my personal assistant rehearsed with me. The lead lawyer from Sam Dash's office, Mike Hershman, a Jewish American, had discussed them with Mo prior. The questions had arisen around White House memos involving my name. Issues appeared that lawyers might pursue for conflicts with the law. (34)

On October 3, 1973, Mike Hershman showed up with three or four lawyers, one of which was Hillary Rodham. The minority side had about three lawyers who hardly spoke. The questions touched on the raising of money, my travel, my support for clemency for Reies Tijerina, the influencing of grants and contracts, my use of my staff for political reasons, and my involvement in political strategizing. One lawyer was unhappy with my answer to the matter of seeking executive clemency for Tijerina: Hillary Clinton. She thought she was a tough questioner as she shot at me incessantly with hostility, "Did you not promise Reies Tijerina an executive pardon *in consideration* for his political support?"

HMR's Personal Files
Chairman Ramirez and Reyes Tijerina discuss
need for a presidential pardon

I answered, but she did not accept nor like my answer. She became brusque and affected an air of superiority over this little Mexican boy that refused to comprehend and understand her simple queries using the word *consideration*. She and I quibbled over the intent and meaning of the word in this context. She probably did not know that I had studied at Loyola University Law School. So I sparred with her as if I was the cat and she, the little mouse. I reverted to the psycholinguistics affected by the relationship between Latin, Greek, and Spanish usage over the centuries. As she persisted in her prosecutorial stance, I lost my composure. I got up and walked around my huge desk to stand directly in front of her and let loose certain gestures and Spanish phrases I had learned at age fourteen from Mexican peasants while we picked oranges from dirty, dusty trees in Orange County. Instantly, one of her cohorts got up and grabbed me by the collar. I ordered him to release me immediately and instructed my personal assistant to call security to take the man out of the building. They did. (35)

But Senator Montoya was not happy at this null outcome, so he had the FBI question me a week later. Again, he was unhappy. Next, he had a high-level FBI agent question me. By this time, I had had it. I instructed the agent to relax and to read the legislation paving the way for the Cabinet Committee slowly, word by word. I said that after that, I would be very happy to answer any and all questions. Minutes after he perused the two-page document, he closed his briefcase and announced authoritatively, "No one will ever bother you again about these matters."

Sadly, he was wrong. A subpoena was served on me ordering me to show up at the Watergate grand jury. I did, and I answered questions from two lawyers for about seven hours. Primarily, they wanted to know what I knew about contracts, bribes, certain irregular business dealings, and the persons connected to them. I answered fully from the reference of the "talk on the street." When they pushed further and asked if I had personally seen so-and-so, was I physically there with so-and-so, did I ever speak to so-and-so about the matters or bribes, my answers were easy: no.

At any rate, when they eventually released me, I gathered myself and proceeded to the stairs at the edge of the raised platform to depart. Some of the approximately thirty-two jurors, almost all of them African Americans (there were two European Americans), clapped thunderously and cheered me. They formed a receiving line. Each one of them smiled widely, shook my hands, and congratulated me. It was exhilarating to hear, "Well done, you have fought for our civil rights," and other such things. Loyola Law School had come in handy. To the informal questions, my answers always added tidbits of my personal history: how I had been called a "Black Carmichael," how I fought discrimination against Blacks, Chicanos, and Native Americans, as well as being a bona fide Chicano civil rights leader since the early 1960s.

From a scared, frightened man without any legal advice to this ending—I was stunned and surprised. I immediately went home to relish and enjoy my gorgeous wife and my adorable kids. I had not yet shared the pain of this day with her. She did not know. It had been such a persecution! So unfair and coming from senators who were such corrupt hypocrites. My knowledge of their corruption was from personal experience. I owe a ton of gratitude to a superbly honest congressman from New Mexico, Manuel Lujan, who taught me so much. I knew about Senator Joseph Montoya's love of bribes. I had seen Senator Humphrey count the dollar bills still in the white legal-size envelope at the Rotunda Restaurant. Senator Magnusen of Washington was always so inebriated when I appeared at the Appropriations Committee that his staff had to walk alongside, firmly holding on to his arms. His questioning of my testimony was so incoherent that the staff director and I decided on the final copy of the hearing. A certain congressman, chairman of a committee, once told me: "Yes, Henry, you saw how I get money from Peruvian ambassador Breckenmeyer; you saw me count the dollar bills. You are shocked and scandalized. Maybe I will get caught. I will have the money for the legal bills and yet have some left. I will do a short time in prison; but then I will live in comfort in Florida. Ta hell with honor and respect. You, on the other hand, will leave Washington a poor man." Chills ran up and down my spine.

I personally knew people in the barrios of Pomona, Riverside, the San Gabriel valley, and Orange County, California who had bought votes for the Democratic Party at the direction of Democratic congresspersons. Yet through it all, it was wonderful to know the honest ones, and I got to know quite a few of them. My faith gifted to me by God and reinforced by my mother and father, my personal relationship to God, to Jesus Christ, to his Church, and my philosophy and theology studies fortified me with courage, wisdom and humility. I realized that divine providence had put me on that hot seat for some good reason. My other mother, *Nuestra Señora de Guadalupe*, never abandoned me.

I would inquire of Mexican American Democrats who came to my office seeking help with the federal government why the European American senators' Select Committee on Presidential Election Activities were only investigating Republicans. I referred to them the fact that the Democratic Party was very well known in the Mexican barrios for buying their votes. I was able from personal knowledge to cite names, chapter, and verse. But these nefarious, scandalous, and patently illegal activities would not be investigated by the Jewish American Sam Dash. No, the American public would never know. The Democrats had declared their own presidential activities off-limits to the investigators. We would never know how the unions bought Mexican votes. I knew!

A certain very, very close relative called it "walking-around money." His Los Angeles County Federated Union headquarters donor, Henry Lozano, would ask me: "Why are you, Henry, so different from [your relative]?" They wanted to get Nixon. We would never discover how Senator Joseph "Little Joe" Montoya had become a multimillionaire, despite the fact that all of his jobs had been with the government. My annual check equaled his from 1971 through 1974: thirty-six thousand dollar. Before that, for many years, Little Joe was paid in the ten thousands and later in the twenties. His sister, Lorella, once told me, "I do not know how my brother became a millionaire. He cannot even do math!" As long as he was the chairman of the Senate Subcommittee that oversaw appropriations for the Internal Revenue Service, he feared them not. After he retired, however, it became a different matter. He suffered a fatal heart attack when informed that the IRS wanted to audit him.

Judges are viewed as vital to an independent system of justice. But Judge Sirica was part of a lynch mob, as we have recently learned from a reading of contemporary newspapers.

Journalists were swarming all over town, plucking tidbits for their stories. In just a matter of days, I received calls for interviews from national newsmagazines and big-city dailies. Frank del Olmo of the *Los Angeles Times* had pitched his tent temporarily in Washington; radio and national television wanted interviews; and finally, my hometown paper, the *Pomona Progress Bulletin*, wanted a story. Spanish-speaking people had finally become players in the national consciousness and awareness. And how! But, what was going to be the price? Were they really looking for good, happy stories relating how well and far Spanish-speaking people had advanced?

The new and unusual confluence of events convinced me to gather Washington's Cuban, Mexican American, and mainland Puerto Rican leaders in a mini-summit meeting. Present at the April 5, 1973 meeting in the CCOSS conference room with me were: Mr. Phillip Sanchez, ambassador-designate to Honduras; Mr. Manuel Carrillo, personal assistant to Pat Hitt, assistant secretary in charge of federal regional offices; Mr. Gil Pompa, director of the Community Relations Service, Department of Justice; Mr. Luis Nunez, deputy director, US Commission on Civil Rights; Mr. Bert Gallegos, general counsel, OEO; Mr. Alex Armendariz, director of the Office of Minority Business Enterprise at the Department of Commerce; Mr. Rudy Montejano, commissioner, Interstate Commerce Commission; Mr. Louis Ramirez, director of community development, OEO; Mr. Ray Telles, commissioner, Equal Employment Opportunity Commission; Mr. Nacho Lopez, special assistant to the secretary of Housing and Urban Development; Mrs. Romana Banuelos, US Treasurer; Mr. Gene Costales, director of the Sixteen-Point Program at the Civil Service Commission; Mr. Tony Rodriguez, Department of State; Mr. Carlos Conde, director of public affairs at the Inter-American Development Bank; and Mr. Mo Garcia, my personal assistant.

I opened the meeting with comments on a briefing given about two weeks prior by the president and John Ehrlichman expounding on the new directions and changes the administration was now implementing. I opined that reorganization for revenue sharing was best for our people, because federal funds would now go directly to the local level: cities and counties. This meant that with the election of Spanish-speaking people to city councils and county government, our elected officials would be directly involved with our communities. Congressman Ed Roybal was considering forming a new organization for that purpose. He was to name it the National Association of Latin Elected Officials (NALEO).

With respect to appointees, I remarked that I felt optimistic. The level of concern inside the White House was pretty high, I related. They were very aware of the unrest and sense of betrayal people were sensing. I, too, was deeply concerned, for I knew that a new crew was taking over at White House presidential personnel. I and my staff gave a briefing on and discussed current activities and priorities at the Cabinet Committee. Everyone departed, I felt, with uplifted spirits, positive attitudes, and knowledge of the administration's direction. They were better equipped to meet the public. (36)

Meanwhile, I had to keep my head screwed on correctly, for I was reading in the daily papers the how, who, and why, of the burglary at the offices in the Watergate Building. Judge Sirica, from the liberal, Democrat-controlled state of New Jersey, was imposing intolerable punishments to compel those confessing guilt to name names. His father had been a peasant in Italy who had boarded a ship to the land where he had been told that money grew on trees. He was raised in a country where torture has been a classic tradition for getting at the "truth." His forefathers, the Romans, had perfected the system with the use of a wooden cross.

Watergate matters were beginning to impinge substantially on my efforts to carry on with my well-defined priorities and directions. The role of Mrs. Anne Armstrong was becoming more public. She needed image development and an introduction to the Spanish-speaking world. I had to carry on with the tender care of this "new kid on the block." I was receiving memos from my staff and also drafting them on how to prepare her for interacting with the Spanish-speaking. Some examples I provide are emblematic of the task:

On March 1, 1973 a PERSONAL AND CONFIDENTIAL MEMO

TO: Honorable Anne Armstrong
       Counselor to the President
FROM: Henry M. Ramirez, Chairman

I am told that you are considering acquiring a Spanish Speaking person as one of your staff assistants to work primarily with Spanish Speaking Affairs. I would like you to consider Carlos Conde. Conde currently has White House credentials and I will be happy to keep him there on detail at your office full time. […] (37)

April 5, 1973
MEMORANDUM FOR: ANNE ARMSTRONG
                 COUNSELOR TO THE PRESIDENT
FROM: HENRY M. RAMIREZ

SUBJECT: Talking points concerning the
                        Administration's accomplishments In
                        the area of the Spanish Speaking (38)

April 5, 1973

MEMORANDUM TO: Ray Maduro

FROM: Henry M. Ramirez
                                   Chairman

SUBJECT: Interview:
                                   Anne Armstrong
                                   Editorial Board,
                                   U.S. News and World Report

We must prepare by Saturday morning a paper with talking points for Counselor Armstrong's interview by the Editorial Board of U.S. News and World Report:

Questions the Editorial Board may ask in relation to the Spanish Speaking, e.g., appointments, grants, directions, Administration's commitments, and other possible key points. [...] (39)

Memo 6 April 73
To Dr H M Ramirez
Fm Mo Garcia
Subj AA's Image

I suggest something along these lines:

A press conference in Washington where Mrs. Armstrong
      would reaffirm...
We should make every effort to get Mrs. Armstrong to attend
      out-of-town gatherings of Spanish Speaking, especially

in places where she would get a good reception, such as Los Angeles.

It might also be well to provide Mrs. Armstrong with a list of active people [...] (40)

Memo 20 April 73

To Dr. H M Ramirez
Fm Mo Garcia and E. B. Duarte

There is no substantive reason for Counselor Anne Armstrong to avoid visiting Phoenix next 4 May 73 [...] (41)

Big-time changes were now arriving at the White House. The current and known affairs and situation of the Spanish-speaking would change. A new chief of staff had arrived.

The needs and newly sparked dreams and aspirations of the Spanish speaking could not wait for the slowly emerging and changing environment of power in the White House. They would no longer accept being a benignly neglected group. Yet that was precisely the new reality. The presidency was weakening, and the corrupt Democrats were on the warpath to destroy it. I comprehended entirely that Anne Armstrong lacked the experience and knowledge essential for leadership over the needs and concerns of Mexican Americans, mainland Puerto Ricans, and Cubans. The White House personnel on whom I had relied for performing the mission of the Cabinet Committee had left.

Of the utmost importance was what I knew about the future of CCOSS. It would cease to exist on midnight, December 31, 1974. The chairman of the Government Operations Committee, Chet Holifield, would not submit the bill to extend Public Law 91-81 beyond its five-year provision. He confided in me privately as he pulled out of his credenza a stack of similar proposed legislation in the interests of Asian Americans, Black Americans, American Indians, and three or more other groups. He commented, "You have been too successful. now everyone wants a Cabinet Committee." Over a cup of coffee, he and his wife chatted very amiably with me about my own future, which was when he mentioned discussing with the president the idea of my running for Congress in his current Congressional District.

It was now action time. With others, Mo Garcia prepared a white paper on the matter of a White House position: "The Importance of Having Spanish-Speaking Person in the White House" in April 1973. (42) He was endowed with knowledge and experience required to write it. He was renowned and highly respected in national and international journalistic circles. He had been assigned to cover all of Latin America for *Time/Life* for several decades. He was fluent in French, Spanish, and English. He had observed dictatorial governments up close. He had a keen mind for analyzing and summarizing his observations. He had been my constant and deeply loyal friend and companion. I asked him to incorporate the thoughts and ideas I had discussed with him on long airplane trips.

I shared the white paper with three persons to get their reactions and support for a White House position. Two of them responded very favorably. My files do not show that the third responded to me.

On May 15, 1973, I wrote to Congressman James Collins (R. TX):

Dear Jim,

I enclose a copy of a position paper drawn up by my office setting forth the reasons why the President should have a Spanish speaking staff assistant in the White House. The paper sets forth the reasons we consider it important to have a Spanish speaking representative in the White House and more specifically why this staff assistant should be the Chairman of the Cabinet Committee on Opportunities for the Spanish Speaking. I would greatly appreciate your writing letters recommending such action, if you are in agreement with this conclusion. I cannot tell you how much it would mean to the Spanish speaking people to have someone in the White House and how important this is when it comes to swinging the Spanish speaking vote toward the Republican Party.

Sincerely,

Henry M. Ramirez
Chairman

Congressman Collins responded:

May 21, 1973

Mr. William Timmons
Assistant to the President for Congressional Relations
The White House
Washington, D.C.

Dear Bill:

I hope that we can do more in developing the standing of the Spanish-speaking people. President Nixon has made tremendous inroads in gaining the respect and admiration of the Mexican-Americans.

Can we have a Spanish-speaking staff assistant on the staff of the White House? I would recommend for this position Henry M. Ramirez who is now serving as chairman of the Cabinet Committee for Opportunities for the Spanish Speaking people.

You are familiar with the last election where we were carrying precincts with the Spanish-speaking people. In Dallas the President carried by a sweeping majority all the precincts where there was a strong Spanish-speaking vote. On the other hand, 95% of the blacks continue to vote a straight Democratic ticket.

With this fine group what can we do to enhance their standing in Washington? Ramirez has been the one who has done the most in Texas in getting results. I would like to see us push him into a strong position.

Best of luck to you,
/signed/ Jim
James M. Collins, M.C. (43)

My letter to Tom Marquez of Dallas received no response. (44)

The third recipient of my May 15, 1973, letter was Mr. Roy Day of Pomona, to whom I wrote: "Dear Roy. It was good to visit with you recently in Los Angeles. Thank you for taking the time to drive from Pomona to Los Angeles for this meeting." In that letter, I enclosed the white paper. (45)

In response to my request, Roy wrote to his dear friend,

May 25, 1973

PERSONAL

The President of the United States,
The White House,
Washington, D. C. 20500.

Dear Friend and President Richard Nixon,

I am enclosed correspondence from the Hon. Henry M. Ramirez, Chairman, Cabinet Committee on Opportunities for Spanish Speaking People. You will recall I recommended this man very highly to you prior to his receiving his present appointment.

In view of the fact I obviously am not informed sufficiently as to the merit of this present request, I am forwarding the information to you just as I received it. I will say that I was very much impressed with this man again on meeting with him in Los Angeles recently, as herein referred to, and believe he will do an outstanding job for you and the country in whatever place you decide to use him.

Meanwhile, Mr. President, my very best to you in this hour of harassment and turmoil. Just remember this from your very first campaign manager—always stay on the offensive, and I know you will be carrying the ball over many goal lines in this day and hour, scoring with the winning touchdowns. I still remember, when a certain representative of a nationally known Corporation, came down from San Francisco and handed me five one hundred crisp bills to present to you personally—from his organization—and I can still see the look of scorn on your face as you handed them back to me, saying—"Roy, I am not impressed with this, and want you to return these and if they want to contribute to my campaign to put money in regular channels, like anyone else."—do you remember this?? I have used this story in many talks I have given around here and in Oklahoma on your beginnings, and very recently.

I like this Ramirez person, and feel he is a real asset to your 1973 team, and also, I am damned proud of you, with very good reason and proof, because I knew you THEN.

Sincerely,

ROY O. DAY

Blind copy to Dr. Ramirez (45)

The "harassment and turmoil," about which Mr. Day comments, slowed considerations of a White House position.

Almost a year later, I received a letter that revealed that Anne Armstrong had recommended to President Nixon the appointment of a Spanish-speaking person to advise him on the problems of the nation's fourteen million citizens of Latin heritage. The February 25, 1974 letter was from Charles R. Esparza to Mr. Louis J. Churchville, assistant administrator at the Federal Aviation Administration. He wrote: "My purpose in writing this letter is to ask that you recommend Dr. Henry M. Ramirez, Chairman [...] to this prestigious post. I consider this appointment to be in the best interests of the many fine Spanish Speaking people in this country." Mr. Churchville then forwarded the letter to his former boss, now ambassador to Honduras, Phillip Sanchez. Phil in turn attached to a copy of the correspondence a nice hand-written cover note dated March 26 with a personal touch: "Dear Enrique, I thought you should see this. It's a good feeling to know you have friends, isn't it?" (46)

On April 3, 1974, Congressman John H. Rousselot (R-CA), wrote: "Dear Anne, In response to your telephone call, I am submitting the following four names of Spanish-speaking Americans for the president's consideration. My first recommendation is for Henry M. Ramirez, Chairman [...]" (47)

Mrs. Armstrong asked me what criteria she should maintain for considering candidates for the White House position. I was adamant in my recommendations that, whoever was selected, that person would have to have a strong and loyal senator from the Southwest supporting him or her. The person selected would have to work with a new president and staff; most, if not all, would have no knowledge of what President Nixon and I had wrought to include us in America, and for that matter, would not care. Events in 1975 and 1976 showed my correct perspicacity. President Gerald Ford filled his White House with his own team, and CCOSS was not extended. CCOSS came to an end on December 31, 1974 as per its enabling legislation. (48)

The crescendo of turmoil and harassment against President Nixon was hitting new highs every day. My "big secret" was climaxing and nearing its denouement. I had some time earlier taken myself off the list of candidates. I belonged to my boss's family—that of President Nixon. I would leave when he left.

In May 1974, a New York monthly, TEMAS, revealed: "According to some manifestations from Dr. Henry M. Ramirez, President Nixon will name very soon a Hispanic to be a White House Assistant." (49) On June 30, 1974, the *Los Angeles Times* also reveals: "House Minority Leader John J. Rhodes (R-Ariz.) reports Nixon will name Latin to Staff." (50) On July 25, 1974, a White House press release out of San Clemente, California announced that the president had assigned Fernando E. C. Debaca to work with Anne Armstrong in the White House. (51) On July 26, 1974, the UPI issued a report that President Nixon had named Fernando de Baca as a special assistant for domestic affairs. (52) Sadly, only days before President Nixon resigned, the third condition of my original appointment, on which they had reneged—a White House position—is finally met, in a timid and lukewarm manner.

Let it be said and known far and wide: President Richard M. Nixon was the *first* president to create a White House position for a Hispanic.

PART IV:

WHY I AM THE ONE WHO CAN TELL THE STORY

CHAPTER THIRTEEN

AT AGE 40, THE "Y" ON THE ROAD THE INGREDIENTS OF MY EDUCATION, FORMATION, AND HISTORY

I had reached midlife: forty-one years of age. Career trajectories are usually well defined and predictable by this point. My own careers as seasonal migrant, laborer, clergy, military, educator, and social scientist, had proceeded along unpredictable (and frightfully, for me), unplanned paths. I do not know if it is usual and customary for a forty-year-old to reflect on past life, searching into his historical psyche for direction, wisdom, counsel, understanding, and knowledge.

An unexpected phone call in December 1970 changed my life, again. I accepted the lunch invitation of Congressman Charles Wiggins. I had been thinking ahead to the next five years, planning my career as an accomplished educator. The congressman had counseled me to look at a high-level political appointment.

It would be a path away from my profession and toward public life as a presidential assistant in charge of all matters Hispanic under the Nixon administration.

I was an American success story. I had risen from a humble, seasonal migrant family to a nationally acknowledged educational professional with a PhD in education from Loyola University in Los Angeles, California in recognition of my contribution to the field. I expected to advance my career as a college teacher, or more likely, a school system superintendent, in California. I was already considering three possible school districts.

But several weeks after the lunch with Congressman Wiggins, I found myself following the instructions of Dr. George Grassmuck. He was quite an important figure: he was an assistant to the presidential counselor and a professor on leave from the University of Michigan. His directions were clear and simple. I was to go to the West Wing entrance and present my ID. The Secret Service guards there would check me by computer and make a call to verify that I had an appointment with the Counselor, Robert Finch.

The guards checked me out, the iron gate opened, and I was directed to walk up the driveway to the West Wing building. A marine attired in dress uniform snapped me a sharp salute and opened the door. I addressed the receptionist and said I was there to see the counselor. She pressed some buttons, quietly announced my presence, and added, "Someone will come for you."

Over the next three and a half years, my footsteps from the West Gate to the West Wing were to be retraced countless times

I had been ordered to come to the White House by my superiors at the US Commission on Civil Rights. I had been for all public purposes an anonymous researcher and bureaucrat who rode buses to work. I was unknown—just another government employee carrying a briefcase. What the heck was I in for? Similar thoughts had raced years before.

Almost three years before, when I arrived at the US Commission on Civil Rights at 19th Street and Pennsylvania Avenue, I had also speculated: *What have I done? What am I getting into? Is this stupid?* And then other thoughts would intrude and assure me, *You can always wash dishes or pick oranges!* Fear would overwhelm me with conjectures and I would ask myself, *What have I done to my little family and my exceptional wife?*

Only two top people at the Commission knew about me personally: one had traveled to Whittier and spent a week checking me out; the other had read about me in the national papers. The Whittier High School newspaper, *The Cardinal & White*, reported on January 29, 1968, "Taylor studies New Horizon." It said that "William Taylor, who works closely with President Johnson, and is the Director of the United States Commission on Civil Rights, came here last week to study the New Horizons Program of this school."

The other person was Eunice Greer, director of research. She also knew a lot about me. She had read about me in clippings taken from the *Los Angeles Times*, the *Whittier Daily News*, the *New York Times*, and the *Christian Science Monitor*. In 1967, Mrs. Greer had traveled extensively to interview about twenty-six candidates for the job I now held. The candidates were Mexican American college professors, all holding PhDs, and authors of articles and books. She showed me the list but sadly would not share it. She considered it confidential information. She told me she and the Commission staff had been searching for a person who had both academic knowledge and successful practical application of educational principles. All twenty-six professors were wanting in the second area, which specifically concerned the education of Mexican Americans. Since she did not explain otherwise, that was the impression with which she left me to understand.

My DC scenario could be described this way: I had never been in the East; I knew no one there. I had no mentor, tutor, or sponsor, and I was an ardent anticommunist Republican working in an agency where, it seemed, everyone was a Democrat and ranged from very liberal to Marxist leanings, at that. I had cursory knowledge of the US government: to me it was the White House, Congress, and the Supreme Court. I bought maps to learn local geography. I became personally cognizant of how deeply Whites and Negroes were divided. It was awesome and yet very real. In the Southwestern states, discrimination against Mexican Americans was institutional, known, and overt; its patterns were vestiges of the victorious conquest of Mexico by the United States. The European Americans living in the Eastern states were not aware that the discrimination Black Americans endured, Mexican Americans likewise endured. When my dear wife and children arrived a few months later, my wife and I happily noticed that their neighborhood playmates in Bethesda, Maryland, did not know what their playmates in the nice suburb of East Whittier, California knew—that they had been objects of discriminatory remarks by virtue of their being Mexican American. In 1968 Bethesda, that was a blessing. Our children were freed from the types of unsavory events I experienced as I grew up in California.

As I waited for someone to escort me, I wondered, where in the White House does the president have his office? I did not realize that the West Wing Building housed his office, the Oval Office.

I was deeply awed at the walk from Pennsylvania Avenue through the iron gates up to the White House, then to be greeted gravely by a soldierly marine with a very sharp salute.

I was not nervous. By midlife, I had already become quite accustomed to pomp and circumstance. Dr. George Grassmuck emerged to escort me past the reception area and through some cramped little offices up narrow stairs to a comfortable and very tastefully decorated office. He introduced me to Counselor Robert Finch, who received me warmly and with no small talk. He got right to why I was there. "I asked you to come here because you're a researcher, right?" I said yes. After he instructed me to design research on what Mexican Americans perceived of this White House, I was on my way back to my office on the corner of 14th and I streets at the US Commission of Civil Rights.

Along the way, I stopped for a cup of coffee to reflect on what was happening. I had not developed any advisor or mentor. My only confidential counselor was my spiritual confessor, and this was not his world of expertise. After almost three years in Washington, I had become a mentor to a wide range of people but still lacked my own. There was no one around who knew my world, who could counsel me on how to make Washington work for my future. My college classmates were now bishops, monsignors, and parish priests, and all were in Arizona or California. My professional colleagues were all in education in Southern California, and almost all of them were knee-jerk liberals.

I still smile and chortle when I recall teacher lunchroom discussions of heavy topics, such as mortality versus immortality. English and history teachers would often take the position that it was the purpose of government to make this society and life as close as possible to a paradise, because after all, this was the only life. Almost all of my Mexican American friends were teachers, truck drivers, and so on.

Thank God, I was blessed with a smart and perceptive wife. She was my talented advisor and counselor. She was my only trusted confidante. What wife would want to leave the known of the pleasant community of Whittier and a fabulous state, California, where the family was indeed very comfortable—with their wide circle of friends and extensive family—to the unknown of Washington DC? But she agreed to the move, even though it would be a great sacrifice to leave the comfort of our own home and great community.

She knew that I had made a significant contribution in education with the New Horizons Program, where I had helped hundreds of students improve their educational achievement. She was mother and father while I spent countless hours developing the New Horizons Program. The program I started at Whittier High School was expanded to the other high schools in the district: Pioneer, Santa Fe, La Serna, Monte Vista, California, and Sierra. I accepted the position with the Commission on Civil Rights as director of the Mexican American Studies Division because in it, I could help not only hundreds of students in the Southwest but millions, and I could make the education experience better for Mexican Americans.

Back to the present: over several cups of coffee, I made three outlines of possible hypotheses for the desired study. I was scheduled to return to the counselor's office in several weeks with them. The finished product would reflect on the perspectives on this White House held by Mexican Americans, with a discussion of each issue followed by recommendations for presidential action. The first outline called for a quick and simple series of telephone interviews of people across the Southwest over a set of commonly known and discussed issues. The second called for a combination of telephone interviews founded on issues arising from a research of the literature. And the third would be based on travel to urban, suburban, and rural areas of the Southwest to execute the "man on the street" approach.

For the next several weeks, I retreated mentally into my personal warehouse of informal and formal education. *Why?* I asked myself. Why was I being tasked to capture the Mexican American mentality toward a national view? Why did Counselor Finch believe I was qualified? Why me? I meditated and reflected.

This country was unique among all others at its origin in 1776. Only this country had declared that God created human beings and endowed them with their own personal inalienable rights to freedom, life, and the pursuit of happiness. (Incidentally, this last word, "happiness," replaced the original word, "holiness," which Saint Robert Bellarmine, SJ (1542–1621) wrote in his *De*

Laicis.) (1) By 1971, the country had achieved another singular attribute: it was structured on a firm foundation of ideas, not on the basis of the homogeneity of its citizens.

As a consequence, if I wanted to fathom the origins of Mexican American cultural diversity, it was necessary to know the history of their country of origin. Given that Mr. Finch wanted me to write a thought piece on what Mexican Americans thought of the Nixon administration, perforce I had to search into my own personal history for answers. And so, while slowly drinking more coffee, I commenced the terribly arduous chore of trying to retrace my roots.

From age one to ten, I lived with Mom and Dad and my five brothers and five sisters in the house on 130 North Gordon Street. The railroad tracks it was near were adjacent to First Street. The downtown of Pomona was one block away on Second Street. Life there was exciting for a little boy. Downtown Pomona was our Disneyland in the 1930s. The stores were the playground for me and my younger siblings: Chalo, Helen, and Inez. As is the custom in Mexican families, authority vested in me as the eldest.

Pomona was the business center for the entire Pomona Valley with its little surrounding villages: Claremont, Chino, Corona, La Verne, Ontario, Walnut, San Dimas, Upland, Guasti, and Cucamonga. The space between these towns was entirely occupied by citrus orchards and vineyards. I still vividly recall the early morning breezes that favored the valley with the sweet fragrance of citrus blossoms from a canopy of treetops that were overseen by the snow-covered peaks of the nearby seventeen-thousand-foot Mount San Antonio and Mount Baldy.

We had no immediate neighbors, but Pomona had four barrios where the Mexicans resided, all at least a half-mile away. My
grandmother, Narzaria Guerrero Ramirez, lived a mile west of us
in the *barrio de Celaya* with her three other sons (Rosendo, Elias,
and Alfonso), a daughter (Marciana), and two grandchildren.
We knew two families in the little barrio east of us, but no one in
the big *barrio de Silao* south of us or in the *barrio del Dompe* (the
dump) in the city's southeast quadrant.

Pomona in 1935, when I arrived at the age of reason, was fresh
and new with a population of twenty-thousand-plus. It had been
incorporated in 1888; European Americans arrived from the
East and purchased land and homes in the 1900s. By the 1920s,
they had built a high school and graded and paved some streets.
The city enjoyed two parks, two railroad stations, a huge Masonic
Temple next to City Hall, and very large Protestant churches situated on the central streets of Gary and Holt. They were Baptist,
Congregational, Episcopalian, Methodist, and Presbyterian. More
distant from the center of town were other temples: Mormon,
Jehovah's Witness, Foursquare, Friends, and so on. (2)

In the 1920s, another large group arrived: thousands of
Central Mexicans. Almost all of them were young families, married couples each with several children. Most were from the state
of Guanajuato; the two big Pomona barrios, Celaya and Silao,
were named after two big cities there. People from other central
Mexican states—Zacatecas, Jalisco, Michoacan, Aguascalientes,
and Queretaro—moved into other cities in the Pomona Valley.

My parents arrived in Pomona in 1929 from the railroad hub
city of Salamanca, Guanajuato. They had fled in 1923, enduring

frightful deprivation and a merciless frigid winter in Juarez, Mexico. Finally, in May 1924, they crossed the border by paying two dollars to the Department of Labor for border passes. They went to Emporia, Kansas.

My memory holds that families went into El Paso and were transported by rail to Emporia. Prospective employers from the Midwest and the West interviewed and hired workers at this place of temporary housing. I recall that it was called *el gallinero* (the chicken coop). Brothers and sisters and cousins became separated for life as some opted for Chicago; others, the West Coast. (I reconstructed my account from bits and pieces of conversations I heard adults exchange from the earliest days of my memory. No one ever sat me down and related, "This is the story of how we came to be in the United States.")

From there, my mom and dad went to the sugar beet fields of Sun City, Kansas, and then to Lamar, Colorado. In both places, my father, Jessie, (12) and Joe (9) did back-breaking work in the fields along the Arkansas River. I remember silently observing my dad lament deeply with tearful sobs his, Jessie's, and little Joe's experience thinning out the beet sprouts in spring with little ten-inch long, six-inch wide hoes. His lament heightened when he later recalled how long the rows of sprouts had appeared. "They seemed to be a mile long!" he would whisper. "We worked stooped, all day," he added. Dad called this phase of working on the sugar beet fields *"Des hay jar."* With a slight smile, he said, "The very hot summers were a little better because we used long hoes to cut the weeds around the bushy beet tops. But the autumn brought another period of stooping, cutting off the leafy tops and heaving them into a truck all in one motion, repetitively." (Dad called this *tapiar*—assuredly a phonetic rendition of the instruction "top it off.") After such comments, he walked away to be alone with his stooped shoulders.

In June 1926, my father's mother, her four single sons, one daughter, and two grandchildren joined the little and suffering Ramirez family in Colorado. My father got a job with the Southern Pacific Railroad, and everyone except my uncle Luis, who had perished in the snows of Kansas, moved to Wilmington, then to Spadra, then to Walnut. Finally, all of the Ramirez clan arrived in Pomona.

The Pomona Valley and the entire Citrus Belt in Southern California saw Mexican barrios sprout next to every citrus-packing house and railroads leading to them. Barrios in surrounding towns had names such as "El Arbol Verde" in Claremont. Dr. Matt Garcia wrote *A World of Its Own: Race, Labor, and Citrus in the Making of Greater Los Angeles, 1900–1970*, a book about his father growing up in this barrio. (3) It is also the barrio where my super wonderful wife was born and raised, a finely educated and cultured lady. In her senior year of high school, she won the Claremont Business and Professional Women's Club scholarship, which she utilized to go to Chaffey College.

A small sampling of other barrio names is "El Barrio del Chile" in Ontario, "Casa Blanca" in Riverside, and "El Jardin" and "La Garra" in Corona. These were *the* communities of the Mexicans. There, they built their Catholic churches, Catholic schools, and community halls. Their own grocery stores were there. The menfolk gathered in their bars and pool halls. The barber shops were in homes. The Mexican American children walked to (or were bused to) segregated public schools, where the English language pervaded classroom life; Spanish lived outside it in the playground and pre- and post-school hours. Their brown bag lunches contained burritos and tacos, not sandwiches. The Mexican way of life was the California barrio way of life. Southern California was Central Mexico.

It seemed that almost everyone was new to California. The parents of the Anglo kids had just arrived a few dozen years prior from the East to live proximate to the Mexican enclaves where the parents of the Mexican kids had also just arrived. As I was growing up, a favorite question was "Where are you from?" Most Anglos would respond that they were from "back East." Ronald Reagan was "from back East." Movie stars were "from back East." Pete Wilson, former mayor of San Diego, US Senator, and governor of California, was "from back East." My classmates had most of their relatives "back East." Their grandparents had come from "the old country" someplace in Europe. (In my primary grades, I framed mental images of US and European geography as if I were in a capsule high above the planet. For that reason, I still do not rely on GPS. I view, imagine, and memorize a graph of geographic patterns below my mental position high above the earth.) Richard Millhouse Nixon was an important exception; he was not "from back East." He was born close to a Mexican barrio in California and was raised between two of them.

The European Americans from east of the Mississippi flocked to Southern California to plant thousands of acres of citrus trees. By 1893, there were forty thousand acres of citrus. Navel oranges were harvested from December to April; Valencia oranges were harvested during the spring, summer and fall, and lemons, all year long. With refrigerated freight cars, high-speed locomotives, and modern marketing techniques, the citrus industry became almost like a gold mine. Workers to pick the fruit were needed. And men were flooding California from Central Mexico. They were of marrying age or already married, with responsibility for a wife and children. They were looking for permanence and stability.

California, from the 1880s to the 1950s, experienced a confluence of two gigantic human currents. European Americans flooded into California, and citrus trees produced jobs and more jobs. And Mexican refugees from a Marxist-Socialist revolution, coupled with persecution of Catholics in the Cristero War, flooded into the California Citrus Belt needing jobs and more jobs.

By January 1971, I could reflect on the historical origins of these Mexicans and on their US-born children, the Mexican Americans. Unlike my earlier experiences, which were linear, I now enjoyed the great advantage of an overview refined by age, education, and travel. Knowledge produced understanding. Analyses of the daily life of Mexicans and Mexican Americans led to findings, perceptions, and summations. The historical origins of my family derived from two fonts: happenings in Europe and events in Anahuac (the name of the lands lying between Oregon and Costa Rica).

For starters, my reflections revealed to my psyche who I am ethnically. I am a Mestizo. The word *mestizo* is formed from the Latin verb *misceo, miscere, miscui, mixtus*. Romans used the last part of the verb, *mixtus*, to define the relationship when someone united with or married a non-Roman. For the conquered people of Britannia (as Julius Caesar knew it—the invading German tribe, the Anglii, renamed it England in the 350s), the Latin word *mixtus* changed into the word "mixture." The concept had acquired the meaning "comprised of persons of different kinds, classes, or races." It came to be used in expressions such as "mixed company" or "mixed neighborhood." To the land of the New World, the Latin word was carried by its Spanish form, *mestizo*. The *Dictionary of the Royal Spanish Academy* defines the verb, *mestizar*, as "to adulterate castes by the copulation of individuals who do not belong to the same caste, only." The child of *mestizar* was called a *mestizo*, which is defined in the same dictionary as a person born of a mother and a father of different races.

Feudal society required records of what today would be termed genetics. Class definitions and differences depended on knowing who was "superior" and who "inferior." In the United States, one finds expressions such as "half-breed" to signify social misfits. Marriage certificates once had to certify whether the parties to the marriage contract were of pure blood, *sangre pura*, or mixed blood, *sangre mesclada*: mestizo. A person of Spanish ancestry was declared to be a person of pure blood, endowed with privileges, social status, and rights unavailable to Mestizos. Sadly, the Spaniards attached very pejorative meaning to the word *mestizo*. Virgilio P. Elizondo explores (and deplores) this topic and its devastating effects on the peoples of Latin America in his *Guadalupe, Mother of the New Creation*. (4)

In my studies, travel, and discussions throughout life, I had already been saturated with knowledge and understanding of the origins of the Europeanness inherent in my *mestizaje*.

Now I had to focus and reflect on the elements of my *mestizaje* that comprised my Mexicanness.

My days, with downtown Pomona as my playground, with all the toys at the five-and-ten-cent store, came to an end in September 1936. Early one morning, I was told to dress for school. I wondered, *Why me? Martin, Manuel, Dolores, and Teresa go to school, and that is good for them, they are older,* I thought. I asked, "Will I also have to learn English?" I was most fortunate and happy, it turned out. My first-grade teacher was Sister Lucy Marie. She was a Holy Name nun and lived at their convent in the Academy. (5) Her brother was a Franciscan priest in nearby Riverside. She could speak with my parents. Her skin color was similar to mine. She was roly-poly, and she hugged me with tenderness and patience. She was also my second-grade teacher.

In the second grade, my grades were almost all A's. I was assigned to the second seat behind Jean-Baptiste Airey, who became my lifelong friend. We were seated at Saint Joseph's School in order of our monthly marks. After the first grade, I recall that I was almost always seated second after Jean in the rows reserved for boys only. (The girls had theirs.) It was because of Jean's family that I added France to my geography—specifically, "la Provence," where the parents of his French-speaking mom "came from."

Little by little, I began to learn to write, read, hear, and speak English only. I became a voracious reader, and my classmates would often question me. "Did you really read all those books that you checked out of the school library?" I still have noticeable scars above my eyes where I struck trees or light-poles as I read while walking the mile and a half from home to school (and vice versa). I almost always walked home alone.

Sometime in the middle of the sixth grade, I decided to buy a diary. I thought, "I need to write about my thoughts and experiences. I think I am an oddball. I speak excellent English with a wide vocabulary, but I now have trouble uttering sentences in Spanish. I am becoming monosyllabic in Spanish. I am mispronouncing Spanish words. I am becoming an object of derision and laughter."

And, of greater significance was the daily experience I lived, where I was becoming a very aware and conscious participant-observer. When I awoke at home, I would make the Sign of the Cross and pray silently. My brother, Chalo, and I were now growing into our second decade of life. I was eleven. Then we were off, after saying good-mornings to all, to do the daily chores. Chalo and I would milk the goats and then take them to nearby fields for fodder, feed the hundreds of rabbits we raised for food and for income, feed the hogs and wash their pens, feed the chickens and gather their eggs, and finally cut some firewood for the wood stove in the kitchen. Conversations with my siblings were all in English; with my mom and dad, usually monosyllabic Spanish.

Then I would walk to Sacred Heart Church one block away to serve daily Mass. My pastor, Father Angel Beta, would then drive me to school. Of course, I was always tardy for class, but the nuns approved and just smiled as I took my seat. Mass was celebrated in Latin, and all discussions at church were in Spanish. The members of Sacred Heart Church came from El Barrio de

Celaya, El Barrio de Silao, and El Dompe. They, the Mexicans and their Mexican American kids, all lived in a society that was completely different from the society of Saint Joseph's Catholic Church and all the residents of Pomona. We knew the European Americans lived primarily in areas north of First Street and east of Garey. The Mexicans and a few Blacks lived almost exclusively in the west and southwest areas of Pomona. Life was peaceful. We knew Mexicans could not buy property north of Holt. We knew that when the plunge or swimming pool was open, Thursday was our day to use it. New water filled the pool on Friday. We knew that only two movie houses permitted Mexicans, and then they had to sit on "their side." We knew all kinds of things.

I was deeply aware that I, however, lived in two societies. As I walked home from school, where I was the only Mexican boy in my class, I had to confront the Mexican kids from El Barrio de Celaya and finally from El Barrio de Silao. They did not like me. I was odd. I did not go to "their" school. The Mexicans from Celaya attended the segregated school Roosevelt, and the ones from Silao attended the other, segregated Hamilton. The two junior high schools Fremont and Emerson were not segregated; there was no need. Few Mexicans survived the sixth grade; almost all dropped out. But from 8:30 a.m. to 3:00 p.m., I was immersed in the European world of history, religion, language, and customs.

I early on perceived the differences in the two societies. The English-speaking world was populated with educated business- and land-owning parents. Their kids, my classmates, were: Ted Tate, the chauffeured son of the Cadillac dealer who lived in Ganesha Hills; Dean Spencer, son of the well-known CPA; Billy

Thatcher, son of the well-to-do citrus rancher; the Sullivans, whose family owned a large construction company; the Aireys, owners of a large ranch; the Kierkoffs, who had citrus groves; and so on. And yet, here I was, achieving better grades than they were. I quickly deduced that education was the key to social differences.

So I yearned to write to my diary on what was transpiring in me. I was living a double life. In the morning, evening, and on weekends, I was a Mexican. During the day, I was learning to be an educated European. I was enduring cultural conflict and, yes, culture shock. I also surmised that I was destined to become famous and well known. I wanted to record the mental conflicts that an emerging bicultural young man undergoes. It is truly amazing how many wonderful older people came to my aid to advise, counsel, guide, direct, and teach me. It seemed I was getting a crash course on what to do and what to avoid.

During my second grade in 1938, I lined up at a facility where nice, new, and warm brown corduroy jackets were being distributed at an office called "the WPA." It was cold. I was rather proud of my achievement: I had a new jacket, and for free. When my father arrived home from work, he asked, "How did you come by that acquisition?" My response was quick and joyful. He ripped it off my body, cut it up into shreds, and scolded me with, "We do not take anything free from the federal government. We work, earn money, and buy what we need." I never forgot! I was to learn and appreciate my father's wisdom about the role of the federal government in our lives. The intrusion of a federal government into the life of his little family had caused his flight from Mexico in search of freedom to a new language, a new culture, and a new country. He had learned the harsh lesson that the more the federal government controls one's life, the more freedom is limited.

In the same fashion, my father admonished me, "We pay for private schooling. We do not get free education at public, pagan, and segregated schools. That is why you, your mom and siblings, every May departed from Pomona for San Jose, where you all cut apricots and gathered prunes in summer—to pay for tuition, books, and clothing for school."

At home, I was acquiring the daily modalities of living a Catholic life. As a family, we prayed the Rosary every night with our parents. When we lived in downtown Pomona at 130 North Gordon Street, my mom would take us to daily Mass at Saint Joseph's Church, from which we would walk to Saint Joseph's Grammar School. My mother would often utter phrases invoking intercession from the saints, the Holy Trinity, and Mary, the mother of Jesus. At every instance of whatever, my mom would invoke "*Jesus, Maria, y Jose.*" My father directed my sister, Guadalupe, and several of her friends to get Mexicans to sign a petition requesting the bishop to erect a church so that the Mexicans could practice their religious rites as they had done in Mexico. Sacred Heart Church was blessed by Bishop Cantwell in 1935; my parents were pillars of it.

My life was rich. By day, I lived in a Catholic European environment. I learned about the Irish Catholics and their esteemed Saint Patrick. The family of Jean-Baptiste Airey Monet spoke French, as I was informed, from the Provence; they never said "France." They assured me that it was different from Parisian

French. Of course, I knew nothing about French or its nuanced differences. My other classmates were Italian, German, and Polish. My parents called them "Americanos." I wondered about my own identity. I was born in California, yet I was not called "un Americano" or "an American" or a "gringo."

At school, I was a student and a Catholic. We were not that aware of ethnicity: we were all Catholics, first and foremost. I knew I was different but did not know in what way I should identify myself. Eventually, my travel to Mexico would provide answers. I would have to go to the country that my parents much praised, lauded, and emotionally missed. Opportunity arrived when the realization hit me with the impact of a violently swinging two-by-four: when I became a priest, I would eventually be assigned to a poor parish with Mexican parishioners. I had to become fluent in two more skills: listening to and speaking the Spanish language.

CHAPTER FOURTEEN

I AM A MESTIZO!

I went to Mexico in 1951 to learn how to speak and hear Spanish with fluency. I had just completed seven years of a classical curriculum. At the end of May 1952, I would receive a bachelor of arts in philosophy. After that, four years of theology would prepare me for ordination to the priesthood. Those four years would also focus on writing and practicing the delivery of sermons and speeches—in fluent English *and* Spanish. Although my lack of fluency in aural-oral Spanish had precluded me from learning more about Mexico, I could read Spanish and English material on Mexico.

My classical education in Los Angeles and Camarillo, California had focused on European affairs, century by century, dating back to the Sumerian period; and literature and history written in Hebrew, Aramaic, Greek, Latin, Spanish, and English. I had studied two courses on US History and one on California history, but none on Mexico or Central or South America. So, I commenced reading books on Mexico and Central and South America extensively, taking a comparative view of the histories of both sets of Atlantic shores. I read a ton of books that allowed me to see the land of my parents and the history of my ancestors through the eyes of Europeans writing in Spanish and English. Additionally, I was able to see the life, the culture, and the history of the original inhabitants of Mexico through the eyewitness of Spanish explorers, missionaries, and government officials.

They were all able to travel through, observe, and write about (and sometimes photograph) Anahuac, which was renamed Nueva España in the 1500s. On August 24, 1821, the Treaty of Cordoba changed the name of the land between Oregon and Panama to Mexico. A sovereign nation was born.

I learned what could have amounted to a major (or at least a minor) in Latin American Studies in any college. I was able to discern the Anahuac, the New Spain, and the Mexico as of 1821 through the observations and insights of writers burdened by their own impedimenta of prejudice and education. And by the 1970s, after years of travel, social interactions, the acquisition of knowledge, understanding, and appreciation of the history and culture of Mexico, I was able to compare them with the historically concurrent affairs of history and contemporary events of Europe. And, in a special way, I was able to discern the patterns of human behavior manifested as both civilizations changed from their barbaric and savage eras to Christianity. (As but one example, I could compare the why and how of human sacrifice in the Druid religion, about which I had read in Latin books, with that of the Aztecs.)

I have been able to perceive these matters as a Mestizo and write about them with the educated insights and perspectives drawn from experiences of a Mestizo. Now, with deep gratitude and appreciation for the gifts with which God endowed me, I write this book as a Mexican American Mestizo. Mestizos can readily recognize perceptions, observations, and prejudices in the writings of Criollos (Spaniards born and raised in Mexico or Latin America), of English or of European Americans.

And so, my adventures in the land of my ancestors commenced. My senses were all on high alert. As they say, I was all eyes and ears. The first night in Monterey, Mexico was a disaster. While my traveling mates were resting, I sought to purchase some post-cards. When two lovely attendants asked in Spanish how they could assist me, I almost froze. I knew not how to request the cards from the glass showcase. I could have asked in English, but I pointed to the merchandise and blurted something. Quizzically and politely, I was asked something else in Spanish. So I pointed again and tried, "*Dos postales, por favor.*" Now they knew. I could not express myself.

They smiled and tried to hold back a laugh, then uttered, "*Un pocho.*" That, I recognized as mocking derision. I looked Mexican mestizo but could not speak Spanish. They bantered about it. I returned to my hotel room, disheartened. They were pretty, they made fun of my deficiency, and they were Spanish Mexicans.

By contrast, on the following day, we stopped at a place to view the beauties of nature. Mountains with dense vegetation were enveloped with fog, and far below the bridge there was a huge and noisy roaring river. Soon, we were approached by a man clothed in white pantaloons, a simple white shirt. He had stiff black hair and was unshaven. He offered us a basket of black avocadoes. I tried to speak two or three words, accompanied by appropriate gestures. Then Raul Tapia spoke to him in Spanish. No use. The man spoke another language and did not understand Spanish too well. Communication was not possible. Years later, I was to learn that the language of the Tamazunchale area was Nahuatl, the native Mexican language.

A few days later, my Mexico City cousins and professional guides escorted me to "the sites of archeology." Every visitor to Mexico is deemed educated on things Mexican so long as they visit, walk over, and know about how and where the Aztecs performed human sacrifice. But truth calls for clarification: I was fed up with studying European archeology, where rocks were piled atop rocks (the Pyramids), and bored with learning about how the Druids in England and Germany also offered up human sacrifice to their humanly invented gods. Did I not know of the religions of the Greeks and the Romans and of their mythology? Did I not teach and test the knowledge of my students on those subjects? But when they took me to Mass at the Basilica of Our Lady of Guadalupe, my real education on Mexico started and has continued unabated.

I had been raised in the culture of Mexico in the town of Pomona, which saw the society of Central Mexico transplanted to the Pomona Valley. Moreover, I lived in the bicultural society of Europe, which was also transplanted from across the Atlantic: one Protestant, the other Catholic. The formal education I received, however, was all Eurocentric. It included Mexico and Latin America almost as if by accident. Internally, I was a European. Externally, I was and would always be "not an American." I did not look like "an American." People from Europe could land in the United States, get a cab, and go downtown anyplace and they would be perceived as "American." I would always be asked the question, "Where are you from?"

In the Basilica de Nuestra Señora de Guadalupe, I finally knew the answer to the questions, "Where are you from?" and "Who are you?" By that simplistic query, the inquirer meant, "What race are you?" I knew "where I was from" in terms of my Europeanness but began to incorporate, to compare, and to analyze Mexico's history in tandem with my knowledge of concurrent events on both sides of the Atlantic. I began to compare the histories of France and Mexico with regard to the French Revolution. The political philosophy of the Jacobins (that is, of Voltaire, Rousseau, Robespierre, Diderot, and so on) was transplanted into Mexico. This French ideology deeply affected Mexico.

A few years later, Napoleon occupied Spain and filled the government with Masons, Jacobins, atheists, and anti-Catholics. This action caused unbearable pain in the Catholic church in Mexico. Catholics were reporting to their superiors in Spain, but the new superiors were not Catholics but anti-Catholic. The situation was not to be tolerated. It was by definition, impossible. (1)

The reason for the discomfort of the Mexican clergy rested on the cultural tradition of three centuries wherein the church had been managed and administered by Spanish Crown pursuant to a papal bull (1508) granting the king of Spain authority over the Church in the New World. (2) The reality that administrative control and management of the temporal affairs of the Church had been wrested from Catholic authorities and given to anti-Catholic

Jacobins was an inherent dichotomy. This obvious contradiction became unacceptable in the provinces, causing parish priests to incite and lead the Mexican War of Independence of 1810.

I marveled at the similarities I saw between the preparations for the arrival of Jesus of Nazareth in Judea's Bethlehem and the historical conditions in Mesoamerica in 1531. Both regions had shared another ruling government's lingua franca, communications, transportation, and law, but not its religious culture. The Romans were polytheistic; the Aztecs were monotheistic. Teotl was their supreme god, who had many aspects.

The Aztecs were a small group. Sometime in the 1200s, they arrived in the valley of Mexico and conquered the Nahuas, adopting their religion and Nahuatl language. The Romans likewise had adopted the language and gods of the Greeks who had settled north and south of Rome. The Aztecs from their citadel, the island city on the lake of Mexico, reached out to conquer Mesoamerica and made tributaries of all its other nations. They communicated via foot-runners; the Romans had the pony express. They built a superior army; the Romans invented the almost invincible Legion. The language of Nahuatl was universally used; the Romans imposed their language, Latin. The Aztec empire embraced all of Mesoamerica from the Pacific to the Atlantic; the Romans had an empire stretching across the known lands in the middle of the world, in Latin, *medius terra (Mediterrean)* The religion of the Nahuas was different from that of the Romans with their many gods; it was monotheistic, similar to the religion of the Hebrews. This thesis is developed at length in Prescott's *The Conquest of Mexico*. Prescott presents a fascinating read in his Appendix, Part I, Origin of the Mexican Civilization—Analogies with the Old World, p. 689-714. (3)

The god of Anahuac had many aspects. Bernardino de Sahagun (1499–1590) was a Spanish Franciscan missionary to the Aztec (Nahua) people of Mexico, best known for his compilation of the Florentine Codex (also known as *Historia general de las cosas de Nueva España*, or *General History of the Things of New Spain*). Scholars regarded him as being the "father of ethnography" and the creator of the first encyclopedia of the new world. He wrote to Saint Pope Pius V on December 25, 1570 that the Mexicans held that there is one God who is pure spirit, omnipotent, creator and governor of all things. They attributed to their god, Teotl, all wisdom, beauty, and good outcomes.

The Europeans arrived to this part of the Western Hemisphere in the 1520s. They found an extraordinarily advanced and complex society, culture, and language. Armed with superior force, they conquered the inhabitants. Whereas fifteen hundred years prior, God sent his only son, Jesus to the other hemisphere, in 1531 God sent the mother of his son, Mary, to appear to the people of the Western Hemisphere atop a hill—Tepeyac—that the Aztecs had dedicated solely for the mother of Teotl, their one and only supreme god.

An Aztec called Antonio Valeriano learned Spanish and Latin soon after the Conquest. In what is now called the *Nican Mopohua*, circa 1551 (about twenty years after the apparitions), he wrote an account in Nahuatl about the "Guadalupan event," drawing from interviews with its participants. However, he transliterated Nahuatl into the Latin alphabet: the original language was expressed in glyphs (drawings). (4)

The *Nican Mopohua* occupies a position of preeminent historical, cultural, and religious significance. It overshadows other well-known documents, such as the Magna Carta, the Preamble to the US Constitution, and the Rosetta stone, among many others.

However, the author himself never published his report; its first five hundred copies were printed in 1649. In 1886, it was translated into Latin. A complete copy, reconstructed from fragments of the first publishing found in libraries, was published in 1946. One of the best translations into Spanish was done in 1978. Janet Barber, PhD translated it into English in 1998 and had it published in Mexico. (5)

Accounts of the Guadalupan event have been handed down over the centuries from Nahuatl oral tradition, independent of Valeriano's document. The *Nican Mopohua* recounts that she appeared, a young lady nine months pregnant, attired as someone from the highest levels of aristocracy, accompanied by celestial songs and flowers. Nahua religion held that Teotl communicated via songs and that his truth was reflected by the flowers, because they were embedded in the earth by roots. Mary proclaimed in Nahuatl that she was the mother of Teotl, and she also used the Spanish equivalent word, *Dios*. She instructed Juan Diego to convey the message that it was her desire for a church to be erected on Tepeyac Hill, where her son could live and help all who were in those lands.

Juan Diego gathered extraordinarily gorgeous flowers in midwinter, tucked them into his *tilma*, and walked about seven miles to the bishop's residence. As he opened and spread out his tilma, flowers cascaded to the ground. On his tilma there suddenly appeared the full-length image of "the Blue Lady," Guadalupe. The position of the stars spread out on her cloak have been determined to have occupied the same positions relative to each other in the universe on the day of the tilma's unfolding. (6) Scientists have demonstrated that the persons reflected in the retinas of her eyes are those who saw her image as it unfolded. (7)

The little church she desired, so that her son could live there, is now the Basilica de Guadalupe in Mexico City. It is the Catholic Church visited by more people than any other in the world, including Saint Peter's in Rome. The chief priests of the Nahua religion decided that her apparitions and the image on the tilma were divine in origin. Indians started to convert Indians. Indians walked hundreds of miles to visit her little church. Ten million became Catholics in a decade. She civilized Mesoamerica. By way of historical comparison, Jesus Christ, her son, civilized Europe. In Salamanca, my ancestors became very devout practicing Catholics.

In order to comprehend the history of the Western Hemisphere post the "Guadalupan happening," one has to understand that the face on the tilma was the face of a Mestiza. That countenance confounded everyone. Prior to the arrival of the Conquistadores, no one possessed that facial appearance. Her appearance as a mestiza was a harbinger of the human outcome of unions, of rape, of the mixture of different peoples, the marrying to come of the two warring, bitter enemies, the Europeans and the native peoples. Her mestiza face would not be commonly seen and known until decades later. (8)

I first learned of the geopolitical significance of the word *mestizo* while pursuing a graduate course in 1958 on the history of

Latin America. I still vividly recall the highlight of the first lecture. The very first words, phrases, and concepts delivered by the professor were, paraphrased: "To understand Latin America is to know its demography. Absence of this knowledge and understanding causes ignorance of everything else. There are five distinct groups: Europeans; native Western Hemispheric inhabitants erroneously named and known as Indians; Mestizos, a mixture of European and Indian; Mulattoes, a mixture of Black and European; and Negroes. Their respective socioeconomic status and location of living are essential for analyzing the history of the respective countries. The languages most commonly spoken are Spanish, French, and English. Some indigenous languages still remain in use."

The usage, meaning, significance, application, and social implications of the word *mestizo* began to occupy my mind. I just had to come to terms with and understand *the essence of my own mestizaje*. I had been raised and educated in two separated societies, one Mexican, the other European. My Mexicanness was subdivided into three groups: Indian, Mestizo, and Spaniard. My Europeanness was divided into classical (ancient), barbarian, and early Christian (300 to 1500) societies, and the modern periods characterized, molded, and facilitated by the printing press, new discoveries, nationalism, transportation, and so on, with a concomitant divergence from Christianity.

The Guadalupan event demonstrates how two peoples in total confrontation and separated by abysmal incomprehension of each other were able to achieve a mental, genetic, and cultural union that gave rise to a new nation comprised of Mestizos. Followers of Jesus Christ have learned over the centuries that "the way" belongs to no one group! It is universal in its application to every human being. Of course, it was extremely difficult for Hebrews, Greeks, Romans, Angles, Celtics, Germans, Franks, and Gauls to leave their way of life, their religions, their worship, and their value systems and replace them with the way of Jesus, who ordered, "You must love your neighbor as yourself," explaining who the neighbor was with the story of the brigands and the Good Samaritan. And, after 1531, the mother of that same Jesus arrived in Anahuac to tell everyone, Spaniard and Indian, to follow the way of Jesus.

The road to the commingling of two peoples to create the current demography of Mexico, of Mesoamerica, and of some countries in South America such that Mestizos predominate, was washed with tears and paved with ugly stones of sadness and human frailties. Today, *mestizaje* is commonly accepted and is no longer a cause for dismay. Time has cured most of the bitterness associated with its creation.

The Guadalupan event with Mary's Mestiza face finally gave me an understanding that provided some tranquility and rationale for previously unanswerable questions, the perpetual "whys." Since early childhood, my parents had related with great care and tenderness the history of Our Lady of Guadalupe. I went to visit her "Little Church" at Tepeyac a half dozen times. I was struck by her tilma, in that her image presented the face of a Mexican girl, yet I knew she was a young Jewish woman from Judea. There were many things I did not understand about her apparitions. Why? Why was she not known as well as Our Lady of Lourdes and Bernadette, or Our Lady of Fatima? Why did the Cubans, Puerto Ricans, and Latin Americans have their "own" Blessed Mary, and why was she not known in the US among the European Catholics? In grammar school, Saint Patrick's Day meant no school. It was very big! But we were not taught about the Guadalupe apparitions at Saint Joseph's School, nor in the seminary! The story of the mother of Jesus, Our Lady of Guadalupe, appearing in Mexico City was relegated to the other society: the transplanted Mexican society, living and alive in the barrios with their customs, religious rites, celebrations, language, and culture. December 12 was super big in south Pomona. It meant piñatas, fiestas, and tamales, and celebrations of her day in church.

It is difficult to recount the myriad of looks, words, and actions I personally endured in living, experiencing and learning about *mestizaje*. I lamented the experience of my mother. I cried when I learned the meaning of the song, "La Borrachita." I could not appreciate the rejection of my mother by my paternal grandmother, an Otomi, who was always unkind to her and never called her by her name. She always asked me, "How is the daughter of the Spaniard?" instead of by her name or "your mother." To this day, I continue my research through documents, visits, and interviews to find out who my maternal grandfather was. From Nazaria, my maternal grandmother, I know he was a Spaniard: "*Como esta la hija del Español?*" Finally, after years of effort and travel, I acquired a copy of my mother's baptismal certificate. It had only the name of her mother. Her father, a very rich owner of haciendas, would in no way have society recognize his responsibility. That is just the way it was. Irresponsible Spanish men caused involuntary *mestizaje*.

At the time in 1948, I brushed the following incident aside. I was a senior in high school studying for the priesthood, and as such, not involved with girls or dating. At breakfast at the home of a well-to-do farming family in a nearby town, the mother, a real *mater familias*, admonished me with, "You know my daughter has fallen in love with you." (I did not know). "Do not pursue the matter. She will marry an Anglo. She cannot marry you, because you are a dark Mexican. We have only White grandchildren." By way of explanation, it should be noted that the farming family were also refugees from the Revolution in Mexico but were from the Spanish landowner class—of *sangre pura*. Maintaining the caste system of the old country was understood as a social imperative by this sadly uneducated matriarch. It did not impinge on my personal life, but the imposition of archaic norms did annoy me.

How did I get to Mexico in the summer of 1951? I was fortunate to have been invited by my classmate, Bob Hempfling of Monterey Park, California, to help him drive a brand-new Buick to Mexico. An upperclassman, Raul Tapia, was delivering a gift to his father in Toluca, Mexico.

My excitement was palpable. I was going to meet my Mexican relatives for the first time. I was to learn, explore, and see things of which I had only mental images formed by conversations with my parents, relatives, and friends. I was going east to Arizona, New Mexico, and Texas! I was becoming a traveler. At last, I would compare the size of Pomona melons and watermelons with those my dad claimed were "much bigger and sweeter" in his *tierra*, his land.

We crossed into Mexico at Laredo, Texas. I was seated in the back. I observed a man following an animal as he plowed very close to the highway. He reminded me of pictures I had seen in books about Mexico. He was wearing a large sombrero and simple white trousers, with a rope around his waist. He appeared barefoot. As the car traveled alongside, I waved excitedly and continued to do so as the man responded by waving with his large sombrero. I was so happy. But, my joviality quickly turned to chagrin, sadness, and confusion as Raul Tapia twisted around from the passenger's seat to confront me in a rage with his outstretched arm. Reinforcing his admonition with a pointed, shaking index finger, he instructed me, "You do not wave at them! They are peasants. You are at a different level. Recognize that! They wave at you, but you do not return their wave. You do not even recognize them!"

Later, when Tapia had calmed down and could speak in a normal tone, he explained at length his rationale. After all, he was only one year away from ordination to Holy Orders! He informed us that a few days after he was born in Toluca, Mexico around 1920, his parents took him to the Spanish embassy in Mexico City. He was officially registered in the book as a member of the Bourbon royal family (as is the current king of Spain). Now, he could always be a Spanish citizen and a member of the Bourbon aristocracy. He had been raised in a proper manner to know his lineage and had been sent away at an early age to be educated in Europe. All of this, despite the fact that his family dated back to the Conquistadores and that the Tapia family had lived in Toluca, Mexico as substantial landowners for centuries!

Bob Hempfling and Raul Tapia had left me in Mexico City and continued on an hour away to the hacienda of Raul's family in the state of Toluca. Just three weeks later, I spent a week with my uncle and aunt in Toluca. Many years later, a reading of *Ulises Criollo* by Jose Vasconcelos revivified feelings, memories, and observations of my very enjoyable days in Toluca. I sensed how daily life was endured in Toluca in 1895, when Vasconcelos attended school there. Things had changed hardly at all in the fifty-plus years from 1895 to 1951 for any of the three societies: the indigenous (Otomi, Mazahuas, and Zapotecs), the Mestizos, or the Criollos (the European Mexicans). One big difference: he writes about "*indios.*" Why could he, an educated man, not describe them by their own names? Did the caste system make them just another blur, as it had done for Raul Tapia, another Criollo?

As a sidebar, Bob Hempfling and I met in Europe in 1973. The European Federation of Military Latino Clubs had invited me and my wife to tour U.S. Air Force Bases in Europe and speak on topics reflecting President Nixon's commitment to equal opportunities for Latino servicemen. General Jones, Commander of the US Air Force in Europe, graciously hosted us with a formal cocktail garden party. At lunch, he had asked me what one thing I most wanted to see or do while on the speaking tour at US Air Force Bases under his command. I replied that, I had heard a former classmate was stationed as an air force officer someplace in Europe and that I had not seen him since 1951. I said that if he was nearby, I would be delighted to see him again. Well, that evening, who shows up in his fatigues, haggard and concerned, but Colonel Bob? Instead of being delighted, he was downright frightened! He had been ordered to report to headquarters immediately by none other than General Jones, without explanation! A helicopter flew Bob from his post on a missile base in the Atlantic Ocean off the coast of Norway.

The general personally brought Colonel Bob to meet up with me and my wife at the party. Bob exclaimed, "You are responsible for this?"

The general chirped gladly and explained, "He asked for you. And he works for the president!" Bob's emotional reactions surged from fear to smiles.

As a participant-observer of the process of *mestizaje*, I benefited greatly from unraveling its lasting impact, its meaning, and its negative effects on mental health. Frequent travels to Europe, Latin America, Central America, throughout the United States, and to Mexico provided me with more observations and experiences on how Europeans perceive Mexicans, and vice versa. I had journeyed to Mexico to acquire audio-aural fluency. And I did. But what was most transformative and significant is that I discovered myself—and my *mestizaje*! It had started as a trip to learn a language and ended a pilgrimage to endure and resolve an identity crisis.

CHAPTER FIFTEEN

POLITICS AND THE LATIN TEACHER IN PICO RIVERA AND WHITTIER, CALIFORNIA

I was so fortunate. Loyola University in January 1957 was preparing students from its School of Education to become credentialed high school teachers. We began the highly tense and nerve-wracking process of being practice teachers. Our future careers were on the line. In addition, we had to initiate job interviews. In 1957, my career as an educator got its start. In February, after practice teaching for only one month and after my very first interview, Whittier Union High School District hired me to teach Latin and Spanish beginning in September at El Rancho High School in Pico Rivera! Loyola had prepared me very well indeed.

The student population numbered about twenty-five hundred, of which about 20 percent were Mexican Americans. My students in advanced Spanish classes and in Latin were almost all European Americans. Since the Mexican American students were not in my classes with but few exceptions (in the Spanish classes), I took only casual notice of their behavior and appearance. However, when the principal, the dean of students, and the head counselor summoned me to a conference to discuss the Mexican Americans and their "problems," I began to observe, introspect, and analyze. I was the only Mexican American teacher on the entire staff. Most teachers had been hired from Indiana and Illinois; they knew next to nothing about Mexican Americans. I was teaching the classics, Spanish grammar, and literature. I had no professional preparation for dealing with the "problems" of Mexican American students. And I knew nothing about what "problems" the administrators perceived. But I was to learn about El Rancho High School.

To their credit, the administrators were searching for answers to the increasing on-campus fighting among Mexican American students. In the conference room, the queries went along these lines: Why do they wear their hair long? Why do they dress differently? Why does the phrase "he 'luked' at me" cause almost instantaneous fighting? Why do the Mexican American students separate themselves from the other students and also from each other, and eat in separate parts of the campus? Why don't they participate in competitive sports, in extracurricular activities, or in student government? Why do they take easy vocational courses? Why do they drop out of school at the tenth grade?

They school was disappointed at my ignorance and lack of expertise. After all, I was a Mexican American. Shouldn't I know? they wondered. (Only God knew then that fourteen years hence, I would commission a national study on the value structures of Mexicans, Cubans, and Puerto Ricans.) Oh, I had some conjectures, but I did not want to become a go-to expert on these matters. I was busy improving my professional standing. I had a new, growing young family and a lovely wife who needed my full attention. We had just purchased a brand-new house in an upscale area: East Whittier. We were engaging our spiritual life as practicing Catholics at Saint Bruno's. I was deeply concerned about my future as a teacher. No one in my Chicano circle of family, relatives, and friends had achieved a breakthrough into a profession as I had just done. Would I make the grade?

After teaching for sixty days, I was promoted! Now I was the chairman of the Foreign Language Department, with a staff of twenty-nine teachers. I was told to hire and fire to upgrade the Department. It was no longer a matter of whether I would succeed as a teacher. It was now a matter of supervising a faculty and innovating educational improvements. Wow, what a change!

A few months later, I was promoted again. I was made a part-time counselor. I continued to pursue courses leading to a doctorate. An entirely unexpected roadblock surfaced, however. Roger Weeks, the school principal, summoned me in a formal manner to his office. He complimented me on my promotions and professional work. He then surprised the dickens out of me. "Do not get any fancy ideas by going out and getting an administrator's credential," he politely informed me. He continued, "You are a Mexican and a Catholic; we in this district do not promote people like you to be administrators." The meeting ended, just like that. I was flabbergasted! I had no interest in becoming an administrator. They were not educators, in my estimation. They held jobs with public relations duties. But ethnic and religious discrimination was strong and prevalent in Pico Rivera.

This unsavory encounter caused me to avoid other educators outside of professional life. In all my years of teaching from 1957 to 1968, I never invited a teacher to my home for dinner. I invited lawyers, engineers, bankers, businessmen, and clergy. I could learn from them, but from teachers? I became one of the incorporators of the Association of Mexican American Educators and was elected president of its local chapter. We remained dedicated to reform and ethnic activism. I looked for more fulfilling challenges in law school, in the pursuit of a doctorate, in political involvement, the church and spiritual development, and eventually, transforming school systems to rid them of educational malpractice. My wife and I founded a club to promote the spiritual, cultural, linguistic, and social needs of the surging Mexican American Catholic community in East Whittier. We called it Club Amistad.

I also commenced incipient involvement with Republican issues. I formed an East Los Angeles chapter of the Young Republicans. I was interviewed by Spencer-Roberts Consultants, Inc., who tried assiduously but unsuccessfully to recruit me to run for office for the Lower House, the Assembly of the California legislature. Spencer-Roberts had managed all of the political campaigns of Nixon, Reagan, and others. I volunteered, nonetheless, to take charge of nineteen precincts in East Whittier for Mr. Nixon's 1960 presidential campaign. At school, despite fierce opposition from the established faculties, I saw to it that the libraries in all eight high schools in the district carried William F. Buckley's new periodical, *The National Review*. The liberal journals would no longer relish a monopoly.

My life was entering a new era. I was no longer a kid from Pomona. I had for all practical purposes, but for our immediate families in Claremont and Pomona, left the Pomona Valley in 1944 when I went off to study for the priesthood for almost ten years and then into the army for two. I married, the belle of the Valley, Ester Gomez Bernal of Claremont, and pursued further graduate studies in Claremont and Los Angeles.

While an educator at El Rancho High School from 1957–1962, our little family and I began to acquire community stature and identity. My wife and I were faithfully attending Saint Bruno's Catholic Church and were trying to live devoted and faithful Catholic lives by living the Commandments. In the pleasant company of other couples, we studied the sacred scriptures and participated in the Christian Family Movement. I focused my efforts on my graduate education, improving my professional standing, and raising a Catholic family. My concern for and awareness of the growing and continuing discrimination against Mexican Americans would explode later.

At that time, national defense and the growing menace of the international communist conspiracy was a topic of conversation, of journals, of editorials, and of a few talk shows. I had already served in the army and was prepared mentally to die fighting the diabolical movement, communism, in Korea. But now what could I do? I began to support candidates in the Republican Party, which I decided was best prepared ideologically to fight Communism.

Besides, my education on the ills of communism had started when I was about ten years of age. My father was my first and highly charged teacher: he would vent his rage after reading something to do with Mexico, the Revolutionaries, the persecution of the

Catholic Church, and the Partido Revolucionario Institucional (PRI). In Pomona, he was the distributor of the organ of the Sinarquista Party. His voice could be heard far and wide. It was strong, resonant, and capable of low and high C. The names Lombardo Toledano, Plutarco Elias Calles, and El General Carranza still ring in my ears.

Toledano was the communist labor leader of Mexico. (1) Calles was the devil incarnate who had tried mightily to eliminate the Catholic Church by killing vast numbers of priests, nuns, and Catholic laypeople. (2) He was the prime cause of the Central Mexican exodus of the 1920s. And General Carranza was the person who made the deal with Marxist Gerardo Murillo (aka Dr. Alt), to bring the assistance of the industrial workers of the world from Chicago and Baltimore to the Mexican Revolution via their organization *Casa del Obrero Mundial* (House of the World Worker), later renamed *Confederacion Regional de Obreros Mexicanos* (CROM). (3) My dad would bellow out that atheistic Communism was destroying his "beloved land," but he could do nothing. He had left Mexico in a self-imposed exile that never ended—he died in California.

He did, nonetheless, hold rallies in our humble house in support of the Sinarquista Party in Mexico. That political party grew out of the Cristero Army that fought the Marxist-Socialist government that resulted from the Revolution, as the latter tried under Plutarco Elias Calles and Alvaro Obregon to eradicate the Catholic Church from 1926 to 1930. The war ended when the pope ordered the Catholics to lay down their arms and surrender. The members of the Cristero Army surrendered out of obedience and rushed to get out of Mexico to avoid the firing squads. Hundreds of thousands of them settled in California and usually next to the citrus packing houses. Their little settlements were called, Barrios. The Sinarquista Party transformed itself into the Partido Nacional de Action (PAN) of today in Mexico. (4) My knowledge of the world of politics grew. The big LA dailies informed us of what the Communists and Nazis were doing in Europe.

In the seminary, students were encouraged to read the official organ of the Catholic Archdiocese of Los Angeles: *The Tidings*. I do not remember the author's name, but he knew China well. He wrote of the struggle between Mao Tse-tung and Chiang Kai-shek. He clearly blamed John T. Service, a senior Foreign Service officer, and John P. Davies, along with others, for aiding and abetting the Communist army that took control of China and established a bloody totalitarian dictatorship in 1949. (5) (Incidentally, both of them were later revealed to be Communist dupes by Senator Joe McCarthy.)

In the 1960's I became an avid reader of *The National Review*. There I found an intellectual home for my opinions on the Cold War that was heating up. I read *Witness* by Whittaker Chambers. The book removed the long dark drapes that had covered reality and the extent of the penetration of the philosophies of Europe into United States society and the world. I was able to understand the roles of writers, actors, movies, professors, opinion makers, government workers, unions, and think tanks in advancing the cause of the new world: the paradise of the proletariat.

Many years later in Mexico City, I enjoyed discussing *How Democracies Perish* with its author, Jean-François Revel. (6) That penetrating book on how Communism is spread and the discussion with Revel encompassed my understanding of the bloody manifestation and outgrowth of ideas. In 1982, I formed a conservative Hispanic breakfast club in Washington and required a reading of that book for membership.

My eminent history professor, Father Newman C. Eberhardt, CM, lectured that the ideas, culture, and behavioral modalities of our "European cousins" would show up in the capitals of the world and in our daily life in the United States twenty-five years (about a generation) later. Some of his examples included: the Church of England would become more homocentric and less theocentric. Church members would begin to vote democratically to decide morality. The followers of the ideas of Nictzschc (socialists, communists, and militant secularists) held that certain people were not human beings, (for instance, a nine-month-old child in the womb). Moral turpitude would become more socially acceptable, and every twenty-five years, morals would become even more decadent.

During those years, I brushed up on my recall of the philosophy I had studied for my major. Since college graduates with engineering degrees are called engineers, I should be called a philosopher, but that would be too pedantic. I had a clearly defined outline of the history and content of philosophy; the Greeks were at the top. The next rung was the period when the scrolls with the philosophy of the Greeks arrived from Alexandria, Egypt. Writers of the English language call this the Mediaeval Period (1100–1500). On that rung, Thomas Aquinas performed a synthesis of the Greek philosophers with Christian thought; this is called Thomism or Scholasticism. On the next line of the outline, we find Descartes, who divided the nature of humanity into mind and body. It was a mistake. And just as when one makes a mistake in the first steps to resolve a theorem in geometry, other mistakes follow sequentially and predictably. The fourth rung is "modern philosophies," replete with mistakes. And that is what the universities today teach. While English writers called the period from 400 to 800 the "Dark Ages," the French coined the name "Renaissance," the rebirth of mankind, for European intellectualism from 1400–1700. After browsing through my memory bank of modern philosophies as taught in this country after the 1930s, my analysis of the trends of American society in the 1960s showed a downward spiral into a new set of Dark Ages and a return to the age of savagery and barbarianism.

My philosophy courses on Hegel, Schopenhauer, Nietzsche, Marx, and their allies and predecessors (such as Kant, Comte, the English Empiricists, and so on) began to come alive with new meanings and applications. I increased my bibliography into the area of the communist conspiracy, the work of the FBI, and copious readings on the penetration of communism into Mexico and Latin America. As I helped elect Republicans, I felt I was doing my part to fight communism. With few exceptions, I was not at all convinced that Democrats were that worried or concerned about communism. My research and reading showed me that in the Democratic Party, socialists and progressives were more comfortable, especially those who had become convinced that there is no life eternal and that therefore, government must strive to make this life a better place—or paradise, if at all possible.

So I worked hard for the election of Richard Nixon. People would ask me in dismay, why did I not support a Catholic? My answer was my awareness of the socialistic tendencies in the Democratic Party.

CHAPTER SIXTEEN

THE NEW HORIZONS PROGRAM: MY CATAPULT TO WASHINGTON

The New Horizons Program was the reason Washington recruited me to leave our beloved California for frontiers unknown, yet it was to advance my career as an educator. I was promised a salary almost equal to that of a famous Senator, Joseph Montoya.

After teaching for five years at El Rancho, I transferred to Whittier High School. The Whittier community wanted a robust teacher of advanced Latin literature. They had heard of my tenure at El Rancho High School in Pico Rivera, where I had been promoted in the first ninety days of my teaching career to chair the Language Department with its twenty-nine teachers (and to part-time counselor). In the second semester, I was declared a Master Teacher and tutored teacher candidates. By the third year at El Rancho High School, the number of Latin classes increased from two in my first year to five. I deeply enjoyed teaching and especially tinkering with new ways of transferring knowledge to students.

During my first seven years, almost all of the students assigned to my Latin classes were European Americans. In my Spanish classes, a few were Mexican Americans. In my advanced English literature courses, all were European American. I was an excellent teacher, and the community and students appreciated that with many awards.

It was, however, my quest for teaching advanced Latin literature that took me on a field trip to the Huntington Library with my third- and fourth-year Latin classes. Upon our return from the library in San Marino, California, I looked out the window of our parked bus discharging the students and observed a scene that would cause my life to change again. It was May 1964.

Whittier's 1963-64 enrollment was one-fourth Mexican American out of a student population of about two thousand. What I saw on that last week of May were Mexican American students gathered in the alley under a very large fig tree next to the faculty parking lot. They had chosen that spot for socializing, isolating themselves from the rest of the campus and after-school life. They came from two barrios, Jim Town and Sunrise Hills, and got along very well with each other.

From my seat on the school bus, I felt as if a thunderbolt had struck me. The stark contrast of the two societies was disappointingly historical and for me, deeply motivating. The students of one society had just completed a field trip to the Huntington Library and Museum in wealthy San Marino to view, study, and enjoy the *Metamorphoses* of Ovid carved around huge vases on the library grounds. They were the privileged offspring of Whittier's well-to-do. They were well on their way to higher education at

Stanford, Princeton, and so on. I had taught them of the highly enriching classics. Their parents—the lawyers, physicians, business owners, and other Whittier leaders—were elated with my performance in the advanced Spanish, English literature, and classics (Latin and Greek) courses. I saw the other society as the same as the one at El Rancho High School: I assumed that the Mexican American students would in time advance and take their place in the college-bound classes, away from vocational shop courses. I knew they tended to drop out of school at the tenth grade, because that was when education was no longer compulsory. I had written a master's thesis on the topic.

That school year, 1963/64, ended a few weeks later. The awkward presence of these two societies would not leave my mind. It would haunt my memories. I knew why those Mexican American kids were in a different and separate society. And yet, I went along blithely as a "professional educator," doing naught about it. I begin to analyze the symptoms and causes of this ugly cancer. In my restless sleep, my subconscious screamed, "Do something about it. You know how!"

The summer of 1964 was devoted to painting the house we had purchased in 1958. It was time for thinking, planning, and reflecting on that traumatic afternoon facing the alley that was home to the Chicano kids, and introspecting on my role as a teacher of the classics at the San Marino Huntington Library with Ovid. 1961 to 1962 had been a hectic year. Our little family had spent the summer of 1961 traveling by car through many cities in Mexico. My mother and father died within months of each other in the succeeding summer in 1962. I had completed the first year of law school at Loyola. By this time, I had also completed education courses on California school law, school finance, curriculum development, school administration, and was a certified remedial reading clinician. I was preparing for a doctorate in education and had not yet applied for admittance into a doctoral program. Doctoral studies and the writing of the required thesis would have to wait. The immediacy of "I must do something" was charting a new course.

I kept a legal-size pad on my desk in the garage. As ideas popped into my mind while I painted, I would climb down the ladder, run to the desk in the garage, and write down questions and some answers on why Mexican American students were not advancing. I reminisced, retraced, and relived my life in search of commonalities and experiences with these Whittier High School Mexican American students. There was a time in my life when I too had lived as they, in two separate societies. There were, however, two big differences. We had enjoyed private schooling that was integrated.

Mom and Dad had been blessed with a primary education in their hometown in Mexico. Unfortunately, most of the hundreds of thousands of other Mexican immigrants were completely unschooled. Mom and Dad vehemently insisted on a Catholic education for us and would have nothing to do with the "pagan" schools. That they were segregated was irrelevant. Mexicans lived, shopped, worshipped, entertained, and socialized in their own "transported Mexico."

As a consequence, we were enrolled in the only Catholic school that taught grades one through eight in the entire Pomona Valley. The Ramirez kids were about the only Mexican

American students at Saint Joseph's Grammar School, which had been built about twenty-five years prior. Since the grandparents of my classmates had all been born "back East," they were new to California. Ethnically, they were Italians, French, Irish, and German. My parents were also new to California, for they too were recent arrivals dating from 1922.

To pay for private school, we all had to work. Beginning in early June of 1935 or 1936, we cut apricots in half and spread them on large redwood trays in Campbell, Santa Clara County, California. We picked prunes until middle or late September. Urbanization came to Campbell, and the groves of apricots and prunes were uprooted. The need for work made us travel to the Fresno area to harvest grapes to be dried into raisins. Upon our return home to Pomona, we picked walnuts, tomatoes, and peaches in Chino; and oranges and lemons in Southern California. The summer of 1947, when I had already finished three years of high school, was my last year of living outdoors in Fresno while harvesting grapes on one-hundred-degree days. Oh, how I relive the evenings when the mosquitoes feasted on my bare arms and legs while my tired body slept.

A final thought occupied my mind: the parents of the "alley Chicanos" had attended *segregated* schools. Their parents were my contemporaries, although my ten siblings and I had attended Catholic schools, all the way through high school. Fortunately, the Supreme Court had abolished school segregation in 1947. That posed a huge contrast.

The Greek and Roman stories of the sculptor who fell in love with the lifeless woman he had carved out of a rock, George

Bernard Shaw's rendition in *Pygmalion* with Professor Higgins, and the Broadway hit *My Fair Lady* steered me to recall who had been my own Professor Higgins. It was the missionary priest, Father Martinez. He was bright, caring, and possessed many other admirable qualities. Above all, he was a very holy and humble man. He introduced me to the "preppy" life and wanted me to eschew my "pachuco" ways. Quietly and without telling me what he was up to, he exposed me to new horizons and new experiences. He would simply admonish me to notice all the details, observe everything, think about what I was going through, and to "Remember, remember what you have learned!" He would take me out of the barrio and into the world of the "haves." I happily and profoundly rejoice, too, in the remembrance of Sister Lucy Marie, who taught me in the first grade with love and hugged me into success. What a saint!

As September and a new school year neared, I completed a plan to transform public schools. I planned how I would bring a halt to malpractice in education and change the lives of Mexican American students at Whittier High School. (As I write these thoughts, I smile at my utter naiveté to think so grandiosely. But I did not know better then.) I had developed some visions on how to improve the system of education—its philosophy, its policies, its practices. In addition to my regular teaching responsibilities, I volunteered to focus on the situations and conditions of Mexican American students.

I conferred with the principal, Seabron Nolin. He was an understanding administrator. He managed Whittier efficiently and problem-free. He knew the Mexican American kids were not great students, but then, they were no problem. They stuck to themselves. I had observed their ethnic cohesion in the alley. Rumbles were easily and quickly quelled. Nolin directed me to discuss my thoughts, ideas, and plans with Jack Mele, the vice principal and head varsity football coach, who had immigrated to California from Cleveland, Ohio. He coached champions. The town of Whittier held him in such high regard that he easily won election to mayor.

Jack Mele approved of my plan. He suggested I also check with another vice principal, Mr. Charlie Cook, the dean of discipline. Mr. Cook was also an immigrant from someplace "back East." He liked the idea that someone was taking interest in "those kids." He and Jack Mele hoped I could get the taller, bigger, and more athletic ones to join the football team. They considered my volunteerism as an additional recruiting tool for quality athletes, never mind the other aspects. They enthusiastically slapped me on the back and clapped hearty applause. After all, they could see no negatives. Little did they know! I was intent on changing everything—no, on transforming it.

I had arrived at a determining, fundamental conclusion about why there were two societies at Whittier High School. The conclusion was also applicable to other areas of California that had similar demography. European Americans had arrived from east of the Mississippi almost at the turn of the century. In 1898, Whittier was incorporated. My hometown 15 miles away, was incorporated in 1888. Most other towns in these areas were incorporated within that time frame. The Mexicans fleeing from the tumultuous disorder of the Revolution of 1910 began arriving in the period of 1903-1930. Their children became Mexican American soldiers in the Second World War. The years of these groups' California arrival differed but slightly: twenty years! Chronologically speaking, it was only the blink of an eye; the migrations were practically simultaneous. The European Americans saw themselves as vaulting over the Rockies, while the Mexicans viewed themselves as arriving in railroad boxcars.

California became the home of two societies: one was European American, English speaking, Protestant, light in skin color. It was educated, landowning, politically knowledgeable; it had a military and capitalist heritage. The other was Mexican Mestizo, Spanish speaking, Catholic, dark in skin color, illiterate, landless, with no political knowledge or legacy, and no military heritage. It was a group of refugees from three centuries of feudalism.

Soon after the school year commenced, I took the boys' gang leader, Johnnie Alvarado, out to shoot pool. Implementation of my ideas called for actions completely "our of and beyond the box. We went to his hangout, where he was king on weekends. I discussed with him what was wrong with the school system and how it was hurting the Mexican American kids. I included the ills of tracking in the lower grades, faulty reading methods, ill-prepared teachers, the superiority syndrome of European Americans and the student off-campus fraternities and sororities, the prejudicial grading para-digms, the unfair "citizenship grading" procedures: the existence of two societies. I exhorted Johnnie to help me help the younger kids who were coming up that would face failure after failure and discreet discrimination. He agreed to help me form a new club. I asked him to send the leader of the girls, Maggie Duran, to my classroom with her buddies after school for a similar chat.

In the meantime and before the first club meeting, I volun-teered to speak during my lunch period before diverse women's groups. I met with them and explained my vision for these Mexican American kids so that they could become "productive members of society and not welfare burdens." The husbands of these women were usually town leaders. I knew that by getting their support, I would enjoy the support of the business community and the school district's superintendents and administrators. After all, they all were brothers in the Lions and Kiwanis Clubs, and so on. By enlisting the enthusiastic support of these segments of the community, when my fellow teachers began to bellow and complain about my unorthodox methods, I could outflank and trump them. When I started sensitivity sessions, they bitterly complained, but I had already won.

Since I realized that the public would want numbers reflecting performance, I immediately defined five outcomes of education and designed evaluation methodologies. I did pre and post measurements. During the summer, I had selected about two hundred students that I characterized as high potential but low achievers. I had studied their scores on the Iowa Test of Educational Development and focused on those in the 110 to 120 range but who were matriculated primarily in vocational classes. These students were predominantly Mexican American.

I anticipated measurable improvements by these students in the basic outcomes of a high school education: average daily attendance (ADA), grade point average (GPA), reading level, extracurricular participation, and graduations coupled with postsecondary education. To obtain these results, it was necessary that I change student attitudes and modify teacher in-service training for attitudinal changes. I wanted parental involvement via a separate, barrio-based Spanish-speaking parent-teacher association. I needed oversight of grading procedures applied to my target population, monitoring of daily attendance by my selected group in all classes, establishment of a remedial reading lab for the exclusive use of anyone in my group that was reading three years or lower than their class, and a review of school policies and practices that might impinge on student performance.

To improve the attitudes of these students, I had Johnnie and Maggie summon (order?) the Mexican American students to my classroom for a lunchtime meeting to develop a club. No one, but no one, dared say no to Johnnie. He ordered with a glance of his eyes. It was agreed: it would be the New Horizons Club. Johnnie liked that.

I begged, borrowed, and got buses for field trips for the New Horizons Club. Over the period of a year, the Club really did view new horizons. We visited a wide diversity of places of work, business, and study. These field trips were not the usual, as to a museum, college, or special event. No, these trips were arranged so that my targeted group would meet people at work: at a bank, an architecture and engineering firm, a junior college, an assembly plant, a multistory building, and so on.

I would select an employee and instruct him or her on how to interact with students as they came by. Whenever students evidenced deeper interest, the employee was to escort them to conference rooms or the cafeteria for further exploration of the job environment. We wanted the students to imagine their working in such places in a few months or years. Their year-long and continuing interaction with these "tutors" would open up "New Horizons."

An article in the *Los Angeles Times* reflected on Mexican American aerospace engineers who had organized to tutor. I reached out to them and brought the New Horizons members to their plants. As a result, tutorial sessions were scheduled at our school. (1) I added other tutoring activities so that students receiving tutoring could also teach others. The school newspaper exclaimed: "Tutoring at Whittier High Start of Something Big." (2)

Up until the occasion of these many trips, these students, poor Anglos and Mexican Americans, had lived their lives in a physical area defined by their barrio, the classrooms, and the alley under the fig tree. The snow-capped mountains were only fifteen miles away, but they had never rolled around in the snow or made a snowball. The beaches were twenty miles away, but they had never been there. Their dads, brothers, friends, and relatives worked at jobs requiring strong bones and muscles but not knowledge or personality. The field trips were like books that revealed the existence of thousands of jobs they could dream of if they had a good education. That was the lesson I had learned at Saint Joseph's Grammar School a generation ago, where I had realized that my classmates lived in nice homes in north Pomona because of their parents' education.

But the most important trip the club made was at the beginning of the year. I requested two buses and had each of the New Horizons kids bring a brown bag lunch. The buses arrived at a beach on a bay. After some relaxation, they murmured: What are we doing here? Is this a field trip? There are no museums, here! Prior to this one, most of their field trips during their schooling years had been to zoos, museums, and buildings. This field trip was going to be quite a turnaround, an epiphany. I had them sit in semicircles on the sloping lawn surrounded by lofty palm trees in front of the sand and ocean bay water. For me, the success or failure of my vision depended heavily on this lesson-plan, on this interaction. Years of experience and knowledge had crystallized in my mind. I knew that two factors debilitated the academic actualization and development of Mexican Americans. One was the ever present and degrading "negative self-image." Mexican feudalism had been the cause and relationships between superiors to inferiors had been the result. The other was the lack of a self-identify. How could they be proud, if they did not know who the heck they were?

Mexican Americans born in New Mexico or Colorado enjoyed the identity of their ancestry from Spain. Those Mexican Americans in the rest of the Southwest, who retained knowledge of their forefathers who had been the landowners of the feudal systems (Haciendas and Ranchos), or were descended from the families of "*sangre pura*" (Spaniards), and were of light skin and hair, also enjoyed knowing about their identity. But, the Mexican mestizos, who were the persons of my efforts, had no clue about their ancestry. They were dark skinned and with clearly identifiable mestizo features: skin color, hair, and face, . They knew they were not Aztecs, nor Germans, nor Spaniards. So what were they?

And so, I started. "My name is Mr. Henry Ramirez, a teacher at Whittier High School. I live in East Whittier. And who are you? We are here alone, away from Whittier High School, from Jim Town, from Sunrise Hills. I have none of you in my Spanish or Latin classes. I really do not know you, and I want to know you." And so on.

And then I delivered a blow to their identity. "Are you gringos?" Laughter.

"No!"

"Are you mejicanos?"

"Maybe," came some responses.

"Are you paddies, soches, americanos, Americans?" I heard many responses: no, no, yes, maybe. "Well, then, are you TJs, vatos locos, Mexicans, Chicanos, Mexican Americans?" More responses came, some agitated, some confused. I walked away from center front and asked them to decide what they wanted to be called. After some discussion, they chose the name "Chicanos." Then I set up the challenge. "Tomorrow, are you going to prove you are Chicanos, or are you going to go to the alley under the fig tree, where you are nothings? Whittier High School is now yours, too. Tomorrow, you will sit and have lunch where Whittier High School students sit and have lunch—in the Quad!" This was all aimed at destroying the students' negative self-image and restoring pride in them. I was on my way to no longer being "just the Latin teacher."

The next day, Jack Mele and Charlie Cook rushed to my classroom, where I was enjoying my lunch in tranquility. "Henry, Henry, the kids! They...they..." They blurted out, "Your kids are eating in the Quad!" They added, "Should we call the cops?"

I calmly answered, "Those kids are Americans and have every right to eat in the Quad." The Quad was the heart of the campus, nicely landscaped with appropriate red-brick seating accommodations under shady sycamore trees and adorned with colorful flower beds. It was the place to gather, to see and be seen.

I had foreseen emotional reactions from the administrators and teachers, but I had already commenced my flanking moves to gain support among the wives of community leaders. I increased the number of my noontime chats. As local newspaper reporters started to call for interviews, I steered them to what I was doing with my Latin club: preparing for the Roman Banquet; the traditional "Slave for a Day" sale, when seniors "purchased" freshman "slaves" for a day; and the Roman chariot races—on tricycles. The community leaders liked the classics, and our activities reminded them of their own student days at their Whittier.

Since the youth are always more prepared for change (their lives change every hour), I called for a meeting with the student body officers. It was easy; most of them were my third- and fourth-year Latin, Spanish, or English lit students. I proposed that they help me develop the theme of mutual acceptance between the New Horizons kids and themselves. A dentist offered the use of his house and pool for a party for my New Horizons kids. With his hands-on assistance and the involvement of the newly formed PTA of Jim Town and Sunrise Hills parents, a nucleus of New Horizons kids and the student leadership had a "mutual acceptance party" in the plush Friendly Hills of East Whittier. The kids from one society met the kids from the other society. At school, they did not know each other. Some ate in the Quad; the others, in the alley. Some attended classes in the established buildings of Whittier High School; the others, in the auto, wood, printing, and metal shop buildings across heavily traveled Philadelphia Boulevard.

The party was an instant success. The kids got to know each other. Most remembered each other from their elementary school days. Peer group dynamics began to work. Student leaders began to invite New Horizons kids to join this and that. Years later, Jack Mele (who had become the school principal as well as the mayor) commented with pride that "the kids are marrying each other." I knew he meant Mexicans and Anglos. The theme of mutual acceptance became a driving force. I discussed it. Panels talked about it. It became the quiet spirit behind actions to bridge both societies.

A most critical objective was to make sure everyone could read. Nothing else could be achieved if that goal was not successful. Since I was also a reading clinician, I devoted most of my attention and efforts there. I acquired an empty classroom, and with the help of the local Lions Club, equipped it as a clinical reading laboratory with simple apparatus for measuring reading action. Attractive magazines were stacked on circular holders. I had each of the New Horizons kids tested for reading level and physical handicaps (such as eyesight, hearing, and so on). Students who tested as reading below a fourth-grade level were reassigned to immersion study in written words. They would get two classes of typing and several hours of clinical remedial reading. After several months, they usually scored as reading three or four grades higher than before. Magically, their GPA and ADA outcomes improved almost overnight. School became fun. They were achieving! There is nothing like success.

Quality teaching is also a function of knowledge, attitude, and understanding. I knew that most of the teachers were ignorant of who these Mexican Americans were culturally. It was necessary to enlighten them in order to improve their teaching skills. Two teachers recorded their impressions, perceptions, and especially what they recalled of other teachers' dialogue about what they thought of Mexican Americans. I had advised them that I would use this information in writing only and promised them anonymity. I created a questionnaire that listed fifty statements from the recording, with columns where each could be marked "agree" or "do not agree" with a check. At one of the compulsory in-service training meetings, the principal instructed each faculty member to check each statement and return the list unsigned.

A highly indignant explosion of objections erupted. Many refused to participate, saying the statements were insulting. When they were told their colleagues recorded the statements as remarks teachers often made, a strange quietude came over the room. In the corner of the large library where I was, I felt invisible but sharp darts racing toward me. I also now knew my standing with my peers was changing permanently. But I also knew that they could complain to no one. There was nothing they could do, other than to look for jobs in Orange or San Diego Counties, in school districts where Mexican American student matters had not yet become a civil rights issue. Many did move on to the nicer suburbs of those counties.

The coaches were a different club. I was invited to a cookout at the home of Vic Lopez, the top assistant coach to Jack Mele. All the coaches were present and dressed in their official coaching T-shirts. I arrived early and was surprised that all the coaches were already there. Jack Mele, the power behind all matters at Whittier High School and at City Hall, was their spokesman. Jack started most amiably and remained so as he chided me for being a "Black Carmichael" in Whittier. He warned me that I could ride over the teachers because the district administrators supported my New Horizons Program, but when it came to athletics dress codes, they settled matters. They admonished me not to try to change the policy that all athletes have short haircuts. They smiled and bellowed, "You all do not understand the hygiene and needs of athletics. Short haircuts are necessary, and that's the way it will remain. Period!"

I retorted, "When the blond-haired athletes start new a style of long haircuts, then you will approve them and rationalize that."

The coaches did not like the fact that my Spanish-speaking PTA had asked for a change in the policy so that Mexican American kids would not be disqualified for having long hair. They continued with other concerns about me trying to change other policies and practices that I thought would enhance my students' advancement and the performance outcomes I had defined.

I finally got up and fired at them, "We are at new crossroads, and you all must decide. Are you going to help me change education for these neglected Mexican American students, about whom you do not give a damn, or are you going to do business as usual? What I am doing is the new vision, the new direction. As I move on and become nationally known for this, and all of you want letters of recommendation for better jobs—when the interviewers ask you what direct work experience you have with the education of Mexican Americans, I will remember." And I did. Several years later, while I was busy at the US Commission on Civil Rights, calls came in from recruiters wanting to know if so-and-so had been involved and helpful with the New Horizons Program.

During the second semester, motivational speakers began to address my New Horizons Club. Speakers included Richard Alatorre, who later was elected to the State Assembly and then to the State Senate; Mike Montez, DDS, later named to the State Board of Education; psychologist Phil Montez, later a civil rights leader; and Herman Sillas, attorney, who was later administrator of the California Department of Motor Vehicles.

The post-measurements of the performance in the five out-comes showed definite improvements. Reading levels improved dramatically. Daily attendance jumped. Kids joined competitive sports. Grades showed improvements, especially from Fs and Ds to Cs. What became most salient and talked about was the fact that five gang members with low grades but high potential enrolled at Long Beach State University. The enrollment of D and F students at Long Beach State was the beginning of the use of the Equal Opportunity Program for Mexican American high school graduates in California.

Doctor Henry Johnson, director of guidance at that University, informed me of the existence of a law that allowed enrollment in all state universities of students with exceptional gifts, talents, or skills. Coaches, drama and arts teachers, and a few others were deeply aware and knowledge-able of its utility for getting star football players and others equally endowed into college who did not have the necessary grades for normal enrollment. Since he was the director of guidance, he could also include Mexican Americans as a special genre. As you may guess, the following year I was able to enroll many of my New Horizons kids at LA State, Fullerton State, and so on.

Exposure to postsecondary education was a most necessary and crowning effort. I knew that few of the New Horizons students would themselves ever attend universities such as USC, UCLA, Loyola, or similar higher-education institutions. Nonetheless, they had to learn what was behind those "ivy-covered walls." So we visited them, duly escorted by university tutors and guides. One particular exposure stands out. My students received a thorough orientation to what to expect and were then left at the local junior college, Rio Hondo, for an entire school day. They were told to visit classrooms where policemen, nurses, accountants, surveyors, and so on were being schooled, and to sit in as auditors. Then they were encouraged to converse with college students in the lounges and relaxation areas. The end result was to acclimatize them to a college environment and dispel the aura of the unknown. Many of my students enrolled at Rio Hondo. It was dramatic. And more graduated from high school. And, whereas in past years, only one or two Mexican Americans went on to college, this year, several dozen went to college (five to a state university)!

Pre and post evaluations demonstrated a resoundingly successful first year. The superintendent invited me to give a report to the trustees on the results. And they voted to spend fifty thousand dollars in the second year of the program, just at Whittier High School. The next year, I was to have a reduced schedule of classroom teaching; our New Horizons activities increased dramatically. Officials at the state Department of Education in Sacramento heard about it. They came, they saw, and they interviewed the district administrators. They liked what they observed and selected the program to receive another nearly fifty-five thousand dollars. What was interesting and amazing was that the entire sum had to be spent as I determined, penny by penny. I had my own budget!

Our five outcomes in the second year were outstanding. Well over fifty New Horizons kids went on to postsecondary education. They were accepted at Pitzer College in Claremont, at Fullerton State College, at Long Beach State, at East Los Angeles State, and at Rio Hondo Junior College. Still others enrolled at trade schools. At the end of the second year, 1965, we were receiving good ink, and a lot of it from the local paper. My superintendent asked me to report on the outcomes for the second year, and this time the trustees increased our budget to a hundred thousand dollars. They released me from full-time classroom teaching. I realized then that what I had started was truly different and needed; it would be an example for the wave of the future.

Teachers at two other district high schools, Santa Fe and Pioneer, were commencing similar programs. They focused on college-bound activities. Eventually their efforts led to the renaming of the program. It was now Expanded Horizons, and it extended to all eight high schools in the Whittier Union High School District.

With the district funds, we acquired a full-time remedial reading teacher and a secretary for the mushrooming New Horizons activities. The parents now had a Spanish-speaking secretary with whom they could interact on school matters.

As the completion of the program's second year neared and our federal funds via the state had become available, the superintendent told me to enrich the Program. Otherwise, he remarked, "the funds would have to be returned to the government." I employed teachers for curriculum development and consultants to provide expertise. For the required course on California history, a team focused on the Spaniards' actions to civilize native Californians, the development of the major cities around the Missions, the contributions of the Mexicans from Acapulco and Mazatlan and the effect of the French Jacobins on the secularization of the Missions in 1834. Another team working on the US history course focused on the work of President Polk to take half of Mexican land.

I had another team design the curriculum for a novel type of summer school for the New Horizons kids. Mathematics was to be taught hands-on at businesses, while English would be taught outdoors. Field trips conveyed the students to the brooks, streams, rivers, and forests at the nearby mountains of San Gabriel. The lessons were simple. On the first day, the students would write a list of things they had seen. The next day in class, they learned that such names for things were *nouns*. They knew the question, "*Que es tu nombre?*" (What is your name?) Transferring this knowledge, they learned that *nombre* also means "noun" in Spanish.

Lessons on verbs were followed by lessons on direct objects, phrases, sentences, and paragraphs. English that these students had either flunked or gotten a D in was becoming easy and fun.

Summer school was fruitful. The trip to the gas company revealed the details of vocational opportunities available through education and exposure to information. But despite our prudent and very worthwhile spending, we still had money left at the end of the summer. I submitted a plan to the administrators for something I called the "California Heritage Tour." The top forty students with the best attendance at summer school would be eligible. This was a great motivator. A bus was chartered. Two teachers and their wives were hired to supervise and be resource teachers. We would use the newly improved course of studies on California history. My wife and I would escort the New Horizons kids on a tour commencing with the Mission in San Diego and ending with the last Mission in San Francisco; the return trip would include a visit to the state capital, Sacramento, and the huge redwood sequoia trees in the mountains. The bus was an active, rolling classroom on US and California history.

I had an underlying, unwritten theme: to confront the negative self-image of my students, once and for all. They saw the names of Lopez from Guadalajara, Hernandez from Mazatlan, and similar names of Mexicans and Indians from other towns like Acapulco and Mexico City who had come to build the Missions on gravestones in the cemeteries within the walls. The pride and positivity in their happy and excited eyes were patent. They saw parents enjoying vacations with their children. They had never experienced that. I reminded them that education causes that result. At the top-of the-line hotels, I told them to walk without looking at their shoes and with their eyes ahead, to focus on details all around them, and to posture themselves as if they owned the place. We taught them how to read menus and how to order with a sense of knowledgeable confidence.

The tour motored from Paso Robles, where the students had enjoyed a great breakfast at a famous travelers spot called the Black Forest. It was known as the halfway place for travelers on the Los Angeles–San Francisco route. Several hours post break-fast when it was time to take care of physical necessities, the bus stopped at a big and ample gas station in the town of King City— the best. No other facilities existed for hours of driving in any direction. I said nothing. As the students raced out of the bus for the bathrooms, I recalled driving past this particular gas station the late 1930s. My mom and my siblings were en route to the San Jose area to camp out during the summer and harvest apricots and prunes. King City did not allow Mexicans; we had to stop on the road and discreetly find inviting tundra before arriving.

And sure enough, some thirty years later, the manager raced out to stop our thundering herd. He yelled, "Mexicans are not allowed!" I gathered my kids and my fellow teachers and appealed to his better angels. With a fifty-dollar bill on my palm, I said, "Allow them to use the facilities and if you find them dirty after-ward, keep the fifty." He liked the wager. After the kids had taken care of their necessities, he checked the stalls and scratched his head. Apologizing, he muttered, "What private school do they attend?" The trip proceeded remarkably, and yet in terms of awful events, unremarkably. It ended a great success.

Needless to say, the third year of New Horizons saw even better outcome scores, and at the end, the trustees voted to expand the program into all eight high schools and a quarter-million dollars for it. The next year, the trustees voted for even more money for us, but newspaper coverage had already gone national. The *Christian Science Monitor* had praised it. (Later, my boss at the Commission on Civil Rights, Eunice Greer, told me that she had read about me and the New Horizons Program in the *New York Times*, though I never could find the mention.) Eventually, the

National Education Association gave the Whittier Union High School District a national award for the program (which had been renamed Expanded Horizons by then) on May 31, 1972.

The director of the US Commission on Civil Rights, William Taylor, came in from Washington in January 1968 to view our New Horizons Program for himself. Later, I learned that he had spent several days in the area interviewing school administrators and community leaders. The Commission wanted me in Washington to do major studies on the education of Mexican American students in the Southwest. The New Horizons Program had become my catapult to Washington. (3)

Then I wrote about how Mexican Americans perceived the Nixon White House for Bob Finch. And because of it, the lives of my dear blessings, my wife and our children, took another turn.

Here I have written of whom I think I am and whom I think people think I am, and oh, so fundamentally, the gifts I received from my faith in God, my parents, my family, my community, and my country.

PART V
SEQUELS

Tranquil and
peaceful moments provide
understanding of events
surrounding the times
and impact of President
Richard M. Nixon.

These sequels are here in these last pages to reflect on what humans have wrought with one of the faculties human beings uniquely possess. That one faculty is the power to imprint their persona, their image, themselves on the world and on people.

And, while looking back on my life as I become more and more public, I realize that reporters and others used their faculty of forging images, Nixon, Ford, Reagan, Mexicans, etc. and mine in this saga of the Nixon era. They had two tools: truth and subjectivism. Let us voyage to see how the press and media created our images with their tools, newspapers, television, radio, and speeches.

We are governed by two sets of laws; one is divine. The first divine law is conscience. It differentiates turpitude from rectitude and is innate; there ain't *nada* we can do about it. It is endowed by God at conception and is busy at every moment of our earthly life, telling us always what is right and what is wrong. Then there are the Ten Commandments. God personally gave us those through Moses. Every human being is subject to the governance of these laws, irrespective of title or circumstance of life.

Conscience is a natural law. It tells us to be truthful. The Commandments specify that it is wrong to speak lies, to say falsehoods, to be mendacious. The reader may rightly ask, "Why are these notions written here in a section dealing with the press?" The answer surges from my personal experiences with the press and are derived from my formation at the hands of my parents, my Bachelor of Arts Degree in philosophy, and my theology studies.

My philosophy studies showed that Marxist dialectic utilized mendacity as a tool for achieving its objective of world domination. The French intellectual, Jean-Francois Revel, showed in his best-seller, *How Democracies Perish,* (1) precisely how communist "journalists" and its fellow travelers were embedded in the press for the sole purpose of twisting facts and truth where needed to achieve the goals of communism.

In our country, my first comprehensive knowledge of this sad Marxist world of falsehoods took deep roots in 1953, when I read *Witness* by Whittaker Chambers. I had read how Alger Hiss lied ever so blithely and snugly to Congressman Richard M. Nixon in House hearings after he swore to tell the truth, and nothing but the truth, so help him God. He appeared an effete follower of the dialectics of Hegel. Since Alger Hiss was a dedicated follower of the atheistic communist conspiracy, he rationalized the act of lying. It was for him a morally neutral human act, a useful means to an end. (2)

I could go on *ad infinitum* with salient examples of how the media has become captivated by an interest in "advocacy," whereby it licenses itself to slander and defame as just "good and tough" journalism. But now I must focus on how the media treated me, and how I learned to cope with the media.

My name appeared for the first time in the local newspaper, the *Whittier Daily News*. It was 1966. A nice reporter assigned to "human interest" stories had reported on an activity called the New Horizons Club at the high school and then did a follow-up story on the fuller New Horizons Program later. Articles over the next several years focused on the extraordinary impact New Horizons was having on the high school community. The reportage was nice, objective, and straight. I sensed that I was acquiring a public image of a striving, well-meaning "Latin teacher."

Then my name appeared in the big metropolitan dailies as the author of a novel educational program. It was a nice, straight-forward retelling. The next time my name appeared was on the radio, on TV, and Southwestern US newspapers. I sensed that I was portrayed fairly and objectively, with a definite touch of favoritism by two writers in particular: Frank del Olmo of the *Los Angeles Times* and member of its editorial board, and Tony Castro of the *Houston Post.* They gave me nice ink because, as they told me, I was fighting for the civil rights of the Mexicans. Advocacy reportage was manifesting itself. They portrayed me as a good guy. These two reporters revealed me nationally to the English-language press.

Tony Castro's early view of me was acquired as he asked questions on our drive from the Brownsville Airport to my meetings with community leaders, schools, and barrios in and around the town. I perceived myself as just a former high school teacher of Latin who was doing some research for the federal government—no big deal. But Tony wrote me up effusively, in a most laudatory manner. I was a dedicated good guy. I was for the people. I was a civil rights warrior.

The press, however, pivoted on August 5, 1971. I was a Republican, a Nixonite! How could I do such a flip-flop? I had joined the enemy. I was no longer a civil rights warrior; I had joined the world of the wealthy. And, what made matters worse; I was a "minority." I became an incomprehensible contradiction. The fact is, I was an Aristotelian-Thomistic philosopher and a practicing Catholic, first and foremost. Republicans who found the killing of humans not yet living outside the womb theologically and philosophically acceptable were certainly not acceptable to me. The members of Congress and the senators who accepted the seven deadly sins as the paradigm of normal Washington behavior were not acceptable to me.

One laughable incident of pivoting stands out: a Spanish-language TV station did a half-hour interview with me. The interviewer, a young, tough, and popular local personality, quietly confided to my special assistant that he hoped he would not mind if he went after this "silver-spoon Republican Mexican." The show would present a real contrast for his poor San Antonio Mexican viewers. He assured my assistant, Mo Garcia, who was from Brownsville, Texas, that the show would be a hit.

Mo encouraged him with great vigor: "Go after him and chew him up as would a hungry tiger."

The young man confidently began, "We have in San Antonio many poor and hungry people." (*60 Minutes* had just done a report on hunger in America featuring San Antonio). He asked, "Do you know what hunger is like?"

I answered: "I certainly do."

His grimace demonstrating incredulity, he pursued, "Tell us in what way. After all, you were raised with a silver spoon in your mouth."

I had him and his viewing audience. "I am one of eleven children. In the 1930s and 40s, we migrated in early summer to pick prunes, apricots, and grapes and returned home to pick walnuts, tomatoes, and oranges at the beginning of autumn. In the deepest of the Depression, in 1937, I vividly remember being hungry daily and going to sleep hungry for a period of three months." Needless to say, the chastised interviewer refocused on my work as chairman.

The modern philosophies of Europe influenced the media who then assumed that their ideas and principles were "middle of the road." They became such avid converts of the new lifestyles, as defined by such philosophers as Nietzche that those who did not share in their advanced and refined ideas were considered odd and even dangerous. I, a student of the Aristotelian-Thomistic school, was a simpleton and therefore "out of it." I was perceived as strolling through the tombstones of the Dark Ages, of the unenlightened times, and of the unreasonable Catholic Middle Ages. The Leftist and the one-sided Walter Cronkite's, the Jack Anderson's, the Tad Szulc's, the Daniel Schoor's, and the Dan Rather's went unchallenged. They defined the shape and condition of the world. A Republican president was anathema in *their* Washington. Yet none of them could say (or perhaps never thought to) that it was patently unfair and corrupt for one political party to wield total power to criminalize the political activities of the other party by subpoenaed investigation.

And so, I plead, by what right did Hillary Rodham investigate, review, and question my travel, my interview of Reyes Tijerina, a civil rights activist of northern New Mexico, and the myriad of my memos to the White House? The press has lived by a double standard. Those who abide by the secular and atheistic modalities are okey-dokey, while those who abide by Christian principles are lower-than. Clinton was impeached for breaking the law. Nonetheless, he is lauded and paraded! They, the definers of the media, say: "Clinton just had a little sex." No! He did lie *under oath* and tried to cover up his actions. Nixon tried to cover up the crime of burglars trying to get information on the other party. He, however, is condemned and ostracized. In the judgment of morality, Clinton's act was intrinsically evil. Nixon's was a venial sin.

The Communists Fidel Castro, Trotsky, Stalin, Lenin, Mao, Che, Alger Hiss, and so on are heroic figures. But Richard M. Nixon, who exposed the nefarious workings of a communist international conspiracy, is derogated and disparaged. Catholic principles and bishops, priests, and nuns are insulted, derided, and mocked. Democrats such as Kennedy, Johnson, and Roosevelt can delight in women and concubines. When Republicans commit the very same acts of turpitude, "they have baggage." Today, at last, opposing voices, views, opinions, and news are available, fairer, and more balanced.

I conclude with a note on the current assessment of how Republicans of today view Nixon's legacy. Their views and assessments are deeply and profoundly warped. Ask any knowledgeable Mexican American. He or she will tell you that President Nixon was the *best*, by far.

This sequel looks into the need for effective tools for organizing Mexican American professionals. When I worked at the Civil Rights Commission, I learned the Black community had developed and matured by imitating the organizations of the White people. I learned a new word, infrastructure. It seemed they had organizations for everything. As chairman of the Cabinet Committee, I received guidance, counsel, and ideas from multiple sources. A constant question and refrain voiced by Chicanos was, "Why don't we have [this or that]? The Blacks do." The realization that these queries were posed to me because the questioners believed I could do something about it, compelled me to internalize: "Yes, I have the power to do something about that." So, one morning, I instructed my driver: "Take the Rock Creek Parkway and drive slowly. I want to enjoy the pastoral sights while I think."

In what specific ways could the Cabinet Committee promote the development of the infrastructure of our people? My mental review pointed to the professional disciplines that had initiated their organizations or had them well underway: for the clergy PADRES; (3) for the Civil Rights, Mexican American Legal Defense and Educational Fund (MALDEF); for small business, the National Economic Development Agency; for educators, Association of Mexican American Educators; for politicians, National Association of Latin Elected Officials; etc. There was a void. The Engineers and Scientists had not yet organized.

I hired John Chapman, PhD as a consultant to plan a conference for science and engineering. We named the invited group the Task Force of Hispanic Scientists and Engineers. About fifty convened in Washington on December 14 and 15, 1973, to discuss whether it was desirable to form an association or associations. As a result, the invitees did form one, under the leadership of Dr. Manuel Castro—a nuclear engineer with Bechtel Corporation's International Nuclear Plant Division. Later on, the scientists formed their own organization.

Another sequel reveals that my life as Chairman was not all sweetness and honey with all Hispanic groups. Mainland Puerto Ricans demonstrated vehemently a few days after I was named, Chairman, and demanded inclusion in the ranks of the Cabinet Committee. They enjoyed full support from their Senators. I had to endure a sometimes hostile community and wondered why the former chairman enjoyed a tranquil relationship with that mainland Puerto Rican community. An interview with the former chairman of the Cabinet Committee, Martin Castillo showed why and how he did it. He revealed how he kept the mainland Puerto Ricans in check so that they would not demonstrate against him or lobby their senators with gripes and complaints.

(4) He simply visited Governor Ferre of Puerto Rico and asked him to maintain equanimity among all Puerto Ricans, including those living in the US. Chairman Castillo enjoyed peaceful relations with the emerging civil rights voices in New York, New Jersey, the Midwest and Pennsylvania. He made sure there would be no surprises. Of course, the polite suppression created pressures and the pent-up feeling that the Cabinet Committee was for Mexican Americans only.

Years later, on June 18, 2009, a Puerto Rican lawyer and member of the Philadelphia City Council by the name of Ortiz regaled Rudy Becerra, a vice president for Latin affairs at the Coca-Cola Corporation; my grandson, Ruben Brown; and me about his role in organizing a huge Puerto Rican demonstration against me that had taken place a few days after my appointment. (5) The demonstration was ugly. This Puerto Rican lawyer had proclaimed the event as the starting date of the mainland Puerto Rican civil rights crusade. I still question if what he claimed was for real, since he is the only one who has ever claimed that event as so important.

It was, however, horrid for several reasons: The mainland Puerto Ricans had gotten together and decided that with me, they would get their share of the Cabinet Committee. They demanded we put a Puerto Rican in the position of executive director or vice chairman. I could not grant nor promise them immediate action, only future consideration; I was only acting chairman at the time, not yet confirmed by the Senate. They had chanted that I would not get it unless they got what they wanted. I personally had no problem acceding to their demand, but William Marumoto had already decided at White House

Personnel that Tony Rodriguez would continue in the position of executive director where he still held the legal power to act, and I could not reveal this fact to the protestors.

Several hundred of what appeared to be hired for-the-day, professional protestors, were bused in from New York and other like places. They rode the elevators to our floor, spilled out into the hallways, crammed into our offices, yelling and showing clear signs of the effects of fortifying spirits. The Spanish-language media was very well represented in full force. A delegation of well-dressed, well-mannered leaders stepped forth and asked for a meeting with me in my office. They presented their demands. I gave them my response and let them vent for quite some time while their unruly cohorts and a demanding media stammered about recording for New York's consumption. I denied them interviews. Finally, I informed the "leaders" that the Secret Service was going to clear all of them out; it was housed in our building. That brought the protest to a quick end.

Cognitively and affectively, I well understood their aspirations and hopes for their Puerto Rican or *Neorquino* ("New York Rican") communities. The deep scars this event created were unnecessary. In me, they had a supporter and a friend. I had already worked the civil rights field in Connecticut, New York, and New Jersey at the Civil Rights Commission. I knew the Puerto Rican civil rights circle; I did not know these Rockefeller Republicans.

The worst part of my hard dealings with them stemmed from the intransigence of a small group of Rockefeller Republicans who insisted I channel my work with the Puerto Rican community through them, and direct political goodies to them only. (6)

The matter of the executive director would plague me for the duration of my appointment. Senator Chuck Percy would never reconcile. Senator Jacob Javits discovered a bone he never tired of chewing on. He even assigned a staffer to ride herd on me. Meanwhile, the senators from the West Coast, who should have shown some scintilla of interest in what I was doing for their Mexican American constituents, manifested none. However, one Texas congressman, Kika de la Garza, became so upset at the grab for power by the Puerto Ricans supported by two senators that he called me to his office to discuss the matter and to let me know he was prepared to do something about it. He was, after all, the chairman of the Agriculture Committee. He ended up giving me his private phone number. Warfare in Congress over this matter was the last thing I needed.

In conclusion, I honestly admit that I never quite understood the insular mentality of the Puerto Ricans. I never really appreciated their class differences, their perceptions of each other, and their own racial and ethnic distinctions. I was perceived by the Anglos in the White House as the ambassador to the Spanish speaking who could handle the Cubans, the Puerto Ricans, and the Mexicans. After all, didn't they all speak Spanish? My personal files are filled with newspaper clippings on the never-ending row with the mainland Puerto Ricans. I became their national civil rights punching bag, with the senatorial support of Chuck Percy from Chicago and Jacob Javits from New York!

With respect to the three national Mexican American organization chartered for the purposes of teaching, and advancing civil rights, the two biggest and oldest Mexican American organizations, LULAC and the GI Forum, were very supportive of my work at the Cabinet Committee. At my instructions, my staff assisted their leadership in their relations with the federal government. I got an appointment for Joseph Juarez, chairman and president of the GI Forum, as a special assistant to the administrator of the Veterans Administration, Don Johnson. There, he was able to make an impact on behalf of Mexican American veterans. Mr. Pete Villa, president of LULAC, was most gracious and helpful. Both of them also spearheaded Project Ser, a joint venture of their organizations that provided federally funded services. In very early 1973, I conferred with the secretary of labor, a member of the Cabinet Committee. He asked me how much LULAC and the GI Forum were requesting for vocational training; the amount was most modest. The secretary said they would be funded for a much higher amount. Since then, both organizations have grown as if on steroids.

The third organization was born in 1968 in the hands of an outstanding person, Herman Gallegos. Herman was a devout Catholic intellectual who founded and named it, Southwest Council of La Raza with a grant of $630,000. He is a historical treasure, a pioneering member of Mexican American movers and shakers. From his home in San Francisco, he came to know and work with other pioneers. He and Dr. Ernesto Galarza were early advisors to Cesar Chavez. Gallegos had been born into a coal mining family in Southern Colorado. He moved to California and earned a B.A. in Social Work at San Jose State University and a Masters in the same field at University of California at Berkeley.

Another Coloradan, Dr. Julian Zamora, edited the seminal book, *La Raza: Forgotten Americans*. It was a compilation of contributions from seven people with whom the Rosenberg

Foundation had collaborated. He was also born and raised in a coal mining town in southern Colorado, close to that of Mr. Gallegos's family. The book stirred the dreams and aspirations of the growing middle class of educated Mexican Americans. Nonviolent unrest became a hallmark throughout the Southwest. Reasonable people began to act on what could and should be done. The civil rights laws of 1964 were only helping reduce discrimination against Blacks. The war on poverty was beginning to flourish with money, but as Herman Gallegos quietly related in one of the three interviews he granted me, "We Mexicans were getting little. The Blacks were getting almost all of it." (7)

Herman approached the Rosenberg Foundation and the Ford Foundation for funds, and with them he started the Southwest Council of La Raza. This organization became the fiscal agent for participating in anti-poverty programs. Herman knew well that this "war" was a money gusher, waged in the Offices for Economic Opportunity in Washington D.C. , Gallegos wrote that the council's purpose was "to provide supportive technical and financial assistance to Mexican American community efforts aimed at upgrading conditions in the Mexican American barrios and eliminating the second class status of the entire Mexican American community. It assists the Mexican American community as a whole in gaining its fair share of both public and private resources. The council concentrates on providing technical assistance in three areas: economic opportunity, housing, and education." (8) These were truly lofty aims.

The Southwest Council of La Raza was to take a clearly distinctive left turn on the highway to becoming a national organization.

To learn how and why this happened, we must compare the California of the very late 1950's and early 1960's through the lens of political organizing.

We have read in the very first chapter of this book, that beginning in the late 1950's and early 1960's, the Republican Party reached out to the Mexican Americans. In contrast, a man from Chicago, financed with a lot of money from who knows where, and by name of Saul Alinsky assisted by his deputy, Fred Ross, camped in Los Angeles, formed an organization called Community Service Organization, concentrated on organizing voter registration, and trained its first leaders Edward Roybal and Tony Rios. Years later, Alinsky and Ross camped in the San Jose/San Francisco area and trained Herman Gallegos and Cesar Chavez. Consequently the world surrounding Gallegos was entirely Democrat. Naturally he selected people to staff his organization who were directly connected with and to the National Democrat Party.

Mr. Gallegos assigned the role of information officer to Miss Polly O. Baca, who was the key person in charge of all Mexican American affairs since the Kennedy presidential campaign of 1960 at the National Democratic Party headquarters. By July 1971, this organization and its affiliates became de facto extensions of the UAW, the Steelworkers Union, and the Democratic Party in matters affecting Mexican Americans. Henry Santiestevan, a high-level United Auto Workers Union (UAW) union boss, was the new executive director.

Meanwhile, Local Councils of the National Council of La Raza were being organized with novel names: in Los Angeles, the East Los Angeles Community Union (TELACU) was led by Esteban Torres, UAW union leader and later a member of Congress; in San Francisco there was the Mission Housing Development Council headed by Herman Gallegos; Chicanos por la Causa was led in Phoenix by Ron Lopez; San Antonio had the Mexican American Unity Council and Juan Patlan; Albuquerque had the Albuquerque Building Cooperative. There were councils in several other cities. Their history reveals that at the beginning, they were engaged in providing community counseling and guidance.

The Southwest Council of La Raza itself, in the person of executive director Henry Santiestevan, visited my office for assistance. We provided the council with the support requested. Mr. Santiestevan requested a daylong seminar so his staff could meet in Washington with program officers from member agencies in specific disciplines: housing, economic development, manpower training, education, and so on. We did this, and successfully. The council submitted proposals, and many were funded. However, in the meeting with Henry Santiesteban, I reminded him that federal funding excluded him and his staff from using money for partisan political activities. I told him he had to remain neutral in the forthcoming presidential campaign. This caution was no different from what I delivered to every organization that sought federal funding through my office. I warned him that if we discovered violations, I would do everything possible to get him defunded. Happily, we found none.

I do not know what assistance the other councils sought or in what political activities they might have participated. This, however, is a fact: by November 1972, President Richard M.

Nixon's vision to appoint a hundred high-level Hispanic executives had accomplished the following at the Office of Economic Opportunity alone: he appointed three regional directors and at headquarters in Washington—the administrator, the general counsel, and the program director for Community Development Corporations. I had heard Herman Gallegos's complaint that the OEO was funding Blacks but not Hispanics in Lyndon Johnson's time.

And, behold, the East Los Angeles Community Center, TELACU, received a grant of ten million dollars from OEO in 1972; and ditto for Chicanos por la Causa in Arizona. Ditto for the Mexican American Unity Council in San Antonio and for other Community Development Corporations (CDCs) for Cesar Chavez, for Brawley, California, for Denver, and for Albuquerque. Seventy million dollars of caring for Mexican Americans is a lot. But did they give any credit to President Richard M. Nixon? Look at the history of these CDCs in Google to get the answer. Do Democrats give this Republican president credit? The answer is easy: NO!

Soon after the 1972 election, the Southwest Council of La Raza moved to Washington and was renamed the National Council of La Raza. A former employee of OEO, Raul Izaguirre, was appointed its executive director, replacing Henry Santiestevan who returned to his job at UAW. This organization embellished it nexus with the unions and with the Democratic National Committee. Izaguirre defined a new direction for the council, which became the Washington home for Mexican American liberals and secular relativists. It constantly issued press releases about the educational, economic, housing, and employment disparities of Mexican Americans as compared with others. They could get their research fingers on copious data that reflected huge disparities by the variables of race and ethnicity. Of course, they never failed to report that the huge disparities were the work of those awful Nixon people.

What is intriguing about their use of readily, newly available data is that the Cabinet Committee under the Nixon administration had seen to its collection! Knowledge of the facts facilitated policy makers to develop ameliorating plans and actions. But for Raul Izaguirre, it was a partisan weapon for denouncing the Nixon administration, and Nixon himself, while promoting the fortunes of the Democratic Party.

The National Council of La Raza was converted into a platform for virulently attacking the Cabinet Committee for being too political. In other words, we were too successful in bringing the opportunities of the federal government to Spanish speaking people. They also became a de facto extension of the Democratic National Party and the unions. Why were they adamantly opposed to amnesty for undocumented Mexicans? At the same time, Congressman Peter Rodino, (D New Jersey) and chairman of the Judiciary Committee, was sponsoring thousands of "little bills" to allow thousands of Italians to immigrate. They were nicknamed "Rodino bills." And Senator Ted Kennedy was making sure that the Immigration and Naturalization Service was looking the other way as hundreds of thousands of illegal Irish were flooding the East Coast.

It is sad to recount that the great regional organization, Southwest Council of La Raza, founded by a faithful Catholic,

Herman Gallegos, had become, a national organization and just another organization of the Democrat Party-more and more Secular and Socialistic.

The next sequel recounts how the Democrats went after Ramirez. Congressman Don Edwards had accepted the job from the Democrat Party: Destroy Ramirez. He carried out the assignment "to go after Ramirez," that is, get rid of the Cabinet Committee in a manner, which appeared to me, gleeful and haughty. As the powerful chairman of the Civil Rights and Constitutional Rights Subcommittee of the Committee on the Judiciary, in the House of Representatives, he held hearings on July 11 and 19, 1973. (9) It was a truly pathetic effort to frame my activities as chairman of the Cabinet Committee as "too political." He paraded "witnesses" of the caliber of Manuel Fierro, brother-in-law of Colorado state Senator Polly Baca, the ageless person-in-charge of Mexican Democrats. She was well known as the permanent Hispanic in the DNC, dating from the Kennedy heydays. He was also married to Polly's sister, Betty Baca, also a DNC employee and a Kennedyite from the 1960's. For the needs of this hearing, Manuel Fierro was suddenly the "Executive Director, Raza Association of Spanish Surnamed Americans (RASSA)!" What a sad joke without humor. The so-called organization, RASSA, did not exist. No matter, Truth was just a subjective word; not an objective reality.

An Alex Zermeno, "Assistant Executive Director" (he had been given that title, also suddenly and temporarily) at the

National Council of La Raza, testified that he was speaking on behalf of Henry Santiesteven, "National Director" of the National Council of La Raza. Oh, yes? Congressman Don Edwards had gone out to the barrio alleys and had brought bitter partisans from the payrolls of either the unions or the Democratic Party. He tried to fulfill the assignment to "get Ramirez," but what can you do with wads of paper? He and Linda Chavez, the then-Socialist and his *Malinche,* did not realize that the world of the unknown and forgotten "La Raza" people had come full circle. Now we, Chicanos and Mexican Americans, were getting national awareness and becoming something else. Don Edwards knew nothing about our progress and advances. He still viewed us from the eighteenth hole at his Saratoga Country Club as low knowledge, ex-migrant mes kins. And, Linda Chavez and the Baca girls?, Well they were not Mexicans; no, they were Colorado *Hispanas with ancestral lineage to Spain.* We Chicanos had ancestral links to Spain and also to one of the many indigenous nations.

Congressman Chuck Wiggins had taken me, an anonymous government employee to a private, exclusive lunch in mid-December, 1970. Three years later, on January 5, 1973, he called me to break the news: Congressman Don Edwards from San Jose, California and chairman of a Judiciary subcommittee had been assigned by the Democrats to "get" me. Congressman Wiggins added, "They are very unhappy at your political success. The over-30 percent Mexican, Cuban, and Puerto Rican vote for Nixon has engendered a high level of bitterness. Edwards has hired a gun slinger from Colorado, Linda Chavez, to help him do you in and destroy the Cabinet Committee. Do you know her?"

To Henry –
With best wishes.
Chuck Wiggins
25th - Calif.

HMR's Personal File

Congressman Don Edwards could not lay a glove on me. He did hurt the fortunes of the Spanish-speaking people as he tried mightily to regain their vote and loyalties. On the other hand, the Senate Watergate Committee could hurt us via nationally televised hearings. Sam Dash and his Watergate gang, including

Hillary Rodham, were in a different league. At the request of Senator Montoya, GAO performed an audit of CCOSS to determine if I had misappropriated funds. What a waste of time! He had seven staff lawyers question me about Watergate. It was another waste. He subpoenaed me for seven hours of grand jury testimony—another waste. As I victoriously strutted out of the huge room of Watergate inquisitors, the jurors had affirmed that Nixon was right on target. The jurors clapped, cheered, and formed a line to shake my hands.

Dash wasted more time having high-level FBI agents question me twice. On November 1, 1973, Mo Garcia memoed me that Mike Hershman of the Senate Select Committee had indicated that I would probably be testifying on national TV on November 8. On November 2, Polly De Mint of the Select Committee called to get a bio and other information routinely asked of the Committee's potential Interviewees. I was never called to testify!

As I watched Marumoto and Rodriguez testify at the hearings on TV, I called Sam Dash's office over and over, adamantly asking why I had not been called. I repeated to his staff that the Democrats did not want a national audience to hear about the many firsts that President Nixon and I had accomplished because Nixon gave a damn about the Mexicans. I taunted him and "Little Joe." I had a story to tell to a national audience, and the Democrats denied me the chance.

Gerald Ford and the Chicanos is the next sequel.

Congressman Ford had replaced the vice president, Spiro Agnew, who resigned on October 10, 1973 and was installed on December 6. The fortunes of and opportunities for the new American group, the Chicanos and other Spanish-speaking people, would eventually fall on him as he became the Oval Office's occupant.

I knew we had the task of introducing him to the world of Spanish-speaking people. We would have to provide him orientations on who we were and on what had been accomplished under the leadership of President Nixon. Mrs. Armstrong had arrived in the West Wing just one year prior, and we provided her with extensive briefings and arranged trips to the field and meetings with Hispanic leaders so that she could learn and cope with her liaison responsibilities to the Spanish speaking. Although she had hailed from an area in Texas with a dense concentration of Mexican Americans, she had lived in a world mentally and physically isolated from them. She seemed to be quite innocently unaware of the pervasive discrimination Texan European Americans imposed on Mexican Americans. Vice President Ford would also need the same orientation, because he too had little experience with us. He did, however, know the Black Americans.

I had, it seemed, spent a lifetime showing European Americans what we Mexican Americans were all about (as the phrase goes). At Whittier High School, I made teachers face their own perceptions of who they thought Mexicans were. I called it "sensitivity training." I did the same with school administrators. It seemed I was always teaching some variety of sensitivity training. In the case of this vice president, whom I could predict would soon be president because of my "big secret," training was an absolute must. I had planned to call on him even before his confirmation but did not want to rush. I assumed that all of a sudden, everyone in the world would be trying to see him. So my close assistant, Mo Garcia, arranged a meeting with the vice president's counselors Kenneth E. Belieu and Richard Burress on January 3, 1974.

The sitting president's evident concern for Spanish-speaking people had resulted in their increased awareness of the real possibility of full inclusion in this country's opportunities. This motivated me to educate the vice president as soon as possible. I opened the meeting, stating that the vice president should be fully briefed about the situation of the nation's Spanish speaking: the Cubans, Puerto Ricans, and Mexican Americans. I added that the Blacks, through Stan Scott (special assistant to the president), had already arranged to meet with the new vice president.

Mr. Belieu responded that Mr. Ford would definitely see me early in February and that he would very much like to be briefed on the situation of the Spanish speaking. I brought up the format for the meeting, stating that I would provide written briefing material prior to it and that I would inform my liaison to the Cabinet Committee, Counselor Anne Armstrong.

My report to Counselor Armstrong resulted in her taking over the entire matter. She managed the details, invitations, the selection of invitees, and so on. The vice president would receive a dog-and-pony show on what the administration had done for the Spanish speaking. The concept of Gerald Ford *knowing about us* was lost. Gerald Ford had been briefed by Blacks, but he was not briefed by Chicanos. He was, however, indeed briefed on what had been done *for us*. By now, Armstrong was angling for a promotion. She became the ambassador to the Court of Saint James's in England. For an aristocratic lady and an Episcopalian, that elevation was only right and proper.

The photo below was taken on July 13, 1974, in the City of Pomona, California, the town where I was raised from infancy. I was born in a little railroad watering station ten miles away: Walnut. Here, I finally had a chance to tell Gerry Ford a little bit about us Chicanos. (The outcome of my still-boiling secret was to show its public side several weeks hence.) We were at the home of a lawyer who was locally loved for his concern for justice for Chicanos. He was a dear friend of my brother. From left to right are: the lawyer, Congressman Vic Veasey, Father Carter, Vice President Gerald Ford, Father Jack Cosgrove (my classmate for ten years in the seminary and then pastor of my hometown church, Saint Joseph's), and myself.

Courtesy Gerald Ford Library

Courtesy Gerald Ford Library

This photograph is of the third of my four presidential meetings in the Cabinet Room. It is dated December 11, 1975. President Ford has invited a group of Hispanics to hear his presidential election plans and receive from us some reactions and suggestions. Seated from left to right were: me (with highly visible bald spot), two unknowns, Manolo Casanova of Florida, Ben Fernandez of California, the president, Fernando C. de Baca (in the White House assistant position for which I had fought so strenuously since April 1971), Rita de Martino of New York, and George Bush (the chairman of the Republican National Committee, facing President Ford).

I had returned to California after my August 1974 resignation from the CCOSS and had resettled with my wife and family in Beverly Hills. I had successfully mounted a business in Los Angeles. President Ford asked for comments on his plans for election. After many comments and suggestions, I finally spoke up and stated clearly and with a few supporting reasons that he would lose Illinois and Texas. I mentioned that the 30 percent vote President Nixon had received from the Mexican Americans was due in large measure to the presidential appointments of so many Hispanics to high-level positions. And, I pointed out that his presidential personnel shop, directed by Rumsfeld and Cheney, had been firing many of those we had worked so hard to recruit and place. He did lose Illinois and Texas. (By contrast, President Nixon won both.)

This sequel records a brief glimpse of another great man, President Ronald Reagan. This is the brief history of my knowledge and experiences with the Irish American, Ronald Reagan. He was raised with the vestiges of a Christian formation. His father had been raised Catholic. He acquired a sound and solid college education on the principles of capitalism. His speeches in 1964 and 1966–67 inspired and motivated me to see in this man a companion to my principles. He possessed a deep knowledge about the communist international conspiracy; he was anti-abortion; he was for the exercise of free will and deep respect for each and every individual. His philosophy was founded on solid Western principles that arose from a Christian civilization. His principles were clearly different and distinct from the modern secular philosophies infesting Western thought. I never asked him, yet I conjectured that he must have read and reread the defining opus, *Witness,* by Chambers. Years later he would gather around himself these personages: for the practical and expedient purposes of politics, he got the veteran politicos: Stu

Spencer, Richard Wirthlin, Lyn Nofsiger, and Mike Deaver. But for profound thinking, he enjoyed the support of two circles: the Kitchen Cabinet and for foreign affairs: Judge William P. Clarke, William Wilson and Bill Casey.

He granted me an audience of almost an hour in 1972 in his California governor's office in Sacramento. The purpose of my visit was to introduce him to what President Nixon and the CCOSS were accomplishing for Mexican Americans. As the taxi took me back to the airport, I tried to analyze what had been achieved, if anything. Was the trip and visit a waste of taxpayers' money? Did he appreciate and comprehend what President Nixon was achieving? Time would tell. He learned and became our big-time amigo. He gave amnesty to two million undocumented Mexicans! His daughter, Maureen, deeply appreciated the votes of the Mexican Americans for Nixon and later helped get even more for her dad.

The most salient bit of memory remaining in my recall is his query, "Why are so many Mexican Americans Democrats?" He brought it to the point: "Senator Ruben Ayala is a close friend. He is a Mexican American from San Bernardino. He is more conservative than I. Then why is he a Democrat?" His focus rattled me. Did he not understand what I had tried to explain about the Mexican Americans and Nixon?

My mind scrambled for clear and convincing declarations. I hemmed and hawed for the right order of thoughts to explain why Mexican Americans like Ayala were Democrats. They finally dribbled out. I assumed the mental posture of a high school teacher and deliberately and slowly enunciated, "Into Southern

California not too long ago came people from the East. These newcomers, who live along the mountains stretching from the Pacific Ocean to Palm Springs, are the owners of businesses in the flatlands. Many, for example, whiz from their Altadena and San Marino homes inside the Arroyo Seco Freeway to their offices in the tall buildings in downtown LA or to their factories in South LA. Neither they nor their children see or get to know Mexicans. The Anglos and the Mexicans live in two separate worlds." My recall is clear; he was attentive. We had good eye contact. He was listening.

My rather lengthy explanation continued: "Most Mexicans are also newcomers from the interior of Mexico. The parents, who fled from Mexico, did not vote, for they were not US citizens. They were refugees from a system of feudalism. Political parties, voting, political education, and political legacies were unknown. Their children, however—and this is where Ruben comes in—heard that Roosevelt was for the poor. They say that seeing is believing, and they saw the fancy, late-model cars parked in the space reserved for the boss, who was a Republican. They, however, had old Chevys parked along the street. There is nothing profound about their decision to register as Democrats. And to top it off, most of them are Catholics, and they were deeply affected by the political campaigns of the Kennedys, also Catholics." Over the years, Governor Reagan's question has occupied a place of deep meditation and reflection in my inner recesses. It is my conviction that I have come up with some firm answers and also educated hypotheses, yet to be researched.

Maureen Reagan, the president's daughter, brought us even closer. One late evening in 1980, a call came to our home. Ester, my wife, answered and heard a voice identify itself: "I am

Maureen Reagan, may I speak with Dr. Ramirez?" The essence of the lengthy conversation was, "My father needs you to update the strategy you designed for Nixon that won him a large percentage of the Mexican Vote. Come over tomorrow, Monday, to the head-quarters in Santa Monica. Lyn Nofziger will be waiting for you."

President Nixon had won over 30 percent of the Mexican American vote in 1972. Eight years later, Governor Ronald Reagan won over 40 percent of it. On the eve of the election, I was nearby him at the Century City Plaza Hotel in West Los Angeles

Several weeks later, I was ensconced on M Street in Washington, an employee of the Office of the President-Elect. There, I worked on presidential personnel. I made selections like Mike Cardenas, a CPA from Fresno, to be the adminis-trator of the Small Business Administration. The director of bilingual education was another key selection. He was an educator from Lansing, Michigan. I reviewed and passed on for further action all the top Spanish-speaking candidates for presidential consideration for appointment to boards, com-missions, departments, and agencies from November 1980 to Inauguration Day, January 1981. Thereafter, I returned to my business in Los Angeles and remained a consultant to the White House.

The following two photographs were taken in the Cabinet Room. In the second, President Reagan met with key Hispanic campaign staff and supporters on March 30, 1981. I note with horror that but a few short hours later, he sustained a near assas-sination at the hands of John Hinckley Jr.

Courtesy Ronald Reagan Library

Courtesy Ronald Reagan Library

At the table from left to right: Dr. Henry M. Ramirez; Fernando C. de Baca (former presidential assistant to President Nixon); Elizabeth Dole; Lyn Nofziger; President Reagan; Dr. Tirso del Junco, California chairman of the Republican Party; and unknown.

President Reagan did not focus on assurances of equal opportunities for the Spanish speaking. We had become—well, like the Italians and Polish, just another ethnic group of Americans. We had arrived. We were no longer a big deal. Two presidents had occupied the Oval Office since President Nixon, and neither displayed any outward sign of care or action directed specifically at the advancement of Hispanics. Under Reagan, we participated in areas of economic improvement at SBA, Commerce, and Procurements.

There was, however, one huge bit of unfinished business: amnesty. President Reagan completed in November 1986 what President Nixon had started in 1973. At least a quarter million illegal Irish were granted amnesty and became US citizens, and so were about two million undocumented Mexicans.

CONCLUSION

President Nixon had taken care of our issues and had made them systemically integral with the enforcement of the civil rights laws of 1964.

Richard M. Nixon was the man who grew up with us Mexicans. He knew us, cared about us, and included us. Let history show that he was the only president who really and truly gave a damn for the Mexicans. He was nefariously lynched by Democratic hypocrites corrupted by power and by a cheering clique, the press, in August 1974. I belonged to his official family. I resigned in August 1974 and with my ever-supportive wife and growing children, now in their teens, returned to God's country, Southern California, with the grace of God and Our Lady of Guadalupe's intercession.

The promises listed in the press release below and made on the day of my presidential appointment, by the grace of divine providence, I state categorically that I fulfilled!

SPANISH SPEAKING NEWS

A NEWS RELEASE FROM THE CABINET COMMITTEE
ON OPPORTUNITIES FOR SPANISH SPEAKING PEOPLE

1800 G STREET, N.W. WASHINGTON, D.C. 20506
TEL. (202) 382-6651

For Immediate Release
August 5, 1971

Clayton Willis
Office of Public Affairs

STATEMENT OF CHAIRMAN RAMIREZ OPENING A NEWS CONFERENCE AT THE WHITE HOUSE
AUGUST 5, 1971

I appreciate the confidence the President has placed in me by appointing me
Chairman of the Cabinet Committee on Opportunities for the Spanish Speaking. I
assume this position with humility for the responsibility is great; but I also
assume it with high hope that the Cabinet Committee will begin to serve the
needs of the Nation's Spanish speaking people faithfully and well.

This Committee will be responsive to all Spanish speaking Americans--Mexican
Americans, Puerto Rican Americans, Cuban Americans and all others who share
Indo-Hispanic origins. We plan to chart a course that will make them an integral
part of the United States in fact as well as in word.

It is time now to re-fashion outworn judgments, to learn to respect one
another's distinct cultural origins. It shall be my goal as Chairman of the
Cabinet Committee to help bring about this understanding from which will come
true opportunities for the Spanish speaking and recognition by their fellow
Americans of the unique contribution they can make as part of the mainstream of
American life.

I do not intend to exploit the hopes of the Spanish speaking population by
offering illusions or retreaded promises which can only lead to disillusion.
If there is skepticism today in the Spanish speaking communities, it is because
we have too often been misled and disappointed by rhetoric instead of being
strengthened by commitment. The President and his staff have given me their
assurance that this office will not be used as a facade of Federal concern or as
a convenient shield against Spanish speaking alienation. This office will be a
working office--working to do what its name specifically says it will do: assure
equal opportunities for all Spanish speaking people.

The cooperation and active participation of the Cabinet members and other
high Government officials who make up the Cabinet Committee are vital to its
effectiveness. The President has pledged their steadfast support to the Committee
in setting up meaningful goals for Spanish speaking recruitment and providing
supportive services by which new programs will be forged to bring greater
opportunity to the Spanish speaking community. Committee members will participate
in the quarterly meetings called by the Chairman to review issues of concern, to
evaluate progress, and to move ahead on expanding horizons.

The Committee has been revitalized. It is a living, functioning part of the
American Government dedicated to turning hope into reality for all those for whom
it has been created to serve.

APPENDICES

APPENDIX A:
THE COMMITTEE AND ITS AIMS

Public Law 91-181
91st Congress, S. 740
December 30, 1969

TO ESTABLISH THE CABINET COMMITTEE ON OPPORTUNITIES FOR THE SPANISH-SPEAKING PEOPLE, AND FOR OTHER PURPOSES.

Be it enacted by the Senate and House of Representatives of the United States of America in Congress assembled, That it is the purpose of this Act to assure that Federal programs are reaching all Mexican Americans, Puerto Ricans Americans. Cuban Americans, and all other Spanish-speaking and Spanish Surnamed Americans and providing the assistance they need, and to seek out new programs that may be necessary to handle problems that are unique to such persons.

Sec. 2.

    (a) There is hereby established the Cabinet Committee on Opportunities for the Spanish-Speaking People (hereinafter referred to as the "Committee").

    (b) The Committee shall be composed of—

        (1) The Secretary of Agriculture;

        (2) The Secretary of Commerce;

        (3) The Secretary of Labor;

(4) The Secretary of Health, Education, and Welfare;

(5) The Secretary of Housing and Urban Development;

(6) The Secretary of the Treasury;

(7) The Attorney General;

(8) The Director of the Office of Economic Opportunity;

(9) The Administrator of the Small Business Administration;

(10) The Commissioner of the Equal Employment Opportunity Commission most concerned with the Spanish-speaking and Spanish Surnamed Americans;

(11) The Chairman of the Civil Service Commission; and

(12) The Chairman of the Committee, who shall be appointed by the President, by and with the advice and consent of the Senate, from among individuals who are recognized for their knowledge of and familiarity with the special problems and needs of the Spanish speaking.

(c) The Chairman may invite the participation in the activities of the Committee of any executive department or agency not represented on the Committee, when matters of interest to such executive department or agency are under consideration.

(d) (1) The Chairman of the Committee shall not concurrently hold any other office or position of employment with the United States, but shall serve in a full-time capacity as the chief officer of the Committee.

(2) The Chairman of the Committee shall receive compensation at the rate prescribed for level V of the

Executive Schedule by section 5316 of Title 5, United States Code.

(3) The Chairman of the Committee shall designate one of the other Committee Members to serve as acting Chairman during the absence or disability of the Chairman,

(e) The Committee shall meet at least quarterly during each year,

SEC. 3.

(a) The Committee shall have the following functions:

(1) to advise Federal departments and agencies regarding appropriate action to be taken to help assure that Federal Programs are providing the assistance needed by Spanish-speaking and Spanish-surnamed Americans; and

(2) to advise Federal departments and agencies on the development and implementation of comprehensive and coordinated policies, plans, and programs focusing on the special problems and needs of the Spanish-speaking and Spanish-surnamed Americans, and on priorities thereunder.

(b) In carrying out its functions the Committee may foster such surveys, studies, research, and demonstration and technical assistance projects, establish such relationships with State and local governments and the private sector and promote such participation of State and local governments and the private sector as may be appropriate to identify and assist in solving the special problems of the Spanish-speaking and Spanish Surnamed Americans.

SEC. 4.

(a) The Committee is authorized to prescribe rules and regulations as may be necessary to carry out the provisions of this Act.

(b) The Committee shall consult with and coordinate its activities with appropriate Federal departments and agencies and shall utilize the facilities and resources of such department and agencies to the maximum extent possible in carrying out its functions.

(c) The Committee is authorized in carrying out its functions to enter into agreements with Federal departments and agencies as appropriate.

SEC. 5.

The Committee is authorized to request directly from any Federal department or agency any information it deems necessary to carry out its functions under this Act, and to utilize the services and facilities of such department or agency; and each department or agency is authorized to furnish such information, services, and facilities to the Committee upon request of the Chairman to the extent permitted by law and within the limits of available funds.

SEC. 6.

(a) The Chairman shall appoint and fix the compensation of such personnel as may be necessary to carry out the function of the Committee and may obtain the services of experts and consultants in accordance with section 3109 of title 5, United States Code, at rates for individuals not in excess of the daily equivalent paid for positions under GS-18 of the General Schedule under section 5332 of such titles.

(b) Federal departments and agencies, in their discretion, may detail to temporary duty with the Committee such personnel as the Chairman may request for carrying out the functions of the Committee, each such detail to be without loss of seniority, pay, or other employee status.

SEC. 7.

(a) There is established an Advisory Council on Spanish Speaking Americans (hereinafter referred to as the Advisory Council) composed of nine members appointed by the President from among individuals who are representative of the Mexican, Puerto Rican American, Cuban American, and other elements of the Spanish-speaking and Spanish-surnamed community in the United States. In making such appointments the President shall give due consideration to any recommendations submitted by the Committee.

(b) The Advisory Council shall advise the Committee with respect to such matters as the Chairman of the Committee shall request. The President shall designate the Chairman and Vice Chairman of the Advisory Council. The Advisory Council is authorized to:

(1) appoint and fix the compensation of such personnel, and

(2) obtain the services of such experts and consultants in accordancewith section 3109 of title 5, at rates for individuals not in excess of the daily equivalent paid for positions under GS-18 of the General Schedule under section 5302 of such title, as may be necessary to carry out its functions.

(c) Each member of the Advisory Council who is appointed from private life shall receive $100 a day for each day during which he is engaged in the actual performance of his duties as a member of the Council. A member of the Council who is an officer or employee of the Federal Government shall serve without additional compensation. All members of the Council shall be reimbursed for travel, subsistence, and other necessary expenses incurred by them in the performance of such duties.

SEC. 8.

Nothing in this legislation shall be construed to restrict or infringe upon the authority of any Federal department or agency.

SEC. 9.

Subchapter III of Chapter 73 of title 5, United States Code, shall apply to the employees of the Committee and the employees of the Advisory Council.

SEC. 10.

There are hereby authorized to be appropriated for fiscal years 1970 and 1971 such sums as may be necessary to carry out the provisions of this Act, and any funds heretofore and hereafter made available for expenses of the Interagency Committee on Mexican American Affairs established by the President's memorandum of June 9, 1967, shall be available for the purposes of this Act.

SEC. 11.

The Committee shall, as soon as practicable, after the end of each fiscal year, submit a report to the President and the

Congress of its activities for the preceding year, including in such report any recommendations the Committee deems appropriate to accomplish the purposes of this Act.

SEC. 12. This Act shall expire five years after it becomes effective.
Approved December 30, 1969.

LEGISLATIVE HISTORY:

HOUSE REPORT No. 91-699 (Comm. on Government Operations).
SENATE REPORT No. 91-422 (Comm. on Government Operations).
CONGRESSIONAL RECORD, Vol. 115 (1969):
Sept. 25: Considered and passed Senate.
Dec. 16: Considered and passed House, amended.
Dec. 18: Senate concurred in House amendments.

APPENDIX B: THE WHITE HOUSE WASHINGTON

May 24, 1971

Dear Henry:

You wrote most thoughtfully in response to my request for ideas and suggestions about the Spanish speaking people and their concerns, and about the related beneficial public action that the Executive Branch of Government should take. Please accept my gratitude and appreciation for this response as well as for your participation in the discussions we initiated in my office last Monday.

This set of exchanges has been both instructive and constructive, as you know, and your contributions helped very much.

With my thanks, and with all good wishes,

Sincerely

Robert H. Finch
Counselor to the President

Mr. Henry Ramirez
Chief, Mexican American Studies Division
United States Commission on Civil Rights
Washington, D.C. 20425

APPENDIX C

August 5, 1971 Minutes of the First Meeting of the
Cabinet Committee on Opportunities for Spanish
Speaking People

Cabinet Room, The White House

The meeting convened at 12:00 noon.

Counselor Robert Finch opened the meeting by thanking the departments represented for their prompt responses to turning in their reports.

The President arrived at 12:10 p.m. Counselor Finch suggested that the President begin, inasmuch as he was considerably behind schedule. The President, however, asked that Counselor Finch say a few words regarding the organization and progress of the Cabinet Committee for the benefit of the Cabinet Committee members present.

Counselor Finch spoke for a few minutes of the activities of the Federal government for Spanish Speaking Americans. He said that the name of the game is to upgrade Spanish speaking people in all areas of Federal activity. He mentioned the proposed regional conferences.

The President then asked about Federal activities outside of the proposed regional meetings. Mr. Finch mentioned that thus far the major emphasis has been on bilingual education programs, which had the greatest impact on Spanish speaking Americans.

The President then addressed his remarks to the members of the Cabinet Committee:

"I have said before around this very Cabinet table–that there has not been enough follow-through in our efforts for the Spanish speaking Americans. There has not been enough pressure from the media, from Congress, and from within Spanish speaking communities themselves compared to the pressure exerted by other minority groups.

In government, only those groups that raise hell and threaten, "You either do something or we will blow the place up", get any attention. This has been particularly true during the 60's and the early 70's. Let me be very candid about this. I am not suggesting that any group which has not had an equal chance should be disorderly. We do not suggest that individuals under any circumstances roll over and be nice guys and not complain. The political reality is that whether dealing with Congress, or Federal agencies, we should make an all-out effort to rectify our record."

The President then turned to Henry Ramirez and commented that they both had started out at the bottom. Mr. Ramirez said that he had picked oranges and made 100 boxes per day. The President said, "You can't afford to be in government!" (laughter)

The President continued: "What has happened here is this: Mexican Americans, Puerto Ricans, etc. are an important factor in our total economic output, and considering what they can do, they are not getting their fair shake with regard to other groups.

This is going to change. It can only change if the members of the Cabinet get off their duffs. I don't want this administration to be one that only responds to those who tear up the place and pound fists. It just happens that in recent times we have had some very disturbing experiences in Los Angeles and other places. I am speaking now to the Mexican American community; for when I lived in Whittier, I had very close ties with this group. They were family oriented, law abiding people. Although they did need attention, the wheel was not squeaking much. This has to change. We owe it to all groups in society to see they get an equal chance, especially those who have been law abiding people.

You have not had an effective lobby. I told Henry that you need a lobby. You should have it, but we should not wait until a lobby is set up. In terms of jobs, we must urge agencies to fill their slots with Spanish speaking people. We have to search for openings–we should g out and find good slots and fill them. We must find the applicants–they don't apply because they think it is hopeless.

The thing I want to get across to those who are non-government is that I urge all minority groups–women, blacks, Mexican Americans–to use your capabilities and improve them. We aren't providing opportunities just as a favor to you. We must keep America competitive. We are pricing ourselves out of the world markets. Twenty-five years ago we were first in everything--today the world is totally changed. Our former enemies are now our major competitors in the free world. The players are new–Western Europe, Japan, China, the Soviet Union, and potentially Latin America and Africa.

Twenty-five years from now, whoever is sitting in this chair will be representing the second or third strongest country unless we develop all our resources. We must develop our human resources. I would like for every American in this country, whatever his background, to have an equal opportunity to develop to the fullest of his capacity. We cannot afford to have any group in this country not have an equal opportunity to develop their capability.

The government must assume this responsibility–private business does not move as fast in developing opportunities. We must provide opportunities not presently available where there is a great need for new talent.

The Mexican American does not have that chance now. That is going to change or the people in the personnel offices in every department are going to change.

Don's wait until the wheet squeaks–or something is blown up in Los Angeles. Provide opportunitity until there is not one scintilla of suggestion that we are not only <u>not</u> discriminatory, but are making positive moves to rectify the situation. Everyone has a better chance in this country to get an equal break. In government, we have an ever greater opportunity.

I want Bob to follow up, and Henry too. It is the only way to work in the future. I want quarterly reports from both of you concerning the progress of each agency–and also their failures.

The President left the room at this point.

Henry Ramirez then introduced the new members of the Advisory Council to the Cabinet Committee on Opportunities for Spanish Speaking People. Mr. Ramirez then gave a brief talk. He thanked the various member departments and agencies for their reports submitted to Counselor Finch. He then outlined his goals and directions for the Cabinet Committee.

MESSAGE TO SECRETARIES

While studying the Annual Report from the Secretaries to the Cabinet Committee, I discovered that many departments and agencies are demonstrating an increasing awareness and sensitivity to the Spanish Speaking population as a distinct minority group. Programs are in progress, dollars are being spent, and many more activities are being planned to meet the specific needs of this group. We should now build on this positive beginning; the Spanish Speaking people of this country have their eyes on this Presidential committee with hopeful expectations for the type of programs and policies that you have begun.

As I see it, the keystones for success of this Committee are threefold:

First, we must seek to define the status quo regarding the Spanish Speaking people and government today. All departments and agencies must begin a concerted effort to assess the status quo – the extent that Spanish Speaking people receive the benefits of your agencies in terms of employment and delivery of services.

Second, these numerical facts must then be compared with other major segments of our population to determine whether they are proportionate and fair. Where discrepancies exist, quantitative goals must be developed to be filled (within a realistic time frame) to eliminate inequalities.

Finally, the third keystone to the success of the Committee is continuing quarterly assessments of our progress towards meeting our predetermined goals. To carry out this three-pronged approach, let me recommend immediate specific actions on the part of all the Secretaries/Committee members.

Each Secretary could appoint a task force with the responsibility of defining quantitative goals in terms of employment and delivery of services to the Spanish Speaking. The resulting task force reports would then be submitted for consideration at our quarterly meetings. In addition, the Annual Report should be updated quarterly to reflect progress of the Committee.

In addition, the regional offices of departments and agencies should be alerted of projected trips by Counselor Finch and myself in order to become acquainted with their specific activities and goals.

Finally, I recommend that substantial sums immediately be set aside for the purpose of active recruitment of Spanish Speaking individuals for Federal employment.

The Cabinet Committee staff also has definite responsibilities to the Secretaries. The staff of your Committee will strive in every way possible to accurately reflect the aspirations and expectations of the Spanish speaking community with mature and sober judgment for your perspective. And just as the Committee reflects community sentiment to you, it also mirrors your images, credits, and downfalls to the community. In other words, the Committee is the community's barometer of the progress or the lack of it, made by your departments and agencies.

It is my firm conviction that we must continue our work in a most business-like manner, with a definition of the status quo, the development of definite strategies and goals, and the charting of our progress from quarter to quarter. We must make this a living Committee–when it is not possible for a Secretary to be present at a quarterly meeting, you should make every attempt to send a high-level policy maker to fully represent you.

I am here as your Chairman to help you make this Committee a success. It has already failed once–we can not fail our President and our constituency a second time. When we success in serving the Spanish Speaking people, the President and our country will reap the rewards of honest service.

MEMBERS OF THE FIRST CABINET COMMITTEE MEETING ON OPPORTUNITIES FOR THE SPANISH SPEAKING PEOPLE

Members of the Committee who were present at the 1st Cabinet Committee on Opportunities for Spanish Speaking People, that President Richard M. Nixon convened, were:

Secretary of Agriculture, Clifford M. Hardin

Secretary of Commerce, Maurice H. Stans

Secretary of Labor, James D. Hodgson

Undersecretary of Health, Education and Welfare, John Veneman

Assistant Secretary of Health, Education and Welfare, Patricia Hitt

Secretary of Housing and Urban Development, George Romney

Assistant Secretary of the Treasury, Charls Walker

Attorney General, John Mitchell

Director of the Office of Economic Opportunity, Phillip V. Sanchez

Administrator of the Small Business Administration, Thomas Kleppe

Chairman of the Civil Service Commission, Robert Hampton

APPENDIX D: THE STUDY

AN OVERVIEW OF SPANISH SPEAKING AFFAIRS FOR WHITE HOUSE PERSPECTIVE

SUMMARY OF CONTENTS

INTRODUCTION

A.   A description of demographic characteristics and geographic concentrations of the Mexican American, Puerto Rican, Cuban and Latin American populations.

B   A brief description of the cultural characteristics which unify all Spanish speaking peoples, such as language, heritage and ethnic pride.

C.   Spanish speaking Americans have been isolated from the mainstream of America and the Federal government has until recently lacked the awareness and sensitivity to deal effectively with the issues of vital concern to this large minority population.

SEVEN MAJOR AREAS OF CONCERN WITH REGARD TO THE SPANISH SPEAKING

I. OFFICIAL RECOGNITION OF THE SPANISH SPEAKING

A. Identification of the Spanish Speaking as a distinct minority group.

    1. It is difficult to determine whether the Spanish speaking are receiving equal opportunities in all areas because of the fact that they were not counted in the 1970 Census and because departments and agencies have not traditionally tabulated their program data on the basis of ethnicity.

    2. It is recommended that all departments and agencies keep uniform records of program eligibility and programs on the basis of ethnicity.

B. Recognition of Spanish speaking religious leaders.

    1. For the first time since the nineteenth century, the Spanish speaking are represented by two very popular and influential Bishops: Bishop Juan Arzube in Los Angeles, and Bishop Patrick Flores in Brownsville, Texas.

    2. It is recommended that the President invite one of these Spanish speaking Bishops to the Nation's capitol to conduct a White House Sunday Service.

C. Recognition of Spanish speaking Representatives in Congress

    1. It is recommended that the President recognize Spanish speaking government officials by inviting

them to a White House meeting to discuss issues of relevance to the Spanish speaking communities.

D.   Recognition of the farm labor issue

    1.   The issue of the unionization of farm laborers is one that is close to the hearts of the Spanish speaking throughout the entire Southwest. This is an issue that has received strong support from the Church.

    2.   It is suggested that the President announce a position sympathetic to the farm workers and initiate steps for the National Labor Relations Board to take jurisdiction over farm workers.

II. THE CABINET COMMITTEE ON OPPORTUNITIES FOR THE SPANISH SPEAKING

A.   A summary statement of the origin, background and present status of the Committee.

B.   A list of the strengths of the Committee, including its importance to the community, its vital role as an advocate for Spanish speaking affairs, and its role as the focal point for the increasing emergence of the Puerto Rican and Cubans.

C.   A list of the weaknesses of the Committee, including limitations imposed upon it by its mandate as an advocacy body, the lack of Administration support, its inability to fulfill the mandate to meet with cabinet officials, and the lack of participation by Spanish speaking groups other than Mexican Americans.

D. A list of recommended actions designed to strengthen the Committee by developing competent leadership, visible support within the Administration and a high level of credibility from Spanish speaking communities.

III. WHITE HOUSE CONFERENCE ON MEXICAN AMERICAN AFFAIRS

A. A summary of the origin of the conference and its present status.

B. A list of advantages of holding the conference from both the Administration and Spanish speaking points of view.

C. A list of disadvantages of holding such a conference at this time including the lack of time for organization, the possibility of disruption, the anger of the Puerto Ricans as a result of being excluded from the proceedings, and the likelihood of producing meaningful results for the Spanish speaking.

D. It is recommended that the conference be held, regardless of size, scope or content, to fulfill the technical commitment to the Spanish speaking.

It is also recommended that the White House Conference not be limited solely to Mexican Americans, and that every effort be made to produce concrete results.

IV. GOVERNMENT EMPLOYMENT

A. A summary of the Federal government's efforts to date to provide increased employment for the Spanish speaking, including the 16-Point Program and the White House Minority Recruitment Program.

B.   Recommended actions include high-level executive appointments by the President, the effective implementation of the 16-Point Program through the fulfillment of specific goals within a time frame, and intensified recruitment efforts.

V. EDUCATION

A.   A statistical description of the low achievement of Spanish speaking students and their propensity to drop out sooner and in larger numbers.

B.   A summary of government activity to date with regard to increased opportunities in education for Spanish speaking students. These efforts include bilingual education, the HEW Office of Civil Rights Memorandum (May 25, 1970), and the U. S. Commission on Civil Rights' Mexican American Education Study.

C.   Recommendations for action include a Presidential statement on quality education for the Spanish speaking, increased emphasis and funding for bilingual education programs, and intensified work on the Mexican American Education Study.

VI. HOUSING

A.   Statistical evidence of the inadequacy of HUD's activities to date with regard to housing for the Spanish speaking.

B. Specific recent activities which indicate increased awareness of Spanish speaking needs and progress toward meeting them. These activities include Spanish speaking appointments, and contracts with Spanish speaking groups, and a description of the Los Angeles Program, a model plan serving Chicanos and Blacks.

C. Recommendations for action include a Spanish speaking housing program at HUD, White House recognition of the Los Angeles Program, and the fulfillment of reasonable quotas for housing for the Spanish speaking.

VII. ECONOMIC DEVELOPMENT

A. Statistical evidence of the low economic status of the Spanish speaking nationwide.

B. Reports from the Office of Economic Opportunity, the Small Business Administration, the National Economic Development Association and the Executive Branch, summarizing their efforts and progress toward providing increased economic opportunities for the Spanish speaking.

C. Recommendations for action include Presidential appointments of Spanish speaking persons to the Federal Home Loan Bank Board and the creation of ten-year goals for the establishment of minority banks and savings and loan associations. In addition, it is recommended that 33% of the SBA budget be allocated for the Spanish speaking, that increased efforts be made to encourage Spanish speaking youth to pursue careers in business.

CONTENTS

INTRODUCTION

SIX MAJOR AREAS OF CONCERN WITH REGARD TO THE SPANISH SPEAKING MINORITY

I. OFFICIAL RECOGNITION OF THE SPANISH SPEAKING

A. Recognition of the Spanish Speaking as a National Minority Population

B. Recognition of Spanish speaking Religious Leaders

C. Recognition of Spanish speaking Representatives to Congress

D. Recognition of the Farm Labor Issue

II. THE CABINET COMMITTEE ON OPPORTUNITY FOR THE SPANISH SPEAKING

A. Background and Present Status

B. Strengths of the Committee

C. Weaknesses of the Committee

D. Recommended Action: Strengthen the Committee

III. WHITE HOUSE CONFERENCE ON MEXICAN AMERICAN AFFAIRS

A. Background and Present Status

B. Advantages of Holding the Conference

C. Disadvantages of Holding the Conference

D. Recommendation for Action

IV. GOVERNMENT EMPLOYMENT

A. Background and Present Status

B. Recommendations for Action

V. EDUCATION

A. Background and Present Status

B. Recommendations for Action

VI. HOUSING

A. Background and Present Status

B. Recommendations for Action

VII. ECONOMIC DEVELOPMENT

APPENDICES

1. Public Law 91-181

2. Cabinet Committee Organizational Chart and Budget

3. White House Memorandum, February 5, 1971

4. Presidential Statement Announcing White House Conference on Mexican American Affairs

5. List of Task Force Members for Proposed White House Conference

6. 16-Point Program for Spanish Speaking Employment in the Federal Government
7. Spanish Speaking Persons Occupying Super Grade Positions in each Department and Agency
8. Bilingual Education Act
9. Bilingual Education Expenditures and List of Programs
10. HEW Office of Civil Rights May 25, 1970 Memorandum

SEVEN MAJOR AREAS OF CONCERN WITH REGARD TO THE SPANISH SPEAKING

INTRODUCTION

There are nearly 12 million persons of Hispanic origin residing in the United States today. Spanish surnamed Americans comprise approximately 5 percent of the total U. S. population, reside in nearly every state in the country, and are increasing at a faster rate than the general population. They are a permanent, substantial and increasingly important segment of the U.S. population and economy.

The Spanish speaking population is comprised of several distinct groups. The largest portion is the 7 million Mexican Americans who find their roots in the Indo-Hispanic heritage of the Southwest. They reside primarily in the five Southwestern states, although there are now sizeable concentrations of Mexican Americans in Chicago, Kansas City, and in the states of Nevada, Indiana and Washington. The second largest group is the 1.3 million Puerto Ricans who represent 16 percent of the total U.S. Spanish speaking population. Primarily urban, 90 percent of the mainland Puerto Ricans live along the eastern seaboard, with about 65 percent concentrated in the New York metropolitan area. The present Cuban population, now estimated at between 500,000 and 800,000 persons, is located primarily in the Miami area (50 percent) and in New York and New Jersey.

In addition to these three large groups, there are nearly 2 million other Spanish speaking persons who have immigrated from Spain and Central and South America. The Washington D.C. area boasts one of the largest Latin communities with an estimated 75,000 persons.

Although there are significant differences among the various Spanish speaking groups, this population demonstrates many unifying qualities. Regardless of origin, Spanish speaking Americans are generally characterized by a strong family structure, deep religious ties, a rather conservative political outlook and an ethnic pride which often takes the appearance of resistance to linguistic and cultural assimilation. The strong cultural identity of the Spanish speaking is largely the result of the physical proximity of the U.S. to Mexico, Puerto Rico and Cuba which is conducive to the constant reinforcement of linguistic and cultural ties to the mother country while providing a steady flow of immigrants.

Because of their language, ethnic pride and skin color, Spanish speaking Americans have traditionally stood apart from the core of American society. Their severe isolation is felt most strongly today in the realm of government, education and economic development. Because they have not yet been "dealt in," the Spanish speaking consider themselves (and are considered by many) to be outsiders. As non-participants, they have neither the opportunity nor the resources to work toward a productive solution to their many unique problems.

Following the pattern of the Blacks, the Spanish speaking are becoming increasingly cognizant of the critical effects of their isolation. Sentiment in Hispanic communities has evolved with time from acceptance of their estrangement to deepening concern and, finally, to outrage among some of the more vocal elements. Unfortunately, however, most policy-makers have remained largely unaware of the untapped potential within Spanish speaking communities. Lacking the necessary knowledge and sensitivity, they have been unsuccessful in dealing with the issues which are of vital concern to this large minority population. Consistent oversights or inadequacies in funding, employment opportunities and the planning of national priorities have generated a good deal of skepticism with regard to the sincerity of this Administration's concern for their welfare.

The President has expressed his desire to see the Federal government respond more effectively to the Spanish speaking. Firm initiative and leadership can be demonstrated toward this end by establishing national goals and priorities and fulfilling them systematically within a time frame. The following discussion of major issues and recommendations for action are designed to provide positive outcomes for the Spanish speaking and maximum visibility for this Administration. It is infinitely more productive to act aggressively now than to have to risk having to react negatively in the future. It is therefore propitious, expedient and in the best interests of the nation as a whole for the Federal government to take swift positive measures to assure the provision of equal opportunities to the Spanish speaking and the incorporation of this population into the American political and economic structure as full participants and beneficiaries.

I. OFFICIAL RECOGNITION OF THE SPANISH SPEAKING

Presidential identification and acknowledgment of Spanish speaking leaders, heritage and culture-related issues is an essential preliminary step toward the full acceptance and incorporation of this population. Through a series of swift highly visible actions, the President can effectively bring the Spanish speaking, and his commitment to them, into sharp national focus.

A. Identification of the Spanish speaking as a distinct minority group

    1. Background

The effectiveness of an organized society to provide fairly for all its citizens irrespective of color or national origin can only be measured statistically. This is part of the rationale of the Census. There at present, however, no adequate accounting procedures to determine whether or not Spanish speaking persons are benefiting equally from the fruits of the commonwealth. The 1970 Census contained only a 5% sample directed toward the identification of the Spanish speaking and is considered inadequate because the questionnaires were printed in English, relied on self-identification and passed over large pockets of migrants and other groups. In February of 1971, the Census Bureau issued a partial survey of Spanish-surnamed population in the United States (Population characteristics, Persons of Spanish Origin in the United States. November, 1969). The survey was based on interviews with a limited number of families but due to the small sample and potential error factor, it contains no breakdown by states.

At the departments and agencies, the situation regarding Mexican Americans is much the same. Most program data tabulations have not been kept on the basis of ethnicity and consequently there are few statistics available to policy-makers to assist them in insuring that the flow of services, contracts and assistance are equitable under the concept of equal opportunities.

2. Recommended Action

a. There is little that can be done at this point about the exclusion of Spanish speaking in the Census. In the departments and agencies, however, each program of assistance of the Federal government should have an established procedure for knowing the number of persons, by ethnicity and income, participating in each project or activity receiving assistance. This data should be collected as a regular part of program operations, and tabulated on both a project-wide and program-wide basis.

b. In support of this effort, the Office of Management and Budget should issue a directive or instructions requiring each agency's budget submission to contain participation data by ethnicity and income for each project seeking funding.

B. Recognition of Spanish speaking religious leaders

1. Background

The Spanish speaking population by and large identifies with the Church; their basic conservatism and moral values are essentially Catholic. Although the influence of the Church is diminishing among Spanish speaking college students as it is throughout the nation, it is still a very strong viable force among mature voters and working-class youth.

For the first time since 1850, there is a Mexican American Bishop, Patrick Flores, in Brownsville, Texas and a Latin

American Bishop, Juan Arzube, in Los Angeles. Both these clergymen strongly identify with all Spanish speaking people and are active advocates of issues which affect this minority. As a result, they enjoy a large measure of warmth, respect, and influence in Spanish speaking communities.

2. Recommended action.

The allegiance of the Spanish speaking to this country "under God" has not yet been recognized in the respected White House Sunday services. An invitation to Bishop Flores or Bishop Arzube to conduct a service for the President would evoke an immediate positive response from Spanish speaking communities, particularly if it were well publicized. Such a gesture would also be a demonstration of great sensitivity on the part of the President, for he would be recognizing the heritage of the Spanish speaking Americans whose traditions include strong religious ties.

C. Recognition of Spanish speaking representatives in Congress

1. It is suggested that the President invite the Spanish speaking senator and congressmen to a White House meeting to discuss issues, concerns, and actions affecting the Nation's second largest minority. The occasion would serve to focus attention on the President's commitment to the Spanish speaking and would further the growth of awareness within the government for the needs of this population. Moreover, such a gesture would sensitize government officials as well as the Spanish speaking to the President's true concern and awareness of the Spanish speaking.

There may be an attempt by some to equate this meeting to the Black Congressional Caucus. The positive salient difference, however, is that this meeting would be an *action*, not a *reaction*, by the White House. Proper publicity could use this distinction to excellent advantage.

D. Recognition of the Farm Labor Issue

1. Background

The vast majority of the Spanish speaking Americans of the Southwest, Midwest and Northeast regions have at one time or another been farm workers. These people have empathy with the plight of the farm workers and are supportive of the unionization of farm workers. The few affluent and middle class Chicanos who have not experienced the hardships of stoop labor have in the past been resistant or indifferent to this cause, but there has been a shift in favor of the movement in the past year or so.

The Catholic Church became involved in the grape pickers' strike in California. The Church supported Cesar Chavez and was instrumental in concluding the strike in that state. Many members of the Catholic Hierarchy became involved in this issue, including Bishop Juan Arzube of Los Angeles, Bishop Patrick Flores of Brownsville, Texas, Archbishop Ted Manning of Los Angeles, and Archbishop McGuchen of San Francisco. Cesar has been successful in enlisting the moral support and leadership of the Catholic Church in California. It appears to be only a matter of time before his drive for farm unionization becomes nationwide with similar support.

2. Recommended Action

Announce a carefully-worded position favorable to the farm workers, and initiate steps for the National Labor Relations Board to take jurisdiction over farm workers. This is the single most dramatic action the President could make to build a high level of credibility with the Spanish speaking population. This single action could swing the critical margins in California and Texas for '72.

II. THE CABINET COMMITTEE ON OPPORTUNITIES FOR THE SPANISH SPEAKING

A. Background and present status

In 1967 the Inter-Agency Committee on Mexican American Affairs was created by Presidential memorandum. Its purpose was to serve as an ombudsman for Mexican Americans and as a liaison between Mexican American communities and Federal officials. So that the Committee might have a greater sense of continuity, legislation was introduced in 1969 to make it a statutory organization. Its earlier mandate was retained, but its programs were expanded to include all Spanish speaking Americans and it was renamed "The Cabinet Committee on Opportunity for the Spanish Speaking." The legislation passed Congress on December 10, 1969, and was signed into law by President Nixon on December 30. (Refer to Tab 1 for text of Public Law 81-191)

The Cabinet Committee now has an annual operating budget of approximately $600,000 and is served by a staff of thirty and by consultants loaned from other areas of the Federal government. (Refer to Tab 2 for organizational chart and budget) The 12-member Committee headed by the Chairman and made of Cabinet members and Commissioners of selected agencies, is required to meet four times a year to review the problems of the Spanish speaking and the progress which has been made toward meeting them. The Committee has been authorized for five years, after which time legislation must be re-enacted to retain its existence.

In spite of laudable intentions and high expectations, it is generally conceded by the Administration and Spanish speaking alike that the Committee has not been effective to date in fulfilling its function for Spanish speaking citizens. As was brought out in a February 5, 1971 White House memorandum, (Refer to Tab 3 for full text) this Administration has considered eliminating the Committee altogether for the following reasons:

    a. It has had no Chairman for several months and, hence, no effective leadership;

    b. It has appointed no advisory council, as is mandated by law;

    c. It has never met with Cabinet members in this Administration, although quarterly meetings are stipulated by law;

    d. It has a dubious track record, although it is admittedly difficult to make a quantitative judgment of an advisory body.

    B. Strengths of the Committee

    1. Public Law 81-191 delineates several functions which are vital to the interests of the Spanish speaking of this country. (Tab 1) The mandate of the Committee is: "to assure that Federal Programs are reaching all Mexican Americans, Puerto Rican Americans, Cuban Americans, and all other Spanish speaking and Spanish surnamed Americans and provide the assistance that they need, and to seek new programs that they may be necessary to handle such persons."

    2. The Cabinet Committee was intended to be a concrete symbol of the Federal government's awareness and commitment to the special problems of the Spanish speaking. Many "grass roots" individuals see it as the most important Federal body which exists solely for their benefit.

    3. Spanish speaking community leaders perceive the Committee as the primary point of contact between the community and the Federal government. It often acts as

a beacon which guides those who might otherwise become lost in the Federal labyrinth.

4. It serves as the focal point for the emerging role of the Puerto Ricans, Cubans and Latins. The Committee can help sensitize government officials with regard to the specific needs of these groups in the same way that it has helped Mexican Americans to some degree in this area during the past few years.

C. Weaknesses of the Committee

1. The Cabinet Committee is crippled by its sole function as an advocacy body. Public Law 91-181 prescribes on the one hand that it is the purpose of the Committee to "assure" that Federal programs are reaching all Spanish speaking Americans, yet it does not give the Committee power to carry out that mandate. The Committee is strictly an advisory body and as such has no power or recourse when departments and agencies choose not to listen. (Refer to Sections 3, 4, 5 of Public Law 91-181). This apparent contradiction is the source of considerable conflict since the Spanish speaking expect delivery of services from this body and have become angry and frustrated at the discovery that the agency which represents them takes on the appearance of an influential mendicant.

2. The fact that the "Cabinet" Committee has never, in reality, met with Cabinet level officials or with their representatives as mandated by law is interpreted by the Spanish speaking as an index of the Administration's lack of responsiveness to Spanish speaking issues and problems.

3. The Committee has not been the responsibility of any specific high-level member of the Presidential staff; hence, no one has felt clearly and solely responsible for its success or failure. The Spanish speaking in government perceive the role of the

Committee in this Administration as one of a neglected step-child, conceived and fostered under another Administration, with no present means of moral support.

4. From the Puerto Rican point of view, the gravest shortcoming of the Committee is that its policies, programs and staffing patterns have consistently favored Mexican Americans to the near total exclusion of other Spanish speaking groups. This issue has generated a great deal of resentment, particularly in Puerto Rican communities, and has been a constant source of divisiveness among the Spanish speaking.

D. Recommendation for Action: Strengthen the Committee

1. Appoint a competent and imaginative chairman. Notwithstanding its role as an advocacy body, the Cabinet Committee could be much more effective with forceful administration and planning on the part of the Chairman and Executive Director. For maximum effectiveness, it is recommended that the Chairman possess the following essential qualities and characteristics:

> a. Respect and support among the various segments of the Spanish speaking community—businessmen, community leaders, professionals, government officials, etc;
>
> b. Acceptance from the different Spanish speaking groups—Puerto Ricans, Cubans, and Latins;
>
> c. Acceptance on the Hill;
>
> d. Verbal and written fluency in Spanish and English;
>
> e. Mexican American ethnic heritage. By tradition and because of the extremely large Mexican American population, the Chairman be Chicano.

2. Assign the Chairman the additional title of Special Assistant to the President, and locate him in the White House.

Regardless of the competence of the Chairman, he must also have the power and influence of the White House behind him at all times to be truly effective. As a Special Assistant, the influence and prestige of the Chairman will be greatly augmented among Federal policy-makers, and the President's commitment to the Spanish speaking will be highly visible in Spanish speaking communities. While the Executive Director assumes the day to day administration of the Committee, the Chairman will assume policy responsibilities over the broad spectrum of Spanish speaking affairs.

3. Include the Chairman in meetings of the Domestic Council. As symbolic head of the nation's 12 million Spanish speaking citizens, the Chairman of the Cabinet Committee should be an active participant in the decisions and policies affecting domestic issues. Again, this is a visible demonstration of the President's commitment to the Spanish speaking.

4. Make an overt affirmation of Presidential support with extensive national publicity. The visibility of the Committee must be maximized in every state and region.

5. Hold the Chairman accountable to *one* high-level individual on the President's Executive staff (e.g., Finch, Erlichman). This will eliminate the confusion and buck-passing which has been so prevalent in this Administration with regard to the Cabinet Committee.

6. The Committee staff must be representative of all Spanish speaking and Spanish –surnamed people in ratio to the percentage each group represents in the population.

7. The Committee must strive in every way possible to communicate to the Chicano, Puerto Rican and Cuban its role and function in order to create realistic expectations from these communities.

8. Energetic and tactful efforts by the Committee will assure awareness and sensitivity toward the Spanish speaking in the critical area of civil rights. The Committee must therefore emphasize its advocacy role with regard to the U.S.C.C.R., E.E.O.C., C, R, S., O.F.C.C. and all civil rights efforts.

III. WHITE HOUSE CONFERENCE ON MEXICAN AMERICAN AFFAIRS

A. Background and present status

1. During the 1968 Presidential campaign, the President promised to convene a White House Conference on Mexican American Affairs "promptly after taking office." (Refer to Tab 4)

2. It was agreed that the Cabinet Committee was the agency with the best resources to organize such a conference.

3. After Martin Castillo left the Committee, Antonio Rodriguez was appointed Executive Director of the Conference.

4. It was suggested that the Conference should be retitled the "White House Conference for Spanish Speaking Americans," so that all Spanish speaking groups would be represented, but no final decision has been made on this question. At present the conference appears to be limited to the President's strict commitment to Mexican Americans alone.

5. Tentative lists of participants have been drawn up and six task forces have been assembled which are studying specific issues of vital concern to the Spanish speaking. (See Tab 5 for lists of task force members) the areas covered by the task forces are: Manpower, Economic Development, Education, Housing, Migrants and Employment. The reports from the Manpower, Housing and Economic Development Task forces have been

completed, and the remaining reports are expected to reach completion by July 1, 1971.

6. A February 5, 1971 White House memorandum (Refer to Tab 3) summarized this Administration's grave misgivings about the desirability of holding such a conference at this time. Although it was acknowledged that the promise to convene the conference was unequivocal and that some concrete benefit might result from such a meeting, the primary argument for not holding the conference was that it is "a sure recipe for trouble: with its myriad opportunities for confrontation politics the inevitable proximity to 1972 would force it toward political theatrics."

B. Advantages of Holding the Conference

1. The concept of "cumplir con su palabra" holds much deeper significance for the Spanish speaking than for most Americans in general. Once a promise has been made, it must be kept if a man, particularly the President, is to be respected by the Community as a man of his word. In view of the fact that the President does not enjoy the full confidence and support of Mexican Americans at this time, the withdrawal of his promise to meet with Chicano leaders to discuss issues of critical importance to the Spanish speaking world is more than likely to cause irrevocable damage to his credibility and popularity with this population.

2. The task force reports already in progress may be utilized as the foundation for a conference. They represent the knowledge and expertise of Spanish speaking experts in each area under consideration. The task force reports not only contain summary statements of critical issues, but also include specific recommendations which, if acted upon soon after the conference, would evoke an immediate positive reaction from Spanish speaking communities.

C. Disadvantages of Holding the Conference

1. Mexican Americans will be cynical. Many feel that they have already been "studied to death" and that nothing tangible has resulted from all the talk. It is rather unlikely that new issues will emerge, for they have been defined and redefined in the past.

2. There will be great difficulty in organizing a balanced and representative conference. The Mexican Americans are splintered into so many factions that it will be next to impossible to have all interests represented. At the same time, the vast majority of Mexican Americans are registered Democrats; the conference would have to be bi-partisan to really represent a respectable number of Mexican Americans.

3. A national conference is wide open to disruptions from radical Chicano groups or other factions which could seriously harm the Administration, as was the case during President Johnson's Mexican American Conference in El Paso.

4. By including only Mexican Americans, the President is inviting severe criticism and possible disruption from other Spanish speaking groups, particularly the Puerto Ricans.

5. It is very likely that such a conference cannot be planned well in such a short time. To avoid the obvious weakness of being perceived as purely political in intent, the Conference must not be held later than January 1972.

D. Recommendations for Action

1. The issue at hand is not the size, scope, or content of a White House Conference, so much as the technical fulfillment of a commitment to the Spanish speaking people. It is extremely doubtful if the people in the communities themselves actually remember the President's campaign promise, but the opposition will most certainly make it an issue and as painlessly as possible. This can be accomplished by inviting a select group of Spanish

speaking businessmen, educators and community leaders to discuss areas of major concern in Spanish speaking communities.

2. It is essential that a gathering of this nature include representatives of *all* Spanish speaking groups; the exclusion of Puerto Ricans would do more harm than good by exposing the President to severe criticism and by fostering severe divisiveness among the Spanish speaking groups. On the other hand, proportionate representation presents a great opportunity for all Spanish speaking people to work together toward common goals with the President.

3. Prove that this Administration really can be an effective problem-solving mechanism for the Spanish speaking by assuring that something concrete results from the meeting. The implementation of task force recommendations, a special message to Congress or grant approvals are all suggested possibilities for action.

IV. GOVERNMENT EMPLOYMENT

A. The fact that the Spanish speaking are severely under-represented in significant policy-making position in their own government is an issue that has merited direct action on the part of the President. This Administration has made a concerted effort to begin filling the vacuum of Spanish speaking policy-makers; as a result, more Spanish speaking persons now occupy key positions than ever before.

To assist Spanish speaking persons interested in obtaining Federal employment the President announced the 16 Point Program in November, 1970. Administered by the U.S. Civil Service Commission as an integral part of the government-wide Equal Employment Opportunity program, the 16 Point Program provides for intensified recruitment, improved training opportunities, upward mobility and other measures designed to improve opportunities in the Federal service for Spanish speaking citizens.

On January 18, 1971, Fernando C. de Baca was appointed Equal Employment Opportunity Adviser to the Civil Service Commission to carry out the Program. The 16 Point Program is regarded as a firm commitment in Spanish speaking communities, and every effort must be made to assure its swift implementation and success. Chairman Hampton has initiated several approaches to (Refer to Tab 6 for full text of 16 Point Program) insure that the program does not fail, but plans are not being implemented effectively by those assigned responsibilities in this area. (Interview, 4/25 Fernando C. de Baca)

In addition to the 16 Point Program, the White House Minority Recruitment Program has been mobilized for action under the direction of Fred Malek. Three minority recruiting teams have been formed to respond to the very high-level Presidential appointment searches. Limited Talent Banks have also been developed, containing information which will be disseminated to each of the departments as soon as they have proposed their specific minority recruiting plans.

Although this Administration has made strides in this area, there is still a great deal to be done before Spanish speaking enjoy an equitable share of the leadership positions in the Federal government. Most of the better-known Spanish speaking Americans in government today do not have line responsibilities, but are staff assistants. Although these individuals play a necessary role in the development of Spanish speaking awareness among the departments and agencies, this function must be regarded as a short term stop-gap measure. At the present time, there are only four Spanish surnamed persons holding high-ranking executive level positions. They are:

Oscar Laurel (Demo.)	Carlos C. Villareal (Repub.)
Member, NTSB	Administrator, UMTA
Department of Transportation	Dept. of Transportation
Level IV	Level III
Louis V. Perez (Repub.)	Vicente Ximenes (Demo.)
Director, Peru	Commissioner
Agency for International Dept.	Equal Employment Opportunities Commission
Level IV	Level IV

Furthermore, in the GS 16-18 super grade positions, there are only 15 Spanish speaking persons in all departments and agencies. This figure represents a mere .2% of the total 8, 125 super grade positions; 5,471 in GS Categories, and 2,656 in other pay systems. (For a complete list of all Spanish speaking persons in super grade and executive positions, refer to Tab 7)

B. Recommendations for Action

1. Require each cabinet member to provide at least one key executive position for a minority person in his department or agency. The machinery is well-tuned to provide able candidates, but these positions have not been made available by the departments and agencies. (Interview 4/26 with Frank Rocco) A Presidential commitment of this nature, successfully carried through, could very well spell out a four year renewal of this Administration.

2. Require periodic review and evaluation of the progress of the progress of the 16 Point Program by Chairman Hampton and the Spanish speaking Presidential Assistant.

3. Require that departments and agencies be held accountable for implementing defined employment goals within a time frame.

4. Utilize the resources of the Cabinet Committee to fulfill the important second point of the Program which reads:

Begin an intensified drive to recruit Spanish surnamed persons, particularly foridentified public contract positions, in areas of heavy Spanish speaking population, including the Southwestern states, and in Chicago, Detroit, and New York, and certain other major metropolitan areas.

The Committee has the resources to reach the Spanish speaking communities nationally in search of competent candidates for positions, and can effectively supplement the recruitment activities of Fernando de Baca at the Civil Service Commission and Fred Malek at the White House.

V. EDUCATION

A. Background and present status

1. Education, the key to economic development and vertical mobility, has the highest priority for Spanish speaking Americans. At present the Spanish speaking student's level of achievement is worse than any other minority group, with the exception of American Indians in some areas of the country. U.S.C.C.R. Statistics reveal that Spanish speaking students in the Southwest achieve at a lower rate than Anglos, their reading achievement is worse, they repeat grades more frequently, and they drop out sooner and in greater numbers than their Anglo classmates. Up to 70 percent of the Mexican American fourth, eighth and twelfth graders are reported to be reading below grade level, compared with 36 percent of the Anglo students.

(U.S.C.C.R. Mexican American Education Study, Unpublished Report, "School Achievement of Minority Students in the Public Schools of the Southwest.") 24 percent of the Spanish speaking twelfth graders in the Southwest are more than three years below grade level in reading. Furthermore, Spanish speaking students have the highest dropout rate of any ethnic group in the country. Of every 100 Mexican American students who enter the first grade, only 60 will graduate from high school, only 1 in 4 continue on to college, while nearly half the Anglo graduates do so. These figures reflect a definite lack of relevance in school curriculum and attitudes for the Spanish speaking student in the American school system.

As a step toward coping with the unique educational problems of Spanish speaking students, this Administration has officially recognized the vital role of bilingual education as a vehicle which permits non-English speaking youth to develop to their full potential as bilingual/bicultural Americans. (Refer to Tab 8) Bilingual education is a concept close to the hearts of most Spanish speaking people and it towers as an example of government sensitivity and concern for equal educational opportunity for Spanish speaking children.

In Fiscal Year 1969, HEW committed 7.5 million for 76 bilingual education programs, sixty-five of which were for the Spanish speaking. (Refer to Tab 9) A breakdown shows that the per-pupil expenditure ranged from $188 in Texas to $1,269 in Colorado. Although this is a laudable beginning, there is a great deal more to be done to provide bilingual education to all students who are in need of it. Most bilingual education today is offered in small scattered pilot programs; U.S.C.C.R. data indicate that in spite of economic support from the Federal government, bilingual education is still reaching only about 29,000 Mexican Americans—only

2.7 percent of the Southwest's Mexican American enrollment. (U.S.C.C.R. unpublished report, "The Excluded Student")

Another significant milestone is the HEW Office of Civil Rights' Memorandum which clarifies the responsibilities of schools with regard to language, tracking, and involvement of Spanish speaking parents (Refer to Tab 10). This office has created a task force to recommend guidelines for bilingual/bicultural education. The Commissioner of Education has also established a task force of prominent Spanish surnamed Americans to submit a report defining specific needed reform for Spanish speaking youth. This report has not been completed at this time.

The U.S. Commission on Civil Rights has conducted a vast comprehensive study of school conditions and practices affecting Mexican American students in the public schools of the Southwest. Although most of the Findings are not yet public, it is expected that this vital information will establish the base line for dramatic educational change.

In the private sector, educators of Spanish speaking background have organized groups such as Aspira, the Assn of Mexican American Educators in California, Hispanic Educators in Colorado and T.E.A.M. in Texas to stimulate improvements in their profession and in their schools. Education is also the highest priority for the quasi-national Spanish speaking organizations such as the G. I. Forum, LULAC and the Puerto Rican Forum.

B. Recommendations for Action

1. The President or the Commissioner of Education should state this Administration's position on quality education for the Spanish speaking.

2. Emphasize the role and significance of bilingual education by increasing the funding of Title VII programs and by requiring

bilingual education components in all funds which are directed toward areas of at least 10 percent Spanish speaking population.

3. Require that all agencies funding educational programs gather data by ethnicity in order to evaluate more effectively the equitable distribution of monies.

4.Encourage the Civil Rights Commission to assign additional personnel to the Mexican American Education Study, to hasten the publication of this significant educational information.

VI. HOUSING

A. Background and present status

Only recently has the Federal government begun to respond to the housing needs of the Spanish speaking Americans, the majority of whom reside in sub-standard, inner-city dwellings. Because program data has generally not been tabulated on the basis of ethnicity, it is extremely difficult to verify the extent to which housing programs are reaching the Spanish speaking.

Statistics recently compiled by the Cabinet Committee indicate that, as a rule, existing Federal programs under the Department of Housing and Urban Development, the Veterans' Administration and the Department of Agriculture are not effectively reaching the Spanish speaking. For example, 51 percent of HUD's Public Housing units are occupied by Blacks, while only six percent are occupied by Spanish speaking families. HUD's estimation of Spanish Americans served in the Neighborhood Facilities Program during the 1970 Fiscal Year was only 3.7 percent. An Indian Housing Program has been established in HUD, yet there is no such program for the Spanish speaking.

On the positive side, however, there are indications of increasing awareness and sensitivity to the Spanish speaking housing problem which have resulted in several specific positive actions:

a. Two HUD area offices (Los Angeles and Dallas) are headed for the first time by Mexican Americans.

b. A 2.1 million dollar construction contract was awarded in October, 1970 to a Mexican American contractor in Denver under FHA's Mortgage Insurance Program. This contract is the largest of its kind ever awarded to a Mexican American contractor.

c. Additional Mexican American sponsored multi-family housing and rehabilitation projects are under consideration in Phoenix, El Paso, San Antonio and Sacramento.

d. A model program has recently emerged from HUD's Los Angeles area office under the direction of Mr. Ray Carrasco. Through the Los Angeles Plan, 10 percent of the total budget was set aside for minority contractors. Black and Chicano contractors in that area benefited equally, with each minority group receiving $11 million. No regional office of HUD had ever before made such significant opportunities available to minorities, yet this is an example which should be followed in all area offices of that Department. In addition, programs of this nature should be strongly encouraged and publicized and given wide White House visibility.

B. Recommendations for action

a. Require that all housing program data be tabulated on the basis of ethnicity.

b. Bob Brown, Counselor Finch and the Chairman of the Cabinet Committee should travel to California as a White House Team to draw public attention to the Los Angeles

Plan as proof that the Federal government can deliver needed services to minorities in an equitable fashion.

c. Determine an administrative goal for the number of housing units that can reasonably be provided to Spanish speaking families under Federal programs and set up a time frame to fulfill that goal.

d. Review for possible adoption the recommendations of the task force paper on housing, which will be completed by July 1, 1971

e. Establish a Spanish speaking housing program at HUD.

VII. ECONOMIC DEVELOPMENT

A. Background and Present status

The Nixon Administration has made a promising start toward relieving the critical economic disadvantage of the Spanish speaking population. OEO data reveal that the poverty incidence of Spanish speaking residents is 64%; in the Southwest, 30.8% of the urban Mexican Americans live in poverty; in rural areas this figure rises to 58.75; in New York City, 61.9% of the Puerto Rican families with five or more members are below the poverty line.

The past few years have seen an intensified effort by departments and agencies to provide much needed economic opportunities for the Spanish speaking. Strides are being made in several areas as the following reports from various departments and agencies indicate.

1. OEO-support for Spanish speaking Americans in the Office of Economic Opportunity is provided mainly through Head Start, Community Action Programs and Health programs, which together account for slightly more than 80

percent of the total expenditures for fiscal Years 1970 and 1971. In FY 1971, out of nearly $1.2 billion, 197 million, or 17 percent of the total, will bring direct benefit to Spanish speaking Americans. (Refer to Tab 11 for full OEO Program report)

2. The Small Business Administration has broadened its scope and increased its services to the Spanish speaking. In Calendar Year 1970, SBA made over 2,000 loans totaling nearly $41 million to Spanish speaking businesses, an increase of nearly 50 percent in number and 53 percent in dollars over the previous year. For the first time, a contract for $125,000 was awarded to a Mexican American management and technical assistance to a new and existing minority owned firm. Furthermore, as of November 30, 1970, there were 331 Spanish surnamed persons employed by SBA; a year earlier there were only 91. Three Spanish speaking persons were appointed to top level positions, a district directorship in Los Angeles, a regional directorship in New York, and a deputy Assistant Administrator in Washington, D.C. One is a GS-16 and two are GS-15 positions.

3. The National Economic Development Association, organized under the guidance of the Cabinet Committee and funded on July 1970 by the Small Business Administration, operates a national office and 11 regional offices. As of March 31, 1971, NEDA had obtained 154 loans for Spanish speaking entrepreneurs totaling $2,220,292, 197 loan applications in the amount of $8,472,018 were pending decision from lending institutions, and loan packages amounting to $21,418,224 were in process. In addition, 10 educational foundations are in organization, and internship programs have been developed. After 8 months, and with only a

$600,000 annual grant, this is an impressive accomplishment.

4. The Office of Management and Budget has spearheaded the Deposit Program for Minority Banks. This office has encouraged the various departments of government to do business with the 25 minority banks in our country, thereby increasing their ability to serve the commercial needs of the minority communities. (Refer to Tab 12 for the list of minority banks)

5. Progress is also being made to overcome the deficiency in Spanish speaking participation in the critical area of finance. Of the 13,500 insured banks, only 4 are controlled and managed by the Spanish speaking (three hundredths of one per cent). Of the 6,350 savings and loan associations, only two are controlled by the Spanish speaking. Two permits to organize federal savings and loan associations have been approved under the Nixon Administration and both institutions are now in organization.

B. Recommendations for Action

1. The President should appoint a Spanish speaking American to the Federal Home Loan Bank Board or the Board of Governors of the Federal Reserve System. Spanish speaking persons have never been represented on these bodies, nor have they been appointed to the Regional Banks Board of Directors or the Regional Banks' Management Team.

2. The Federal Home Loan Bank Board and the Comptroller of the Currency should be instructed to facilitate the formation of Spanish speaking commercial banks and savings and loan associations. By 1980, it is estimated

that approximately 15,000 commercial banks will be in operation in the USA. In order for the Spanish speaking to control a proportionate number of these banks (5 percent), it will be necessary to charter 750 commercial banks over the next ten years—an average of 75 per year. By 1980 there will also be approximately 7,000 savings and loan associations chartered in USA. In order to control 5% of these institutions over the next ten years, it will be necessary to charter 350 associations, an average of 35 per year.

3. SBA contracts awarded to minority groups are expected to exceed $55,000,000 in FY 1971. The projection over the next 10 years is estimated at $2 billion. As 33% of the total U.S. minority population, a sum of $660,000,000 (33 percent of the total) should be specifically allocated to the Spanish speaking. To further implement this program, a Spanish speaking Project Development Officer should be assigned to each SBA District and Regional Office to deal specifically with the Spanish speaking businessmen.

4. Every effort should be made to encourage Spanish speaking youth to pursue education programs leading to a career in business. Business Administration scholarships and internship programs should be established to train Spanish speaking persons for eventual installation into the mainstream of SBA, Department of Commerce, and other governmental agency operations.

5. A computerized Spanish speaking minority enterprise capabilities directory should be established and maintained on an up-to-date basis. This listing, issued monthly, as well as for private sector business subcontracting on private or government projects, and would also serve as a statistical measuring stick.

Members of the Committee who were present at the 1st Cabinet Committee on Opportunities for Spanish Speaking People, that President Richard M. Nixon convened, were:

Secretary of Agriculture, Clifford M. Hardin

Secretary of Commerce, Maurice H. Stans

Secretary of Labor, James D. Hodgson

Undersecretary of Health, Education and Welfare, John Veneman

Assistant Secretary of Health, Education and Welfare, Patricia Hitt

Secretary of Housing and Urban Development, George Romney

Assistant Secretary of the Treasury, Charls Walker

Attorney General, John Mitchell

Director of the Office of Economic Opportunity, Phillip V. Sanchez

Administrator of the Small Business Administration, Thomas Kleppe

Chairman of the Civil Service Commission, Robert Hampton

ENDNOTES

CHAPTER ONE

1. The Mexican-American War of 1846–1848: A Deceitful Smoke Screen, Humberto Garza, 2006, Sun House.

So Far From God, The U.S. War With Mexico 1846–1848, John S. D. Eisenhower,1989, Random House.

The Year of Decision, Bernard De Voto, 1942, Little, Brown and Company.

2. War of the Rebellion, Series I–Volume L–in Two Parts, Washington, GPO, 1897.

3. Report I: Ethnic Isolation of Mexican Americans in the Public Schools of the Southwest, The Mexican American Education Study, United States Commission on Civil Rights, April 1971.

Report II: The Unfinished Education, Mexican American Educational Series, United States Commission on Civil Rights, October 1971. Report III: The Excluded Student, Educational Practices Affecting Mexican Americans in the Southwest, United Commission on Civil Rights, May 1972. Report IV: Mexican American Education in Texas: A Function of Wealth, Mexican

American Education Study, United States Commission on Civil Rights, August 1972.

Report V: Teachers and Students, Mexican American Education Study, United States Commission on Civil Rights, March 1973. Report VI: Toward Quality Education For Mexican Americans, Mexican American Education Study, United States Commission on Civil Rights, February 1974.

4. AN OVERVIEW OF SPANISH SPEAKING AFFAIRS FOR WHITE HOUSE PERSPECTIVES, Dated May 1971; Submitted to Counselor Finch on March 1971; and a companion memo on suggested political actions for Presidential Decisions.

5. A thank-you letter to Henry from Robert H. Finch, Counselor to the President, on May 24, 1971.

6. Personal letter to the President of the United States from Roy O Day, dated May 25,1973.

7. Memorandum dated May 18, 1971 TO: BOB FINCH FROM: George Grassmuck RE: Henry M. Ramirez—Report from Tom Bewley in Whittier.

8. A faxed Freedom of Information Request to the FBI.

CHAPTER TWO

1. White House Memo summarizing misgivings, dated Februry 2, 1971.

2. White House memo to establish the Inter-Agency on Mexican American Affair, dated June 9, 1967.

3. Interview with Martin Castillo at his Los Angeles Law Office on September 11, 2000.

4. Interview with Congressman Edward Roybal in his Congressional Office in 1971.

5. Newspaper article, Tony Castro, November 13, 1972..

CHAPTER THREE

1. James Polk, Inaugural Address, Tuesday, March 4, 1845

2. Op cit: The Year of Decision 1846, page 8.

3. Opt. cit. The Mexican-American War of 1846-1848,

4. 1930 Census Questionnaire—Population

5. Ten Days of Interviews of Leading South Texas Mexican Americans by USCCR Staff, in my Personal Files, October 7-15, 1968.

6. Hearings before the USCCR, San Antonio, Texas, December 9-14, 1968.

7. Op. cit. Questionnaires for the Mexican American Education Study in Report I: Ethnic Isolation of Mexican Americans in the Public Schools of the Southwest, pages 67–89.

8. Reporting Form, Office of Civil Rights, Dept of HEW

9. The Federal Civil Rights Enforcement Effort, November 1971.

CHAPTER FOUR

1. Article from Cardinal and White, the student newspaper of Whittier High School, *William Taylor visited Whittier High School,* January 29, 1968.

2. Article from Christian Science Monitor, *No more F grades for "New Horizons" Pupils,* February 10, 1968.

3. White House Memo from Tony McDonald, RE: *Spanish Speaking Medal of Honor Winners,* May 12, 1972.

4. Dept. of Labor Memo from Dr. Bette J. Soldwedel, *A Progrsm for Spanish-Speaking Americans, February 5, 1971.*

5. HEW Memo from J. Stanley Pottenger, *Identification of Discrimination and Denial of Services on the Basis of National Origin,* May 25, 1970.

6. Op. cit. Hearing before the U.S. Commission on Civil Rights, San Antonio, Texas, December 9–14, 1968.

7. Interview with Attorney Henry Zuniga, former Special Assistant to Hilario Sandoval, SBA Administrator, August, 1971.

8. White House Memo from Robert H. Finch, *Administration Programs for Spanish Speaking Peoples (P599),* in National Archives, Authority FO 12958-4-3-08, dated October 17, 1970.

9. CCOSS Memorandum dated August 23,1971

10. Letter from Southeastern Federal Regional Council Chairman, Frank J. Groschelle to Frank C. Carlucci, OMB, *Implementation of Regional Spanish Speaking Program*, March 24, 1972. In Archives FO 12958 4-3-08.

11. Letter from Groschelle to The Honorable Robert H. Finch, *Action Plan for the Spanish in Region IV*, Archives FO 12958 4-3-08, March 22, 1972.

12. Jose Rojas Garciduenas, *SALAMANCA, Recuerdos de mi Tierra Guanajuatense*, Editorial Porrua, S. A., Mexico, 1982.

13. Interview with E. B. Duarte, U.S. Immigration Official, December 18, 2010

14. Press release dated October 12, 1971 in my personal files.

15. WLS-TV, TV news clip, October 14, 1971, 10:00 p.m., RADIO TV REPORTS, INC.

16. HEW Regional Memorandum of Sept 30, 1971.

17. Article from *El Puertorriqueno*, Chicago, Ill. Dated October 7–13, 1971.

18. Article from *El Informador*, Chicago, Ill, Dated 17 October, 1971.

19. CCOSS Memorandum to Raymond Hanzlik from Henry Ramirez, Subject: Questionnaires for Regional Directors, dated December 15, 1971.

20. Archives two documents that summarize the president's plans and accomplishments derived from the plans, Authority: FO 12958, dated April 3, 2008.

CHAPTER FIVE

1. Article from *La Luz* Magazine of December–January, 1980.

2. White House press release, November 5, 1970.

3. The *Washington Post*, Elsie Carper, August 26, 1971.

4. *Scripps-Howard*, Seth Kantor, August 14, 1971.

5. *Los Angeles Herald-Examiner*, September 26, 1971.

6. *Los Angeles Times*, Frank del Olmo, Sept. 13, 1971.

7. *Los Angeles Times* editorial, August 23, 1971.

8. Federal Personnel Manual System Letter 713-18, January 23, 1973.

9. Manpower Report of the President to Congress, March 1973.

10. Testimony at hearings of the Government Operations Committee on July 23, 1973.

11. President's New Summary, *Ramirez, Chmn of the Cabinet Comm. on Opportunities for Spanish Speaking, August 8, 1972.*

12. White House Memo from Rayburn Hanzlik to Henry Ramirez, August 9, 1972.

13. Committee for the Re-election of the President memo from Alex Armendarez to Fred Malek, *SPANISH-SPEAKING FEDERAL EMPLOYMENT*, August 31, 1972.

14. Letter from Robert E. Hampton to Senator John V. Tunney, *Federal Government Employment of the Mexican American in California*, December 29, 1971.

15. Letter from Robert E. Hampton to Congressman Robert McClory, *Congressman Edwards' Statements on President Nixon's Sixteen -Point Program, March 29, 1972.*

16. Ibid. Committee for the Re-election of the President memo.

17. CCOSS Memo from Henry M. Ramirez to Anne Armstrong, *Presidential Memorandum on Equal Opportunity for Spanish Speaking People,* June 17, 1974.

18. Article in magazine, *Critica,* p 7, 1976.

19. CCOSS Memo from Roy O. Fuentes to Chairman Ramirez, *List of S/S Program Coordinators,* July 26, 1974.

20. E-Mail from Carlos Esparza to Henry Ramirez, March 5, 2009.

CHAPTER SIX

1. List of Appointees, *SPANISH SURNAMED PRESIDENTIAL AND SUPERGRADE APPOINTEES AS OF JANUARY 7, 1972.*

2. White House Memorandum, Subject: High-level Spanish Speaking Appointments, June 20, 1972.

3. White House printout, Spanish Surnamed Presidential Supergrade and Key Appointees Under the Nixon Administration as of November 1972.

4. Article in the National Journal, *Republicans Woo Mexican Americans,* Section on Politics, September 25, 1971

CHAPTER SEVEN

1. Secretary Maurice Stans, *Nixon's Economic Policy toward Minorities,* at Hackensack University, November 20, 1987.

2. Ibid., Stans speech

3. Executive Order No. 11458, March 5, 1969.

4. Interview with Leonard Manzanares, SBA staffer.

5. National Economic Development Agency, funded on July 1, 1970

6. Letter, Federal Home Loan Bank Board Letter from Raymond D. Chavez, April, 1973.

7. Article by Ruben Salazar in Los Angeles Times, *The Mexican Americans NEDA Much Better School System,* August 28, 1970

8. SBA 8(a) Contract Award Distribution by Minority Code as of January 31, 1972.

9. Op cit: Guanajuato, chapter four.

10. La Cristiada, in Volumen 1, 2, 3, 4 by Jean Meyer, siglo veintiuno editores, Mexico, D. F., 1973.

CHAPTER EIGHT

1. Copy of internal note for the record, with initials: gg, July 6, 1971.

2. Copy of the Program of the White House Sunday Service, November 14, 1971.

3. Article from *Philadelphia Inquirer*, "Johnsons visit Nixons," November 15, 1971.

4. Articulo de *Diario Las Americas*, November 15, 1971.

5. Article from *La Opinion*, November 14, 1971.

CHAPTER NINE

1. CCOSSP press release in Spanish, June 16, 1972.

2. Article in *Los Angeles Times*, July 28, 1974.

3. Letter to the Papal Nuncio, Jadot, November 15, 1973

CHAPTER TEN

1. Op. cit. Meyer, *La Cristiada.*

2. Newspaper article from *News-Examiner*, April 1972.

3. Newspaper article from the *San Diego Union*, July 1974.

4. E-Mail from E. B. Duarte confirming his telecom of 1975, January 11, 2007.

5. Article on Chapman in *Seattle Daily Times*, July 23, 1974.

6. Article on Chapman in the *San Diego Union*, July 15, 1974.

7. Article in the *San Diego Evening Tribune*, Frank Saldana, February 21, 1974.

8. Mexican Articles on treatment of its workers, June and July, 1974.

9. Article in the *Sentinel* of Hanford, CA, July 9, 1974.

10. Article in the *San Diego Evening Tribune*, Frank Saldana, February 21, 1974.

11. Article in *El Nacional*, Chicago, Ill., January 11, 1974.

CHAPTER ELEVEN

1. Committee for the Re-Election of the President Memorandum, Alex Armendariz, *SPANISH SPEAKING PHOTOGRAPHS,* July 18, 1972. Alex wrote: :the campaign is in desperate need of pictures of chicanos..."

2. CCOSSP Memorandum for Counselor Finch, September 3, 1971

3. CCOSS Memo, *200 namea for National Hispanic Heritage Week Proclamations,* September 7, 1973.

4. Copy of Presidential Proclamation of September 1973.

5. Photograph of Vice President Agnew Proclaiming on behalf of President Nixon

6. White House Press Release, *Remarks by the President,* September 13, 1988.

7. Treasury Department, Internal Revenue Service, Booklets in Spanish, Dec. 1971.

8. Copies of *Hoy*

9. Op. cit. Zamora

10. Interview with Martin Castillo in his Law Office in Los Angeles, September 4, 2010.

CHAPTER TWELVE

1. *New York Times* Article, Tad Szulc, June 19, 1972.

2. Telecom Interviews with Herman Gallegos, Don Morales, and E. B. Duarte on separate days and years on the subject: Maturation and recognition of the Chicano Cause

3. Article from *The Evening Star*, June 19, 1972, "Echeverrias Arrive in White House"

4. White House Memorandum, *Names of Twenty Invitees to State Dinner for President Echeverria*, May 4, 1972,

5. White House Memorandum, *Names of 80 Post Dinner Invitees to Festivities*,. May 25, 1972

6. US Senate Watergate Hearings, *on Presidential Campaign Activities of 1972*, November 5, 1973 , p. 5605–5606.

7. White House Memo *Names of invitees for the following activities: State Department Luncheon, Mexican Embassy Reception, Mrs. Agnew Luncheon, May 24, 1972*

8. White House Memo, *Names of Invitees for Blair House Dinners, May 24, 1972*

9. The State Department: The State Visit of Echeverria, Members of the American Party, June 1972.

10. CCOSS Letter of Resignation to the President, November 10, 1972.

11. Ibid. *Watergate Hearings,* p 27-33.

12. White House Press Release on *Appointment of Anne Armstrong,* December 18,1972.

13. *Civil Rights government ID card.*

14. Telecom note, from Erhlichman, February 21, 1973 .

15. Obituary on Anne Armstrong, the *Washington Post,* July 31, 2008

16. White House Memorandum, Bill (Mo) Marumoto, on *Need for Liaison Office,* November 30, 1972.

17. Memo for the Record, November 1972.

18. Memo from Mo Garcia, November 1972.

19. Memo from Carlos Conde, November 1972

20. Letter from Frank Gamboa, retired naval captain.

21. Article from *Stars and Stripes,* November 15, 1973

22. Aide-memoire from Mo Garcia on George Bush meeting, January 12, 1972

23. Article of January 13, 1973 from the *San Antonio Express-News.*

24. Interview of Ben Fernandez by Tom Bryan for San Juan of UPI, January 20, 1973.-20-73

25. Article, UPI, Peggy Simpson, January 19, 1973.

26 Article, *El Sol de Houston*, February 25, 1973.

27. Article, *Los Angeles Times*, Frank del Olmo, February 26, 1973.

28. Confidential Memo to Armstrong, RE: Presidential Meeting, March 5, 1973.

29. Article, *The Register*, March 11, 1973.

30. Open Letter to the President, California by Fidel Gonzalez, Jr., California LULAC State Director, Feb–Mar 30, 1973.

31. Article from *ABC de las Americas*, Pam Terry, March 31, 1973.

32. Note of a telecom informing us of an audit, April 14, 1973.

33. Questions from Sam Dash's Watergate lead lawyer, Hershman, October1971.

34. Secretarial notes transcribed on questioning by lawyers, October 3, 1973.

35. CCOSS Memo *on the Briefing Chairman Ramirez gave the Hispanic Supergrades on the Briefing President Nixon gave the PAS'*, April 5, 1973.

36. CCOSS Memo *recommending Carlos Conde for assistant to Armstrong*, March 1, 1973.

37. CCOSS Memo to Armstrong on *Hispanic Discontent*, March 5, 1973.

38. CCOSS Memo to Armstrong: *We Need to Meet on Discontent*, March 22, 1973.

39. CCOSS Memo to Armstrong on *Talking Points*, April 5, 1973.

40. Memo from Mo on *Armstrong's image*, April 6, 1973.

41. Memo from Mo and E.B on *Armstrong's trip to Phoenix*, April 20, 1973.

42. In my Private Paperes, *Thought paper by Mo Garcia on White House position*.

43. Letters to (May 15, 1973) and from (May 21, 1973) Congressman James Collins.

44. Letter to Tom Marquez, May 15, 1973.

45. Op Cit., *Roy O. Day* letter to the president.

46. In my Private Papers, *Letter from Ambassador Phil Sanchez.*

47. Letter from Congressman John Rousselot, April 3, 1974.

48. First leak from HMR *on Appointment by Nixon of White House Assistant,* May 1974.

49. *Los Angeles Times* reveals Nixon will name Latin to staff, June 30,1974.

50. White House press release, *Nixon appoints Special Assistant De Baca,* July 25, 1974.

51. UPI revels, *Nixon designated De. Baca, Special Assistant.* July 26, 1974.

CHAPTER THIRTEEN

1. Article from Catholic Citizen.org, Karl Maurer, July 4, 2003

2. Pomona Centennial History, Pomona Centennial—Bicentennial Committee, August, 1976

3. Matt Garcia, *A World of its Own,* (University of North Carolina Press, 2001)

4. Virgilio Elizondo, *Guadalupe, Mother of the New Creation,* (New York: Orbis Books, 1997)

5. A HALF CENTURY'S HISTORY OF THE ACADEMY OF THE HOLY NAMES POMONA, CALIFORNIA, 1898 TO 1948, Mrs. M.C. Kennedy, (Pomona: Historical Society of Pomona Valley, 1949)

CHAPTER FOURTEEN

1. Neumann, Eberhardt, C.M., *The Summary of Catholic History, Vol. II,* St. Louis, MO, Herder Book Co., 1962.

2. Jose Luis G. Guerrero, *EL NICAN MOPOHUA,* (Mexico City: Realidad, Teoria y Practica, S.A. de C.V., 1998, P. 479.

3. William H. Prescott, *History of the Conquest of Mexico,* (New York: Random House, Inc.) p. 689.

4. Ibid. Guerrero, Vol. I, p. 89.

5. Ibid. Barber, Vol. I, p. 90

6. The Bellarmine Report, *New Discoveries of the Constellations on the Tilma of Our Lady of Guadalupe.*www.catholicintl.com

7. Christopher Rengers, OFM Cap, *MARY OF THE AMERICAS,* (New York: ALBA HOUSE, 1991, p.86.

8. Op. Cit. Elizondo,

CHAPTER FIFTEEN

1. Robert Paul Millon, *Mexican Marxist-Lombardo Toledano,* The University of North Carolina Press, 1966, p. 27.

2. Op cit. Meyer, *La Cristiada,* Vol. 2, p. 232.

3. *Testimony at Hearings of the U.S. Senate Foreign Relations Subcommittee, 1910-1920,* p. 769.

4. Article in *Reforma.com,* February 23, 2003.

5. Articles from the *Offical Organ of the Los Angeles, CA, Archdiocese, The Tidings,* in the 1940-1950's.

6. Jean-Francois Revel, *How Democracies Perish,* (Garden City, New York, Doubleday, 1986).

CHAPTER SIXTEEN

1. Article from *The Los Angeles Times,* 1967.

2. Article from the *Whittier* High School Newspaper, *Cardinal and White,* April 28, 1967.

SEQUELS

1. Op. cit. Revel, *How Democracies Perish.*

2. Op. cit. Chambers, *Witness.*

3. Martinez, Richard Edward, *PADRES,* The University of Texas, 2013.

4. Op.cit. Interviews with Martin Castillo,

5. E-Mails, *Re: Rudy Becerra and Ruben Brown Recollections,* June 18, 2009, in my Private Papers.

6. Memo from Mo Garcia to H.M. Ramirez, *Re: Meeting in Dulcinea Restaurant in New York City,* March 31, 1972.

7. Op. cit. Interviews with Gallegos, July 31, 2009.

8. Ibid. Interviews with Gallegos.

9. Op. cit. House Hearings of the Committee on the Judiciary conducted by Congressman Don Edwards, 1973.